Daily Wisdom for Women

Print ISBN 978-1-62836-866-6
Special Edition ISBN 978-1-61626-001-9

eBook Editions:
Adobe Digital Edition (.epub) 978-1-63058-622-5
Kindle and MobiPocket Edition (.prc) 978-1-63058-623-2

Published by Barbour Books, an imprint of Barbour Publishing, Inc., P.O. Box 719, Uhrichsville, Ohio 44683, www.barbourbooks.com

Our mission is to publish and distribute inspirational products offering exceptional value and biblical encouragement to the masses.

 Member of the
Evangelical Christian
Publishers Association

Printed in China.

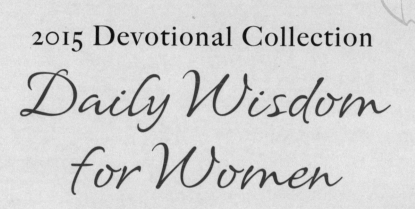

2015 Devotional Collection

Daily Wisdom for Women

BARBOUR BOOKS

An Imprint of Barbour Publishing, Inc.

Introduction

Experience an intimate connection to your heavenly Father with the *Daily Wisdom for Women* devotional collection. Featuring a powerful devotional reading and prayer for every day of 2015, this beautiful volume provides inspiration and encouragement for your soul. Enhance your spiritual journey with the refreshing readings— and come to know just how deeply and tenderly God loves you.

Only One Thing

*One thing I do [it is my one aspiration]: forgetting what
lies behind and straining forward to what lies ahead,
I press on toward the goal to win the [supreme and heavenly]
prize to which God in Christ Jesus is calling us upward.*

PHILIPPIANS 3:13–14 AMP

The start of a new year is filled with anticipation of what is
ahead—a sense of getting to start over, make a fresh start—and
with relief that some things are best left behind. Some make
resolutions, only to break them within a few days or hours. Some
set goals, both realistic and unrealistic. Many stay up New Year's
Eve in order to welcome in the New Year; others value their
sleep more and really couldn't care less.

Luke records a story in his Gospel illustrating our need
to resolve to do only one thing. Jesus and His disciples came
to Bethany and were invited to stay with Martha, Mary, and
Lazarus. When Martha came to Jesus, complaining that her
sister Mary wasn't helping her, Jesus spoke to her in loving
concern: "There is only one thing worth being concerned about.
Mary has discovered it, and it will not be taken away from her"
(Luke 10:42 NLT).

Maintaining a close relationship with the Savior is the
only goal Paul would set. He wasn't perfect at it, but he single-
mindedly pursued it. And he encourages us to do so today. Life
is much simpler when we choose to pursue only one thing—
the race before us. Don't look back.

*Heavenly Father, keep our eyes on
the goal, forgetting the successes
and failures of this past year.*

Run with Endurance

*Let us strip off every weight that slows us down,
especially the sin that so easily trips us up. And let
us run with endurance the race God has set before us.
We do this by keeping our eyes on Jesus.*

HEBREWS 12:1–2 NLT

Running was the first and, for many years, the only event of the ancient Olympic games. So it is no wonder that the New Testament writers use the metaphor to describe the Christian life. The first races were two-hundred-yard sprints. These gradually increased in length as the Olympic games continued to develop. The modern marathon commemorates the legendary run made by a Greek soldier named Pheidippides, who ran from the battlefield outside Marathon, Greece, to Athens to proclaim a single word: victory! Then he collapsed and died.

The Christian race lasts a lifetime, with Christ Jesus as our goal, the prize that awaits us at the finish line in heaven. It can't be run all-out as a sprint or no one would last the course. Though there was one race in the ancient games where the runners wore full armor, most of the time the ancient runners ran naked, stripping away anything that would slow them down. Obviously the writer of Hebrews was familiar with the ancient sport of running when he advised believers to run with endurance the race God set before them.

*Father, as we run the race You set
before us this year, let us run with
endurance, not allowing anything to
distract us from the goal of Christ-likeness.*

Life Is Short

*Teach us how short our lives really
are so that we may be wise.*
PSALM 90:12 NCV

A pastor tried to illustrate the brevity of life to his congregation. "Think of a straight line stretching into infinity on either end. Anywhere on the line, place a dot, smaller than a pinprick. That is your life, your 'threescore and ten' years Moses spoke of."

James describes our life as "a vapour, that appeareth for a little time, and then vanisheth away" (4:14 KJV). In reality, given our finite minds trying to wrap around an infinite concept, these examples don't really come close to describing the brevity of life. But in spite of that, God does have a purpose for each one of us, a purpose He designed uniquely for each individual.

As a new year stretches ahead, many tend to procrastinate, thinking that time stretches into enough time to accomplish their goals and still "enjoy life." But Moses likens our lives to grass that springs up fresh in the morning, but by evening it dries up and dies (Psalm 90:5–6). What seems a long time to us is really very little in the eyes of an eternal God. No wonder Moses' prayer was for wisdom to live a fulfilling and purposeful life in the brief time allotted to mankind. We would be wise to make this a daily prayer as we walk forward.

*Father, teach us to number our days, to live
each day with purpose and wisdom as You
lead us to fulfill Your purposes through us.*

Singing a New Song

He has given me a new song to sing,
a hymn of praise to our God.
Many will see what he has done and be amazed.
They will put their trust in the LORD.

PSALM 40:3 NLT

For many, the New Year is a good time to reflect on the events of the past year, to review what God has done, to praise Him for deliverance and safety, and to thank Him for His provision—both individually and corporately. Some of the social networks online have software that will look at the posts and pictures an individual has made and put together a year in review, hitting the highlights and major events. But those "reviews" don't always pick up on the praise and thanksgiving to God that should result from such an accounting.

Take a moment to reflect on all that God has done in the previous months. Then proclaim the works of the Lord, be amazed at His outpouring of love, grace, and mercy. Break out in song, spontaneous and free. Praise God in hymns, praise songs, and scripture songs. Even those who can't "carry a tune in a bucket," as the saying goes, can praise God with a joyful noise. If God's people don't proclaim the glorious works of their God, how can they expect the world to ever have a right view of Him? Sing a new song of praise to God for His many and varied works, and renew your trust in Him for the new year ahead.

Father, thank You for the new song of
praise You have placed in my heart.

Courage!

"Be strong and courageous. Do not be afraid;
do not be discouraged, for the LORD your
God will be with you wherever you go."

JOSHUA 1:9 NIV

Israel was on the verge of a new era in the life of their nation. Forty years before, God had delivered them from their four-hundred-year slavery to the Egyptian pharaohs. But when given the opportunity to enter the Promised Land, they instead saw the giants in the land and wouldn't trust God to give them the land in spite of the obstacles. Only Caleb and Joshua had the faith to believe God.

Now, after forty years of wandering in the wilderness, Joshua is tasked with the job of leading the children of those naysayers to take the land God promised long ago to Abraham. It's interesting to note that between Moses' charge and God's direct communication to the new leader, Joshua is told to "be strong and courageous" no less than seven times (Deuteronomy 31:6–7, 23; Joshua 1:6–7, 9, 18). And no wonder. Joshua faced a task that would be impossible to accomplish without God's help.

The challenges of a new year may seem impossible. Some may be old, familiar hurdles or battles; others may be hidden from view right now. Whatever is ahead, take courage from these promises given to Joshua and claim them for whatever lies ahead. "Be strong and courageous. . .for the Lord your God will be with you wherever you go."

Father, thank You for the promises of
Your Word that You are always with us.
We never need to face anything without
Your presence and constant help.

Be Strong

*Be not grieved and depressed, for the joy
of the Lord is your strength and stronghold.*
NEHEMIAH 8:10 AMP

Nehemiah, Ezra, and other religious and civil leaders of their
day had been given the job of leading the Jews back to Jerusalem
after seventy years of exile. It hadn't been easy work for those
who had made the long journey. Solomon's beautiful temple had
been destroyed, and the attempts to rebuild it had resulted in
something very inferior to what they remembered. Rebuilding
the walls and reestablishing their homes were tasks made more
difficult when they only had one hand with which to build.
They held weapons in their other hand in order to defend their
right to live in the land. At one point the work of rebuilding was
stopped after their enemies wrote a letter to the Persian king
pointing out the unsuitability of the Jews to live out from under
the immediate control of their captors.

Now the work was done, and the people wanted to hear
what the Law of God said so they could avoid making the same
mistakes again. All the Jews in the land came to Jerusalem and
listened as Ezra read from the Law and Levites explained what
they were hearing. The renewed understanding of God's Word
caused them to weep. Finally Nehemiah stood before the people he
now governed and begged them not to be grieved and depressed.
God was pleased with their desire to do what He commanded. It
was a day for rejoicing for they were back in the land.

*Father, joy gives us strength
to do Your will. Let us find
our joy in You today.*

Well-Watered Gardens

*"The LORD will always lead you. He will satisfy your needs in
dry lands and give strength to your bones. You will be like a
garden that has much water, like a spring that never runs dry."*
ISAIAH 58:11 NCV

Exhausted and weary to the bone, the writer walked into
the prayer time barely able to summon any pleasure in the
proceedings. The previous year had been grueling, and while
she still clung to her faith in Jesus Christ, she had very little
strength left. Empty and dry, she could barely make it through
the motions of living. She came to the prayer room from a
meeting with her agent, who had refused to drop her as a client.
Frustrated at her lack of purpose and unable to write out of her
desert-like existence, she sat facing the friend who had agreed to
pray for her.

Soon after prayer began, the dam holding her emotions
hostage broke deep within. Tears flowed, and the Lord poured
assurance after promise after confirmation over her head in the
form of more life-giving water. God wasn't done with her yet.
Hope pushed through the dry soil, turning lush and green in the
showers of life-giving water.

Two months later she stared in amazement at Isaiah 58:11.
Almost word for word, the verse matched what her friend
had prayed, proving once again that God's Word is living and
powerful.

*Thank You so much, Father, for sending
Your Holy Spirit to wash us with the
water of Your unchanging Word and to
refresh us in the showers of blessings and
mercies that are new every morning.*

Confident Peace

*I have told you these things, so that in Me you may have
[perfect] peace and confidence. In the world you have
tribulation and trials and distress and frustration; but be
of good cheer [take courage; be confident, certain, undaunted]!
For I have overcome the world. [I have deprived it of
power to harm you and have conquered it for you.]*
JOHN 16:33 AMP

The apostle Paul called the peace Jesus spoke of in this passage
incomprehensible, not easy to comprehend or understand with
our finite minds (Philippians 4:7). Part of the armor of God that
Paul later describes in Ephesians 6 is the footwear, the sandals—
the gospel of peace. God has much to say about peace in the
Bible. A quiet spirit, a peaceful spirit, is what God desires for
each of His children. Yet worry in the midst of our busyness is
much more common.

The scriptures tell us all we need to know in order to live a
life of peace, of contentment, free from the worry and distraction
of the world. Replacing the worry-thoughts with things that
are true, honorable, right, pure, lovely, admirable, excellent, and
worthy of praise (Philippians 4:8) will make room for the peace
from God that transcends human understanding. Jesus gives it
freely to all who desire to follow His example. Claim it today.

*Father, as I take every thought captive to
the glory of Jesus Christ, help me to think
on the things Paul listed in Philippians.
May Your peace reign in my heart and life today.*

Thirsting for God

*O God, you are my God; I earnestly search for you. My soul
thirsts for you; my whole body longs for you in this parched
and weary land where there is no water. I have seen you in
your sanctuary and gazed upon your power and glory.*

PSALM 63:1–2 NLT

David wrote many of the psalms in the middle of difficult times.
Biblical scholars believe this one was written when David fled
Jerusalem when his son Absalom took the throne from him.
Even in the midst of David's breaking heart, he sought the Lord
with a deep, soul-parched thirst. He was the deer being hunted
by his son; he was the one longing to be filled, to be completely
satisfied through the only source who truly satisfies.

Many years later, Jesus said, "God blesses those who hunger
and thirst for justice, for they will be satisfied" (Matthew 5:6
NLT). The thirst Jesus describes is the same thirst David spoke
of. Charles Spurgeon, a nineteenth-century pastor in London,
explained it this way in his Treasury of David: This thirst is
"the cry of a man far removed from the outward ordinances and
worship of God, sighing for the long loved house of his God;
and at the same time it is the voice of a spiritual believer, under
depressions, longing for the renewal of the divine presence,
struggling with doubts and fears, but yet holding his ground by
faith in the living God."

*Father, I, too, thirst for You in the dryness
of my soul. Thank You for Jesus who
alone is able to satisfy this thirst.*

Perfect Rest

*Come to Me, all you who labor and are heavy-laden
and overburdened, and I will cause you to rest.
[I will ease and relieve and refresh your souls.]*
MATTHEW 11:28 AMP

One day the crowds pushed against Jesus as He taught. So
instead of allowing them to push Him into the deeper waters
of the Sea of Galilee lapping at His feet, He got into one of the
fishing vessels His disciples owned. When the evening came, He
asked His disciples to take Him to the other side of the lake. So
they did. While the majority of the crowd couldn't follow Him, a
few did who had boats.

Jesus, tired from the day's teaching, healing, and casting out
demons, went to the back of the boat and fell asleep. Even when
a severe storm blew up, He slept on. Finally, afraid the huge
waves would swamp the ship, the disciples woke Jesus with their
shouting: "Teacher, don't You care that we're going to drown?"

Jesus woke, heard the disciples' fear, and rebuked the wind
and waves, and they instantly calmed. This is the kind of rest the
Lord desires to give to His children when He said, "Come to
Me, all you who labor and are heavy-laden and overburdened."

When we go to Him for rest, He eases, relieves, and
refreshes our souls. He gives the best kind of refreshment we
could ever wish for.

*Father, please remove the burden that
weighs me down and give the rest that
eases, relieves, and refreshes my soul.*

Trust God

Roll your works upon the Lord [commit and trust them wholly to Him; He will cause your thoughts to become agreeable to His will, and] so shall your plans be established and succeed.
PROVERBS 16:3 AMP

Many people make resolutions at the beginning of a new year . . .only to break them before the month is complete. Others set goals, then lay out detailed plans to accomplish them. In fact, January sees a plethora of self-help courses, webinars, blog posts, and other venues that emphasize how goals and/or resolutions will lead to success if we can manage not to break them or throw out the goals. There's nothing wrong with these things, except too many times we forget to include God in our plans.

In the first chapter of Joshua we read of God's charge to Joshua after Moses was dead. It was time to lead the children of Israel into the Promised Land. God tells Joshua the secret to success: "Be sure to obey all the teachings my servant Moses gave you. If you follow them exactly, you will be successful in everything you do. Always remember what is written in the Book of the Teachings. Study it day and night to be sure to obey everything that is written there. If you do this, you will be wise and successful in everything" (Joshua 1:7-8 NCV).

Solomon writes that we are to roll all our plans and goals onto the Lord. If they are in accordance with God's plan, then He will establish our plans and help us make them reality.

Father, I commit my plans to You today.

Renewed Strength

But those who hope in the LORD will renew their strength.
They will soar on wings like eagles; they will run and
not grow weary, they will walk and not be faint.

ISAIAH 40:31 NIV

Several times throughout scripture, the Lord had the writers use the eagle as a comparison to His people. Moses, speaking to the children of Israel just before his death, draws a beautiful picture of the eagle caring for her young. He then compares it to the Lord's leading in our lives. "He found them in a desert, a windy, empty land. He surrounded them and brought them up, guarding them as those he loved very much. He was like an eagle building its nest that flutters over its young. It spreads its wings to catch them and carries them on its feathers. The LORD alone led them, and there was no foreign god helping him" (Deuteronomy 32:10–12 NCV).

Isaiah carries that metaphor a bit further in Isaiah 40. Women seem to be most involved in nurturing their children, and as a result we tire easily. Starting in verse 27 in the Isaiah passage, Isaiah wonders how God's people can say that God is too busy or tired to care for His people. Instead he turns it around and says that even young men and children get tired. Only those who hope in the Lord will He carry on His wings, renewing their strength.

Father, thank You for these comparisons
that show Your loving heart in caring
for Your children. I praise You for enabling
us to do the work You have called us to do.

God's Superabundant Work

*Now to Him Who, by. . .the [action of His] power that is
at work within us, is able to [carry out His purpose and] do
superabundantly, far over and above all that we [dare] ask or think
[infinitely beyond our highest prayers, desires, thoughts, hopes,
or dreams]—to Him be glory in the church and in Christ Jesus.*
EPHESIANS 3:20–21 AMP

God is a lavish God who delights in doing much more than the
human mind can dream or hope for.

A short time into his reign, King Solomon went to Gibeon to
worship the Lord because the temple in Jerusalem wasn't built yet.
One night the Lord came to Solomon in a dream and said, "Ask
for whatever you want me to give you" (1 Kings 3:5 NIV).

Solomon didn't hesitate: "Now, LORD my God, you have
made your servant king in place of my father David. But I am
only a little child and do not know how to carry out my duties. . . .
So give your servant a discerning heart to govern your people and
to distinguish between right and wrong. For who is able to govern
this great people of yours?" (vv. 7–9).

God was pleased with Solomon's request and gladly granted
it. But then He showed His superabundant nature. He gave
Solomon wealth and honor and a long life (vv. 13–14). No other
king in Solomon's time or even after has ever surpassed God's rich
blessing on his life.

*Father, keep my eyes fixed on You so
I don't miss when You want to
bless me in superabundant ways.*

God's Joyful Love

The Lord your God is in the midst of you, a Mighty One,
a Savior [Who saves]! He will rejoice over you with joy;
He will rest [in silent satisfaction] and in His love He will be
silent and make no mention [of past sins, or even recall them];
He will exult over you with singing.

ZEPHANIAH 3:17 AMP

The first time a mom holds her newborn, a grandmother holds her grandchild, or an aunt holds her newborn niece or nephew, their hearts fill up with overwhelming love for that child. You look into the baby's eyes, check all the fingers and toes, and marvel over the perfection of this child. You can't imagine anything they do or say as the child grows up will lessen the love you have for him or her.

This scenario is just a tiny glimpse into how much God loves His children. Paul wrote in Romans 8: "I am convinced that nothing can ever separate us from God's love. Neither death nor life, neither angels nor demons, neither our fears for today nor our worries about tomorrow—not even the powers of hell can separate us from God's love. No power in the sky above or in the earth below—indeed, nothing in all creation will ever be able to separate us from the love of God that is revealed in Christ Jesus our Lord" (vv. 38–39 NLT).

Zephaniah says that God's love for His child is so overwhelming that He breaks into singing. Music is a spontaneous expression of many emotions, but especially love.

Father, thank You for Your arms of
love holding me close to Your heart.

To Know Him Is to Trust Him

Those who know your name trust in you,
for you, O LORD, do not abandon those who search for you.
PSALM 9:10 NLT

Names often reveal the character of a person. This is true in biblical times, especially when it comes to the names of God. A study of His names often brings a deeper awareness of God and who He is. Isaiah, in predicting the birth of Christ, listed several of His names: "For a child is born to us, a son is given to us. The government will rest on his shoulders. And he will be called: Wonderful Counselor, Mighty God, Everlasting Father, Prince of Peace" (9:6 NLT).

In other places He is referred to as Lord Jehovah, Almighty God, Shepherd, Priest, King of kings, and Lord of lords. He is the God who Sees, the Righteous One, Master, Redeemer, the All-Sufficient One. Each name describes a little different attribute or includes the many sides of His character. All are perfectly true about Him.

A study of the names of God, Jesus, and the Holy Spirit not only gives us a deeper insight into the nuances of who He is, but it also strengthens our ability to trust Him implicitly with every detail of our lives. He has promised to reveal Himself to those who truly seek Him out, who truly desire to "know Him [that I may progressively become more deeply and intimately acquainted with Him, perceiving and recognizing and understanding the wonders of His Person more strongly and more clearly]" (Philippians 3:10 AMP).

Father, reveal Yourself to me through
Your names, so I will trust You more.

The Lord Gives Victory

"See, God has come to save me.
I will trust in him and not be afraid.
The LORD GOD is my strength and my song;
he has given me victory."

ISAIAH 12:2 NLT

The first time we see the phrase "the Lord is my strength and my song" is in the book of Exodus in the song Miriam and the women danced to as Moses and Miriam and the children of Israel sang. The reason for their rejoicing was their deliverance from Pharaoh and his army. When the Israelites left Egypt, they came to the Red Sea. They realized the army of Egypt had followed them. Then the Lord opened the Red Sea, and the Israelites crossed on dry land. The Egyptians followed. But once the last Israelite was safe on the other side, the Lord closed the waters over the Egyptians who had followed them. It was a great deliverance, and the people celebrated.

Later, Isaiah not only predicted God's judgment on the people of Israel because of their sin and desire to go their own way, he also predicted that God would send salvation and deliverance once their time of judgment was complete. As God had delivered the nation of Israel in ancient times, so would He deliver His people in the future. All would know His name; all would trust Him and not be afraid; all would find strength in praise and rejoicing. And therein lies true victory.

Father, faith in You brings victory in
the battle against sin. May we sing
praises to You for Your salvation.

Be Still and Know

Let be and be still, and know (recognize and understand)
that I am God. I will be exalted among the nations!
I will be exalted in the earth!

PSALM 46:10 AMP

September 11, 2001. A day Americans will remember forever.
Terrorists took over passenger planes and ran two of them into
the World Trade Center towers in New York City. Another
crashed into the Pentagon in Washington, DC. Yet another
plane headed to the nation's capitol crashed into a Pennsylvania
field when the passengers took out the hijackers, refusing to let
them fulfill their purpose.

While the whole world watched the horrible events
unfold, many turned to the Word of God to find comfort in
this unprecedented carnage. Psalm 46 is one of the passages
promising peace in the midst of cataclysmic events. The psalmist
starts the song with "God is our refuge and strength, always
ready to help in times of trouble. So we will not fear when
earthquakes come and the mountains crumble into the sea" (vv.
1–2 NLT). No matter what happens, God is standing ready to
help. Later in the psalm, the reader is invited to "see the glorious
works of the LORD" (v. 8), to watch as the Lord destroys all those
who stand in opposition to Him.

Then the reader sees the command: "Be still, and know that
I am God." In another version the phrase is translated, "Cease
striving" (NASB). No matter what happens, God has it all
under His control. There is no need for fear.

Father, quiet my spirit before You
today so I may know who You are.

Stand Strong

But we thank God! He gives us the victory through our Lord Jesus Christ. So my dear. . .sisters, stand strong. Do not let anything move you. Always give yourselves fully to the work of the Lord, because you know that your work in the Lord is never wasted.

1 CORINTHIANS 15:57–58 NCV

Women today wear Superwoman capes as they juggle schedules, maintain their homes, work outside the home or from a home office, and stay active in the ministries at church. It's no wonder that so many are tired. They joke that once the children leave home, they'll have time to rest. But that doesn't always happen. Adult children still desire the "Mom touch"—decorating their homes, cooking meals, giving out hugs. So the Superwoman cape stays on even though it's a little tattered.

When the pressures of life crushes Superwoman into the ground and tears her cape off and tramps it into the mud (and it will happen to everyone), thank God for the victory He will give when we surrender our schedules, plans, and dreams to Jesus Christ. Don't give up. Thomas Edison said, "Many of life's failures are people who did not realize how close they are to success when they gave up." God has already given us the victory. Stand strong in that knowledge. In God's economy nothing is ever wasted.

And that Superwoman cape? Women in every generation since Eve have worn it. The circumstances differ, but with Superwoman only the circumstances differ.

Father, the victory is already won.
But I can only stand strong in Jesus Christ.
Keep my eyes focused on the goal ahead.

God Is the Boss

*Work willingly at whatever you do, as though you
were working for the Lord rather than for people.*
COLOSSIANS 3:23 NLT

Over the centuries, many men and women have accomplished
amazing things. Things that have won them recognition from
the world in the form of Nobel prizes, Olympic medals, literary
awards, books on the bestseller lists, honorary doctorates, and
much more. Most pursue these awards and titles to bring glory
to themselves; a few make their accomplishments less known,
seeking God's direction, following His leading. Earthly medals
and awards, recognition and acclaim only last a few years at best.

Jesus said, "Don't store up treasures here on earth, where
moths eat them and rust destroys them, and where thieves
break in and steal. Store your treasures in heaven, where moths
and rust cannot destroy, and thieves do not break in and steal.
Wherever your treasure is, there the desires of your heart will
also be" (Matthew 6:19–21 NLT).

It's so easy to fall into performance and/or approval traps,
but they usually suck the joy out of the job. When we recognize
that we work for the Lord, not for the approval of man, we are
freed from man's laws and expectations. We are free to be the
people God created, fulfilling the purposes He had in mind for
us. Remember something C. T. Studd, British cricketeer and
missionary, wrote, "Only one life, 'twill soon be past. Only what's
done for Christ will last."

*Father, help me put aside any desire
for man's approval, but only seek to do
those things that will last for eternity.*

Knowing God's Will

*I plead with you to give your bodies to God because of all he
has done for you. Let them be a living and holy sacrifice—
the kind he will find acceptable. This is truly the way to
worship him. Don't copy the behavior and customs of this
world, but let God transform you into a new person by
changing the way you think. Then you will learn to know
God's will for you, which is good and pleasing and perfect.*

ROMANS 12:1–2 NLT

Frank Sinatra popularized the song "My Way," written by Paul
Anka. The lyrics tell the story of an old man looking back on
his life. He's satisfied with how he lived. He has no regrets for
anything, even when he failed, because he alone controlled his
life and he "did it my way."

It's a sad song, really, when the lyrics are analyzed in the
light of God's Word. Paul wrote to the church in Rome, laying
out in the first part how all people are born with a sin problem,
one about which they can do nothing. Their only hope is in
Jesus' work on the cross. Finally he comes to the last section
of the letter, and he pleads with his readers to give themselves
entirely over to God's control. Because He has done so much for
us, total surrender—a living sacrifice—is the only way to truly
worship Him.

God's will is clear: turn away from the world's behavior and
customs, and let God transform our thinking.

*Father, I desire Your way over
"my way." Transform my thinking.
Godly actions will follow.*

Approach God with Confidence

Let us then approach God's throne of grace
with confidence, so that we may receive mercy
and find grace to help us in our time of need.
HEBREWS 4:16 NIV

The dictionary defines confidence as the "faith or belief that one will act in a right, proper, or effective way" or "the quality or state of being certain." Both definitions fit the admonition written by the author of Hebrews.

In this passage, Jesus' work on the cross and a description of why He is our great High Priest gives us the means to "approach God's throne of grace with confidence." Jesus—100 percent God, 100 percent man—is the only one who fulfills God's demands for holiness and righteousness in those who approach Him. When we accept Christ's sacrifice on the cross, we believe that He paid the blood ransom required to remove our sins from us, making a relationship with God a reality. We do not have to adhere to a set of dos and don'ts or jump through a lot of hoops that man requires in order to gain an audience with our Father God. We have confidence in Jesus Christ's ability to make us able to stand before a holy God.

With that restored relationship, we are also certain that when we approach God's throne in need of grace and mercy, we will receive it. What a great and precious promise we can cling to as we run the race set before us.

Father, thank You for the confidence that
is ours because of the work of Your Son,
Jesus Christ, on the cross.

Content in Christ's Strength

*I have learned how to be content with whatever I have. . . .
I can do everything through Christ, who gives me strength.*
PHILIPPIANS 4:11, 13 NLT

Sometimes Paul seems like a giant of a man, way above everyone else on the spiritual scale. Granted, it is a manmade scale, certainly not one God uses.

Paul wrote his letter to the Philippian church from a prison in Rome. Prisons in the ancient world were nothing compared to those in our country today. In chapter one, we learn that Paul was guarded day and night by the emperor's own elite guards—the praetorians. Because Paul never backed down from sharing the Gospel with whoever crossed his path, many among the guards believed in Christ and then carried the Gospel into Nero's palace. Because of this unique opportunity to spread the Gospel, Paul rejoiced.

In the latter part of the letter he declared that the gift the Philippians sent him was welcomed with rejoicing. But even without it he could rejoice because he had learned to be content in whatever situation and condition he found himself. So how was Paul able to do this when so many of God's people today never learn his secret? Before Paul ended the paragraph, he told us: "I can do everything through Christ who gives me strength." Paul couldn't generate contentment in all situations, but Christ in him could. The same "secret" enables God's people to do the same nearly two thousand years later.

*Father, thank You for enabling us to live joyful,
contented lives through Jesus Christ.*

Trust God, Be Blessed

*"But blessed are those who trust in the LORD
and have made the LORD their hope and confidence."*
JEREMIAH 17:7 NLT

The believer's hope is founded on Jesus Christ alone, for He alone was able to pay the sin price for all mankind. Implicit trust in God's provision should be a natural result if a person has trusted in Christ for salvation. But sadly it isn't always. In Jesus' parable of the sower, He tells of four different kinds of ground the seed falls on and compares it to sowing the seed of the Gospel on human hearts.

Jesus told the parable of the wise man and the foolish man, saying all people go into one of those categories. The wise woman listens to Jesus' teachings and follows Him. Her life is built on a solid foundation so that when the storms come with the high winds and floodwaters, she will not collapse and wash away. She stands firm in the hope of the Lord. But the foolish woman is the one who hears Christ's words but doesn't obey them. Her foundation is laid on shifting sand, so that when the winds and storms come, her house collapses and she has nothing to hope for.

Determine to be the wise woman and be blessed because you place your confidence in Jesus Christ alone for salvation and a future.

*Father, I thank You that my hope is built
on the firm foundation of Jesus Christ.*

With God, Why Fear?

*What time I am afraid, I will have confidence in and put
my trust and reliance in You. By [the help of] God I will
praise His word; on God I lean, rely, and confidently put my
trust; I will not fear. What can man, who is flesh, do to me?*
PSALM 56:3–4 AMP

God chooses the most improbable people to do His work (1
Corinthians 1:27–29).

Gideon was threshing wheat in a winepress when an angel
from the Lord spoke to him: "The Lord is with you, you mighty
man of [fearless] courage" (Judges 6:12 AMP). Gideon worked
alone, but he may have looked around to see if there was anyone
else who'd sneaked in. Now Gideon knew he was the epitome of
fear. After all, who threshes wheat in a winepress when he needs
the winds of the hills to blow the chaff away? But fearful Gideon
listened to what God had to say and gathered an army to fight
the Midianites. But then God told him to pare his army down to
three hundred. Three hundred against the vast Midiante army?
But by this time, God had shown Himself trustworthy and
Gideon obeyed. Because he trusted God, he put his fear aside
and relied on God for the outcome.

God wants followers who will obey His leading in spite
of fear.

*Father God, sometimes my fears threaten to
overwhelm me and shut me down. Help me
give my fears to You as I obey Your will.*

God's Word Accomplishes His Purposes

*"As the rain and the snow come down from heaven,
and do not return. . .without watering the earth and making
it bud and flourish, so that it yields seed for the sower and
bread for the eater, so is my word that goes out from my mouth:
It will not return to me empty, but will accomplish what
I desire and achieve the purpose for which I sent it."*
ISAIAH 55:10–11 NIV

Farmers and ranchers settled this country, especially in the move
to the West. Many immigrants came into the country looking for
land, which was plentiful here. With a general population shift to
the cities where people can find jobs, farming and ranching isn't
as prominent. For many the experience of planting a field with
seed, waiting on God to send the rain at the right times, giving
the plants the moisture they need to bud and flourish, and seeing
the crop through harvest is only something they read about.

The Lord uses this analogy to describe what happens when
God's Word goes out in a sermon, in verses memorized, or in the
written word. God promises that when His Word is planted in
someone, it doesn't go to waste. It may take a long time to see it
take root and grow and be harvested, but it will. For it will not
return to God until it has achieved the purpose for which He sent
it. So moms of wayward children, take heart. God is still working.

*Father, thank You for the promises
of Your Word that we can hang
on to when life gets hard.*

Be Strong and Courageous

"So be strong and courageous! Do not be afraid and do not panic before them! For the LORD your God will personally go ahead of you. He will neither fail you nor abandon you."

DEUTERONOMY 31:6 NLT

In *The Horse and His Boy*, one of the books in the Narnia series by C. S. Lewis, we see a beautiful picture of how the Lord gives us strength and courage to do His will. The boy, Shasta, runs away from home. Along the way he meets up with a talking horse from Narnia and a nobly born girl, Aravis, with her talking horse. They decide to take their horses to Narnia, but their plans fall apart when they have to go through the Calormene capitol city, Tashbaan.

Several times as they travel, they are chased by lions, harassed by cats, and generally persecuted by various members of the cat family. Finally, on one particularly dark night, Shasta crosses over a mountain pass alone. In the dark and fog Shasta senses rather than sees a creature walking along beside him. And he's terrified.

Later, when he meets Aslan, Shasta learns that all the cats were Aslan, guiding them, pushing them, and yes, terrifying them into doing what they needed to do. Aslan was also his protector as he crossed the steep and dangerous mountain pass in the dark. Shasta is angry until he realizes that Aslan did everything out of love, even hurting Aravis when her pride was keeping them from the mission they'd been given.

Father, thank You for the beautiful picture of Your protection and courage to those who are Yours.

Nothing Is Impossible with God

*For with God nothing is ever impossible and no word from
God shall be without power or impossible of fulfillment.*
LUKE 1:37 AMP

Gabriel, the archangel tasked with telling Mary that she would
be the mother of the promised Messiah, spoke these words to
her when she asked how such a thing could happen when she
wasn't married. She responded with humility and submitted to
the Lord's will.

Two other times in scripture an angel announces a birth
to couples who in human years were too old for such a thing
to happen. When the angel told Abraham that Sarah would
conceive and have a son within the year, Sarah laughed. When
the angel asked why she laughed, she denied it at first and then
said she was too old. The angel responded that nothing was
too hard for God. And it happened as God said it would. Then
Sarah's laughter of unbelief turned into joy.

Several months before Gabriel appeared to Mary, he showed
up in the temple where a priest named Zechariah was sacrificing
the daily offering. Gabriel told him that he and his wife,
Elizabeth, would have a son in their old age. The child would
be the forerunner to the promised Messiah. Zechariah's unbelief
led to losing his voice for the next nine months until his son was
born and he gave him the name the angel had said.

God delights in doing the impossible, waiting until the perfect
time to fulfill His Word.

*Father, give me faith to believe Your Word
as Mary received the news of Jesus' birth,
knowing that nothing is too hard for You.*

God's Grace in Weakness

"My grace is all you need. My power works best in
weakness." So now I am glad to boast about my weaknesses,
so that the power of Christ can work through me. That's
why I take pleasure in my weaknesses, and in the insults,
hardships, persecutions, and troubles that I suffer for Christ.
For when I am weak, then I am strong.

2 Corinthians 12:9–10 NLT

The apostle Paul had many amazing experiences over the years
after his conversion, and he saw God bring him through many
experiences, each designed to draw him ever closer to his goal to
be like Christ. One such experience was getting to visit heaven,
whether in the Spirit or out of the Spirit—either in reality or in
a vision—he didn't know. But in order to keep Paul humble, the
Lord sent a "thorn in the flesh."

Scripture doesn't say exactly what that "thorn" was, but it
caused Paul enough pain and trouble that he asked the Lord to
take it away, not once but three times. Finally God told him,
"My grace is all you need. My power works best in weakness."
In other words, "No. All you need is My grace to help you
cope with this thorn. For in your weakness you are forced to
depend on Me for strength to get you through and still be able
to proclaim My Gospel. Others can see Me in you, when your
'thorn' should keep you from doing anything at all."

Father, help me to rely on Your grace as
Paul did, knowing You allow weakness
to keep me from working independently.

God's Provision

*And my God will liberally supply (fill to the full) your every
need according to His riches in glory in Christ Jesus.*
PHILIPPIANS 4:19 AMP

Sometimes the littlest words in our language pack a lot of meaning into them. All is one of those words. Three letters encompass the total extent of the whole. Everything is in the word all.

In the letter to the Philippians, Paul is wrapping up a discussion of how God had used the church to provide for Paul's need while he was in prison, even though many of them didn't have much to give. Paul spoke out of experience when he told them God would supply all their financial needs because they gave sacrificially to help another person with a greater need.

But God meeting their financial need isn't all that is encompassed in the meaning Paul intended to convey when he chose this particular word. When Jesus taught this principle to His disciples, Luke recorded it in his Gospel: "Give, and you will receive. You will be given much. Pressed down, shaken together, and running over, it will spill into your lap. The way you give to others is the way God will give to you" (6:38 NCV). Jesus indicated that whatever people have to give, when they give it, they will receive as they have given. Emotional, spiritual, physical, material—whatever the need, God will supply it abundantly, "pressed down, shaken together, and running over."

*Father, thank You for this promise that You
will abundantly supply for every need I have
through the riches of heaven in Christ Jesus.*

God Has a Plan

*For I know the thoughts and plans that I have for you,
says the Lord, thoughts and plans for welfare and peace
and not for evil, to give you hope in your final outcome.*
JEREMIAH 29:11 AMP

When Jeremiah wrote this, Israel was already in captivity in Babylon. Things looked pretty bleak, and many held no hope of returning to the land God had given them generations before under Joshua's leadership. It was because they refused to listen to the prophets, telling them to repent of their sin of consistently turning away from God's plan and living the way they wanted to, that they were in this predicament.

After the majority of the Jews were taken to Babylon, Jeremiah wrote them a letter telling them to accept where they were. Since they were going to be there the full seventy years God had predicted, they were to settle down, build houses, establish communities, plant gardens, marry, die, celebrate their special days—in other words, live life to the fullest while they were there. The sooner they accepted God's punishment, the sooner they could begin living again. The letter concluded with a reminder that God had not forgotten them. He still had plans for His people. Good plans, not evil. He wanted to give them hope that this punishment wasn't for forever.

God still has a plan for each one of His children. They are still plans for peace and good, hope-filled plans.

*Father, thank You for the thoughts and plans
You have for each of Your children. Help us to
live life to the fullest in the hope of those plans.*

Jesus Never Forsakes

*Be satisfied with your present [circumstances and with what
you have]; for He [God] Himself has said, I will not in any
way fail you nor give you up nor leave you without support.
[I will] not, [I will] not, [I will] not in any degree leave you
helpless nor forsake nor let [you] down (relax My hold on you)!
[Assuredly not!] So we take comfort and are encouraged and
confidently and boldly say, The Lord is my Helper; I will not
be seized with alarm [I will not fear or dread or be terrified].*
HEBREWS 13:5–6 AMP

Count the negatives in these verses. Nine times—including
four I will nots—God assures His people He has everything
under control. What a wonderful "comfort" verse, filled with
the promise of God's protection, help, and provision. Because
of what God does, we have no reason to be dissatisfied with
anything God allows into our lives—either good or bad.

Study the book of Job. Listen to Job's statements of
faith throughout the book. But none are so convincing as his
statements in chapters one and two, refusing to sin against God
with his words. Even after his wife—his closest companion
here on earth—urged him to curse God and die, Job refused to
comply. He acknowledged that God had the right to give and to
take away. And he blessed the Lord throughout, accepting that
God never revealed the whys to him.

*Father, I don't need to know the whys.
You are in control no matter what
happens. Thank You for this promise.*

God's Joy

*Nehemiah said, "Go and enjoy choice food and sweet drinks,
and send some to those who have nothing prepared.
This day is holy to our Lord. Do not grieve, for the
joy of the LORD IS YOUR STRENGTH."*

NEHEMIAH 8:10 NIV

The beginning of each month brings a daunting mound of things to accomplish. However, looking back to God's provision during the past month gives His children hope. Nehemiah encouraged the Israelites after they finished rebuilding the walls of Jerusalem to enjoy themselves (in a godly manner). They endured scorn, weariness, and threats from the nations around them as they were rebuilding their homes, but God protected them and blessed their work. When they were tempted to wallow in regret over past wrongs they were told not to be burdened by guilt, but to go forward doing what is pleasing and joyous to God

God's joy is in the faith of His children, and staying close to God is what gives His creation joy and strength no matter what may come in the future. The Israelites were also told to give to those in need as part of their celebration so that everyone could share in the joy. The passage says that when the people understood what they were told—God's message of hope—they rejoiced greatly. This month is another opportunity to repent of wrong doings and enjoy the Father's ever-present goodness.

*Father God, thank You for the redemption
hope You give through Jesus. Help Your
daughters to leave the burdens of the past
and the worries of the future in Your
hands. In Your joy we find true joy
and lasting strength.*

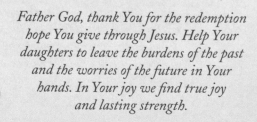

He Chose

*The Lord did not set His love upon you nor choose you
because ye were more in number than any people, for ye were
the fewest of all people; but because the Lord loved you.*
DEUTERONOMY 7:7–8 KJV

In the book of Deuteronomy God tells the people of Israel that
they are unique. Who else has "heard the voice of God speaking
out of the midst of the fire" and lived? What other nation
could claim that Jehovah was on their side as they saw all the
miracles God did for them? However, God says that this special
treatment, this unique relationship with the one true God, was
not a result of anything done by the Israelites. They did nothing
to deserve this love; it was freely given to them. They were
actually a terribly rebellious and ungrateful people. However,
God still reached down to them and constantly assured them
of His love and presence. Women today, and men as well, seek
to do things to gain acceptance or affection. They judge their
worth by their accomplishments, looks, possessions. But God
says He loves His people and it is nothing they do which makes
them right with God. It is only God's grace, evidenced most
powerfully through the death and resurrection of Jesus that
produces the Maker's love. He chose to love and to save. What's
more, He chose to love the least.

*Father, humble us when we think we can reach
You by our own strength. When we are discouraged
and weary, let us remember that You love us still.*

Set Aside for God

*And they made the plate of the holy crown of pure gold,
and wrote upon it a writing, like to the engravings
of a signet, Holiness To The Lord.*
EXODUS 39:30 KJV

The Israelites were on their way to the land promised to them
by God in the book of Exodus. During their journey across
the desert, they were continually brought to recognize that this
God wanted them to personally know Him. God taught them
how they should live differently from the surrounding nations:
to be just, merciful, humble. He gave them instructions on
how to set up a place of worship and on the activities and attire
of the priests, so that the people could be in fellowship with
God—as they were created to be originally. One aspect of the
priests' clothing was a headpiece on which was written: HOLINESS
TO GOD. It was a seal, like that of a king, which showed they
belonged to the Creator and Lord of all. God also wants this
for His children today. The image of Israel as set apart and of
the priests as even further set apart symbolizes God's desire for
the Church to be distinct and bear the seal of Christ. Christian
women must show through their attitude, dress, words, and
work that they honor an amazing God. When others see their
testimony, they, too, will be irresistibly drawn to be set apart
for God.

*Holy God, let Christian men and women
radiate the light of Christ because they
are set apart to bring Your good news of
reconciliation to a dark and broken world.*

A Woman's Boldness

*Achsah answered, Give me a present. Since you have set me
in the [dry] Negeb, give me also springs of water. And he
gave her the [sloping field with] upper and lower springs.*
JOSHUA 15:19 AMP

Most critics have labeled the Bible to be an oppressive book,
which has contributed to the marginalization of women
throughout the centuries. Those critics never truly read the
Bible. Many who called themselves Christians, unfortunately,
have twisted parts of scripture and pulled passages out of
context to justify their otherwise unbiblical view and treatment
of women; but God reveals a beautiful picture of women in
His Word. Achsah, the daughter of the faithful warrior Caleb,
married the valiant Otniel. This bold woman approached her
new husband and urged him to ask her father for a field. Otniel,
not only a mighty warrior but also a kind husband and wise
judge, seems to have respected his wife. She received land as her
dowry but found it to be a dry place. Achsah petitioned Caleb
again, but this time she went herself. Caleb knew the justness of
her request, and he gave her both the upper and lower springs of
water. God included this brief story of Achsah perhaps because
He wants His daughters to be bold. If God calls someone to a
special task, He will also mold the hearts of those around her—
just like He did with Caleb and Otniel.

*Father, guide Your daughters to know that
true submissiveness means to do the right
and just thing. Give more women the
boldness and respectful heart of Achsah.*

Bitterness

*"Don't call me Naomi," she told them. "Call me Mara,
because the Almighty has made my life very bitter. I went
away full, but the Lord has brought me back empty.
Why call me Naomi? The Lord has afflicted me;
the Almighty has brought misfortune upon me."*
RUTH 1:20–21 NIV

God has unseen beauty hidden in the midst of trials. Naomi, whose name means pleasant, poured out her sorrow to the women of Bethlehem, her hometown, in the scripture reference above. She lost her husband, two sons, and her home for a second time. However, God shows throughout history that He heals both physically and spiritually. He gives beauty for ashes and joy for the spirit in distress. For Naomi the answer was right beside her: her loyal daughter-in-law Ruth. Naomi, this old and tired woman, did not realize what happened would be used by God in His great rescue plan for humanity. In her confusion and despair, she was bitter; but El Shaddai, God Almighty, had everything under control. He used the death of Naomi's sons and her return to Bethlehem to bring Ruth and Boaz together. Otherwise God would have used another family to be the ancestors of Jesus. God once again brought pleasantness to Naomi by giving her a new home and hope. Although she did not personally see the blessing of kingship that came to Boaz's great-grandson David, Naomi was an important part of God's great plan for the little town of Bethlehem.

*El Shaddai, give Your daughters perseverance
to trust in Your greater plan. Turn bitter
and angry hearts to see Your work of
redemption and reconciliation.*

Strength

Then Hannah prayed and said: "My heart rejoices in
the Lord; in the Lord my horn is lifted high. My mouth
boasts over my enemies, for I delight in your deliverance.
There is no one holy like the Lord; there is no one
besides you; there is no Rock like our God."

1 SAMUEL 2:1–2 NIV

Hannah was filled with sorrow because she could not have
children; and her husband's other wife taunted her because of
this. Even though Hannah was the favorite wife (her name
means favored), she still longed to be a mother. So she brought
her suffering heart before God in prayer and God graciously
answered. He gave her a son whom she named Samuel, and
who became one of the greatest judges and prophets of the Old
Testament. God did not stop there. He also gave her five other
children after Samuel. In the scripture reference above, the word
horn means strength. Hannah acknowledges that Jehovah God is
her strength. In her deepest pain and overwhelming despair she
first turned to God. His answer filled the longing in her heart
and drew her to a deeper worship of God. He is the only one
who can give strength to overcome the worries of this world.
God calls His children to seek deliverance from their burdens
only in Him because any other option is futile and fleeting.

Rock of Ages, help Your children to rejoice in
You as their strength. Keep us from trusting
in ourselves, and remind us that You answer
prayers, often in unexpected ways.

Written on Him

*"Can a mother forget the baby at her breast
and have no compassion on the child she has borne?
Though she may forget, I will not forget you!
See, I have engraved you on the palms of my hands;
your walls are ever before me."*
ISAIAH 49:15–16 NIV

God's people, during the life of the prophet Isaiah, were under threat of captivity, and they saw impending doom. They knew their dark and rebellious hearts brought this about, and they feared that Jehovah would forget or forsake them. God responded by likening Himself to a mother—the ultimate symbol of love and devotion. Mothers care for their children to guide and protect them. However, in this fallen world there are also women who abandon their children. God says that unlike weak and broken earthly parents, He will remain steadfast. He can do no less when He says that He engraved His children on the palms of His hands. Carved into His hands! This image comes to life when Jesus took nails through His hands to save sinners and make them children of God. What a powerful promise: He will never leave us nor forsake us.

Holy God, thank You that we can call You Abba, or Daddy. Thank You that Jesus suffered, died, and rose again so that people of all tribes and nations could know You as Father. Thank You that You never forget Your children. Help us to never doubt Your compassion, provision, and love.

His Likeness

As for me, I will behold thy face in righteousness:
I shall be satisfied, when I awake, with thy likeness.
PSALM 17:15 KJV

Throughout the ages women were given an ideal image of
womanhood, which society encouraged them to emulate. The
ideal woman constantly changed, as is seen through the history
of fashion, women's rights, and changing social and cultural
traditions. One of the wonderful things about God is that He
never changes; neither does Christ as the only example of what
it means to be the perfect human. Society today, both Eastern
and Western, places much of a woman's value in her appearance:
clothes, makeup, and body type. It is easy for a woman to make
idols out of these things. However, a Christian woman should
bear the image of Jesus. If she loves Jesus with her whole heart
she will seek to please Him; He is the only person who has
already poured out more love on her than any earthly man ever
will or can give her. The holy and pure characteristics of Jesus are
the only things that produce satisfaction: His joy, peace, patience,
goodness, love, faithfulness, etc. So, when women allow the Holy
Spirit to work in them these characteristics, they will have true
beauty, not the fleeting beauty and popularity of the world.

Father, protect Your children from looking to the
world for affirmation or from seeking the false
beauty of the world. Help Your daughters to wake
up each morning being more and more like Jesus.

Unashamed

I sought the Lord, and he answered me;
he delivered me from all my fears.
Those who look to him are radiant;
their faces are never covered with shame.

PSALM 34:4–5 NIV

Christians in communist countries around the world were
portrayed as less intelligent, their children were ridiculed at
school, and their family members were refused leading roles in
various institutions. Many others were tortured and killed for
their love of Jesus. Though marginalization does not occur to
the same extent in Western countries today, Christians are still
ridiculed for their beliefs throughout the world. However, when
ridicule comes, as Jesus promises that it will come to all believers,
it is important to first seek God's strength. Christians must pray
and trust in Christ's love, which casts out all fear. This love will
then be poured over and into the Christian by the Holy Spirit,
so that no matter what kind of persecution comes their way,
the person will remain strong in his or her faith. God will help
them not to be ashamed of the Gospel. They will shine with the
life-giving truth and love of Jesus. Several years ago, the Voice
of the Martyrs, an organization that helps Christians who are
persecuted, held a conference entitled "Unashamed." Seeing the
boldness and radiance of persecuted sisters in Christ should spur
other Christian women to unashamedly follow Jesus.

Glorious Lord, forgive us when we water-down
Your message to avoid scorn from others. Jesus
was not ashamed to die for me. Let me also
be unashamed to live or die for Him.

Life in the Light

*How priceless is your unfailing love, O God! People take refuge
in the shadow of your wings. They feast on the abundance of
your house; you give them drink from your river of delights.
For with you is the fountain of life; in your light we see light.*

PSALM 36:7–9 NIV

David packs so many beautiful metaphors in the verses above
that reveal to readers important aspects of God's character.

His love is unfailing, and no price could ever be put on this
love.

People find comfort and protection when they turn to God's
love and when they seek to do everything according to God's
will—this is what it means to be in the shadow of His presence.

It is in the presence of God that people have a veritable
feast for the soul that is evidenced materially or physically. God
fills the spiritual thirst of people by giving them of Himself—
knowledge of Himself, instilling in them His love, and giving
them His characteristics.

Just as Jesus preached in the Sermon on the Mount in
Matthew 5 (where He also provided physical bread), God will
bless and fill those who hunger for and thirst after the goodness
and purity of God. The Creator God is the source of all life, and
it is only through Him that humans can understand the meaning
and purpose of existence. It is His Light—Christ—that gives us
life.

*Great Refuge, illuminate the minds and hearts
of Your daughters to see the light that is Christ
and to be beacons from which this light shines
onto others who are in darkness.*

Fragrant Prayers

May my prayer be set before you like incense;
may the lifting up of my hands be like the evening sacrifice.
PSALM 141:2 NIV

Coming before God in honest prayer is often difficult. There are many distractions offered by the world. Prayer is also easily corrupted into something it should not be, which is why Jesus spends so much time emphasizing the need to dispel previous conceptions of prayer. He presents prayer as a very personal and intimate conversation with the Father. The Bible is filled with examples of the importance of heartfelt and sincere prayers. God asks His children to bring Him something beautiful in their prayers; and if His children love Him then they long to give Him sweet-smelling prayers. What makes prayers beautiful? Throughout the Bible God reveals that prayers should be a mixture of praise, confession of sins, and petitions. The humble heart of the one praying, who lets the Holy Spirit work in him or her, makes the most beautiful of prayers. It is not the use of clever words that draws God's ear, but words that show a desire to know Him at a deeper level. When His children pray with their whole being, the position of the heart, mind, and body are all affected. The beautiful fragrance of Christ will follow His daughters wherever they go.

Father, we echo the voice of the psalmist in saying
that we want our prayers to be drenched in Your
Word and to be like sweet-smelling incense before
You. Let us continue both day and night
to fellowship with You in prayer.

Lover

*You are as beautiful as Tirzah, my darling, as lovely
as Jerusalem, as majestic as troops with banners.*
SONG OF SOLOMON 6:4 NIV

Some Bible scholars believe the Song of Solomon is a picture of
Christ and the Church. If readers follow this symbolism then
Jesus is again presented as the ultimate and purest form of love.
In the love poem written by Solomon, the Beloved still loves the
distracted and wandering woman. However, she becomes more
like him because of the love he shows her. The children of God
take on beautiful qualities when they enter into a relationship
with Jesus because the Holy Spirit works the character of the
Bridegroom into their hearts, making them more like Jesus.
Tirzah means "delightsomeness" or "my delight is in her." God
calls His children beautiful, darling, and lovely. He compares
them to the prosperous and royal cities of Tirzah and Jerusalem.
Followers of Christ are children of the King and therefore
inheritors of the kingdom of God. Alongside all of the previous
descriptions, Christians are also likened to majestic troops.
God gives His people strength and victory to conquer the lies
and temptations of Satan. All of heaven rejoices when His
children come out victorious. With Christ as our heavenly lover,
God gives us the beauty of the most delightful things, the rich
character of nobility, and the strength of all armies.

*Let us raise Your banner high, O Lord, because You
have chosen to love the sinful and unlovely. We pray
that You continue to transform Your people into
something beautiful in which You can find delight.*

Perfect Husband

*For your Maker is your husband—the Lord Almighty is
his name—the Holy One of Israel is your Redeemer;
he is called the God of all the earth.*
ISAIAH 54:5 NIV

With the approach of Valentine's Day, it is important for
Christian women in particular to remember that only in Christ
can one find perfect and fulfilling love. This does not mean true
godly women should become nuns, but rather that they should
not seek to have a man fill the longing in their hearts that only
God can fill. Some women enter into marriage while others
do not; both have the promise that God acts as their perfect
husband. The different metaphors throughout the Bible of
God as husband, father, friend, and brother seem strange and
contradictory. However, God seeks to show His people that in
Him they can find the best and purest of everything—especially
of relationships. Tomorrow, Christian women should not let
their emotions be manipulated by the commerciality of the "love
holiday." To avoid any disappointment they must first remember
that the Redeemer lavishes His love on His people, and they
must strive to show this love of Christ to others. No earthly love,
friend, or spouse is perfect. But the Maker is perfect, and He will
take care of His own.

*Almighty God, help us to understand how You
fulfill the different roles of husband, father, and
brother in our lives. Let Your daughters face
tomorrow ready to pour out their love on others
as Your love is abundantly given to us.*

Bridegroom's Love

As the bridegroom rejoiceth over the bride,
so shall thy God rejoice over thee.
ISAIAH 62:5 KJV

Legend has it that Saint Valentine was a third-century priest who defied Caesar's edict to outlaw marriage. Valentine was executed when he was discovered performing clandestine wedding ceremonies for Christians. Valentine knew marriage is a symbol of Christ and the Church, and he died protecting this sacrament. Although it is important to lovingly acknowledge significant others on this holiday, the most exciting love is that which was poured on us by God through Christ. As a woman, there is no greater feeling than to love and be loved, to feel accepted, appreciated, and admired. In the 1998 BBC adaptation of Charles Dickens's novel *Our Mutual Friend*, the main character justly tests the woman he loves. When she humbly passes the test, he joyously proclaims, "My dear girl! My gallant, courageous, and noble Bella!" Any woman would love to hear a man speak so highly of her. The prophet Isaiah reminds his readers that God does just that. He rejoices over His people just like a bridegroom who is completely enamored with his bride. Nowhere is this love more clear than in the fact that God sent Jesus to die for rebellious creation. When God sees His people trust in Him for strength to gallantly and courageously fight against temptation and sin, all of heaven rejoices.

Lord, let Your children find complete joy and peace
in Your love today. Thank You for Your patience
with us when we are sinking and Your delight in
us when we live the way we were created to live.

True Love

*Little children, let us not love [merely] in theory or in speech
but in deed and in truth (in practice and in sincerity).*
1 JOHN 3:18 AMP

With so much talk about love the past few days, it is easy to
forget what "love" means in everyday life. There are a plethora
of books, blogs, and movies on the topic; however, going from
the theoretical to the practical is incredibly difficult. Comfort,
pride, and ignorance hinder a person from going out to do an
act of love. Then it is even more difficult to make sure that one's
acts of love are done out of a pure and sincere heart, that they are
not done to receive recognition or for any other selfish motive.
Paul writes to the Colossians that they must put on love, which
is the bond of perfection (Colossians 3:14). It may not come
easily, but with prayer and an earnest desire to change, the Holy
Spirit energizes God's children to love people in a practical and
wholesome way, which brings reconciliation and deeper faith.
This is the kind of love that emulates Jesus as the ultimate
example of love. No one loved in deed and in truth more than
Jesus. From the religious leaders to the prostitutes, from the
noblemen to the lepers, Jesus spoke to, touched, and healed
them. It ultimately comes down to how much one is willing to
sacrifice. Jesus proved that His is the truest of loves.

*Greatest Love, thank You for giving Your life
for Your friends. Help Your daughters understand
and act upon their knowledge of true love.*

Governing Authorities

I urge, then, first of all, that petitions, prayers, intercession and thanksgiving be made for all people—for kings and all those in authority, that we may live peaceful and quiet lives in all godliness and holiness.

1 TIMOTHY 2:1–2 NIV

On President's Day Americans honor their leaders and in particular two of the most influential presidents, George Washington and Abraham Lincoln. The first and sixteenth presidents achieved monumental strides in their battles for freedom and justice in the Revolutionary War and in the Civil War respectively. Honoring those in authority is a biblical principle, and Christians are reminded that they must also bring the current leader of the country before God in prayer. It is much easier to respect and give thanks for a good and strong leader, but the challenge comes in praying and interceding for a less-than-likable leader. Whatever the opinions or political leanings of a Christian, the Church body is instructed, urged, to petition, pray, intercede, and give thanks for those in authority. The actions of state leaders affect the lives of all citizens, and seeking the salvation of a leader will bring peace and joy in the hearts of those who intercede even if the country itself is in turmoil.

King of Kings, thank You for the leaders of our country. You are using them to shape Your children to be more like Christ. May the government leaders come to saving faith in Jesus and be used as a powerful arm in Your work of redeeming the lost and broken.

Wisely Spent

*Why spend money on what is not bread,
and your labor on what does not satisfy?
Listen, listen to me, and eat what is good,
and you will delight in the richest of fare.*

ISAIAH 55:2 NIV

In anticipation of Lent, the forty days prior to Easter, it is crucial to remember the importance of feasting on God's Word and letting it fill us. Often so much energy and money is put into tasks and objects that provide no benefit for the soul. God knows the tendency of His people to be drawn by the things of this world, so He sends wake-up calls like the verse in Isaiah. He even emphasizes the need to focus on what He is saying: "Listen, no really, stop and listen!" Creation will never be satisfied unless it is in fellowship and constant communication with the Creator. Lots of time in prayer, in reading and studying God's Word, and in being a fruitful part of the Church body is the bread and labor that satisfies our souls. Many decide to give something up, to fast from something, during Lent. Whatever this thing is, it is important to give it up in order to spend more time on things that are truly nutrients for the soul.

*Father, guide Your children to use their time
and money wisely and to Your glory. Open our
hearts to hear You calling us to a feast, and help
us identify the good things on which we should
spend our energy. Let the next forty days before
Easter be rich in fellowship with You.*

Fasting

*"Is not this the kind of fasting I have chosen: to lose
the chains of injustice and untie the cords of the yoke,
to set the oppressed free and break every yoke?"*

Isaiah 58:6 niv

Whether someone chooses to observe Lent or not, the issue
of fasting is a reccurring theme in the Bible. It is one of the
most misused and misunderstood modes of worship. God
reminds His children that fasting does not mean to deprive their
bodies of good things or to present a holier-than-thou image.
He makes it clear that fasting done properly means battling
injustice, bringing freedom to the oppressed (both physically
and spiritually), and breaking the bondage of sin. This requires
a great deal more faith and self-sacrifice than giving up sweets.
The key to such fasting is acknowledging and doing away with
sin in one's life. Ash Wednesday, the start of Lent and the first
day of fasting for many, should be a day of repentance and of
looking forward to the victory of Christ's death and resurrection.
Jesus spent forty days fasting in the wilderness prior to the start
of His public ministry as an example to Christians of the need
to spend time in communion with God. John Piper says that by
fasting either of their time spent on various things or of food,
Christians show that "this, O God, is how much I long for You."

*Redeemer, humans are nothing but ashes; yet in
Christ they become Your children. Guide us to
fast in the way that brings healing to this broken
world and that makes us more like Jesus.*

Beauty for Ashes

*To appoint unto them that mourn in Zion, to give unto them
beauty for ashes, the oil of joy for mourning, the garment of
praise for the spirit of heaviness; that they might be called trees of
righteousness, the planting of the Lord, that he might be glorified.*

ISAIAH 61:3 KJV

Repentance calls a believer to mourn for her sin. This mourning
requires Christians to recognize their sin and to feel remorse
for their actions that offended God. God will use this humility
and love of Him to give His children freedom and joy. Ashes
were a sign of death and mourning—of being overcome by
grief. However, God takes away death and the destruction of
sin and instead gives the beauty of His presence. He molds the
hearts of Christians to be more like the beautiful heart of Jesus.
The second gift mentioned in the verse, oil, was an important
medicine of antiquity; when Christians mourn their sin, God
gives the medicine of joy by reminding His children that He
cleanses them of the darkness in their hearts. When burdened
by the cares of this world, He removes the spirit of heaviness
and depression and clothes His people with praise and blessings.
God then makes His children stand tall and firm like trees who
have inherited the righteousness of Christ because they realize
they have no righteousness of their own. The great Gardener
does this work of healing and reconciliation because He is good.

*Jehovah, let us glorify Your name for all Your
gifts and trust only in You for lasting joy.*

Hunger for God's Word

When your words came, I ate them;
they were my joy and my heart's delight,
for I bear your name, LORD GOD ALMIGHTY.
JEREMIAH 15:16 NIV

Why does God tell people to read His Word? He commands
this because it is His primary means of communication with His
children. Believers are inexorably bound to Him, and because
of this great bond only the will of the Father gives the greatest
comfort. Jeremiah's words may seem extreme, but God wants to
give a startling picture of what it means to hunger for His words.
Jesus while on earth knew the Old Testament scriptures by heart;
Paul as a Pharisee may have spent years poring over the books of
the law (the first five books of the Bible written by Moses). The
disciples, too, although mostly poor, came to a deep and saving
knowledge of God's words as they listened to Jesus. If people
are God's children then they also should find delight in reading
His Word. They should wrestle with it, analyze it, let it convict
and change them; it should be their sustenance just as food and
water. Just like earthly hunger cannot be satisfied by eating once
a day, His children also continually desire more spiritual growth
until they are finally united with Jesus in heaven.

Great Provider, let Your words be sweet as honey
to Your daughters. Give us diligence to read—
to eat—from the Scriptures daily, even when we
are tired or our spirit rebels. Thank You for the peace
You fill us up with when we spend time with You.

Rend Your Heart

"Even now," declares the LORD, "return to me with all your heart, with fasting and weeping and mourning." Rend your heart and not your garments. Return to the LORD YOUR GOD, for he is gracious and compassionate, slow to anger and abounding in love, and he relents from sending calamity.

JOEL 2:12–13 NIV

One of the most dangerous things about religion is how easily one can pretend to be faithful. Jesus spoke to the religious leaders of His day, saying that they were beautiful goblets on the outside but on the inside they were dirty and broken. God's children need to have truly repentant hearts to avoid becoming spiritually dead on the inside. It does not matter if people put on a façade of holiness and of feeling sorry for their sins. If their hearts are not truly changed then their lives will remain unchanged and far from God's blessings. Believers are told to break their hearts of sin so that God can fix them and make them work properly. When His children show remorse for the bad they committed, God is gracious to forgive and compassionate to heal and to restore. People can only begin to understand God's colossal love when they understand the depth and darkness of their own sin. Confess the brokenness and then rejoice in God's salvation.

Gracious Abba, reveal to Your children even the most subconscious of wrongs, and let Your daughters confess their sins knowing You are the Father who forgives. Thank You for Your great patience and Your abounding love.

Declaring Righteousness

I do not hide your righteousness in my heart;
I speak of your faithfulness and your saving help.
I do not conceal your love and your faithfulness
from the great assembly.

PSALM 40:10 NIV

A person cannot help but proclaim God's undeserved goodness in everything that she does when she sees what God has done in the lives of the broken. Richard Wurmbrand spent a total of fourteen years in communist prisons. Despite incarceration, he used every opportunity to tell fellow prisoners of the perfect, holy God who came to earth to die for the broken and sinful. Even in solitary confinement Wurmbrand used Morse code to spread the good news of the resurrection and the hope of life after death through Jesus. These are truths that should not and cannot be hidden. If a person refuses to speak God's truth, God will make His Word heard through someone else. The first person will sadly miss out on the beautiful partnership with God and the fruit that is produced. So many things try to discourage Christians from saying confidently that God is completely good and that only He can give lasting help. However, the psalmist encourages Christians to not conceal the great love and awesome faithfulness of God. Personal testimonies have proved to be a powerful tool for revealing the truth. Many prisoners dedicated their lives to Christ through Wurmbrand because he refused to keep silent.

Righteous God, let Your daughters boldly
declare Your grace. Remind us daily of
Your faithfulness, and let the joy in our
hearts spill out wisely through our words.

Let the Light Judge

Therefore judge nothing before the appointed time;
wait until the Lord comes. He will bring to light what
is hidden in darkness and will expose the motives of the heart.
At that time each will receive their praise from God.

1 CORINTHIANS 4:5 NIV

Dr. Helen Roseveare served as a medical doctor and missionary
in the Congo from 1953 to 1973. When civil war erupted she
refused to leave the country and endured horrific treatment,
including rape at the hands of rebel soldiers. It could have been
easy for her to doubt God's goodness, but she instead looked to
her pain as sharing in the suffering of Jesus. How simple it is to
jump to conclusions about certain situations or certain people.
However, God says that creation is to wait for His judgment.
Since Jesus is the Light of the world, only He can make things
clear and judge justly. Christians should not remain passive but
should wisely seek justice through the guidance of God's Spirit.
Love should replace the spirit of judgment. God's love is the
strongest of weapons, and when this dwells in and flows from
His children then they can endure times of uncertainty and
darkness without falling into the trap of judging God or others.
When they endure they will in the end also reign with Jesus, just
as Paul tells Timothy (2 Timothy 2:11–13), and they will receive
praise from God.

Light of all creation, give Your daughters patience
to wait for You to expose the darkness and to
bring Your perfect justice. Keep us from pride
and from wrongly judging others.

Fellowship

*Let us hold unswervingly to the hope we profess, for he who
promised is faithful. And let us consider how we may spur one
another on toward love and good deeds, not giving up meeting
together, as some are in the habit of doing, but encouraging one
another—and all the more as you see the Day approaching.*

HEBREWS 10: 23–25 NIV

Two days prior you were encouraged to declare God's
righteousness and faithfulness "to the great assembly." Both in
Psalm 40:10 and in the above verse the need to meet with fellow
believers is evident. What is so crucial about fellowship, and
isn't faith about a personal relationship with God? The personal
relationship with God is of utmost importance, but it must play
out in one's interaction with both Christians and others. If a
person is really close to God he or she is a healthy member of the
Body of Christ, the global Church, and as such should help the
other parts of the Body. The Church's ability to work properly
and according to God's plan depends on the entire Body. Such
a unity brings great blessing. All of God's children, no matter
how weak or strong their faith, have blessings to offer other
Christians. But this mutual encouragement only happens when
they meet and form relationships. Some family members are less
likable than others, but they are still family. Christians become
more like Jesus by loving and fellowshipping with each other.

*Father, help Your daughters to build up
other believers, and open our hearts to
willingly accept the convicting voice of
the Holy Spirit spoken through others.*

The Great Wealth of the Poor

*Listen, my dear brothers and sisters: Has not God chosen those
who are poor in the eyes of the world to be rich in faith and to
inherit the kingdom he promised those who love him?*
JAMES 2:5 NIV

The great phenomenon of this era is the explosion of Christianity in the developing world. There are many more poor Christians than there are rich Christians. Jesus said that it is easier for a camel to pass through a needle's eye than for a rich man to go to heaven. Trusting God is a lot more difficult for a woman or a man when they are surrounded by comfort and material wealth.

Amazingly, when one is in a dry place—physically, emotionally—that person is more likely to have a sincere and total dependence on God. The marginalized followers of Jesus often see their various forms of poverty as a blessing. They are following in the steps of their Rescuer who also lived in poverty. Jesus had little in the world's eyes, but He had the Father. In His Sermon on the Mount Jesus blessed the poor in spirit by saying that they will have the kingdom of heaven. God not only gives endurance and rich faith to His children who are poor here on earth but they have assurance of a final reward—being in the presence and fellowship of the One they love—their Maker, Father, and Friend—for eternity.

*Father, thank You for Your love and provision
for Your needy children. Help us to always
remember our greatest wealth is Christ.*

Trust the Good News

*We also have the prophetic message as something
completely reliable, and you will do well to pay attention
to it, as to a light shining in a dark place, until the day
dawns and the morning star rises in your hearts.*

2 PETER 1:19 NIV

The beauty of the Old Testament is that it foreshadows the
coming of Jesus through the histories that depict humanity's
great need for God as rescuer. The apostle Peter knew that God's
message was true. Like any good Jewish boy, he had learned
the Torah, the first five books of the Bible, and then he actually
saw Jesus as the One who made all those images and promises
come true. However, there was a time when Peter doubted the
role of Jesus as Savior. His denial was the darkest moment of
his life. Peter's letters were most likely written to other Jews of
his time who also were well acquainted with the Old Testament
prophecies about the Messiah. Peter tells the readers to believe
the good news of Jesus Christ. It is completely reliable. In the
darkest moment of Peter's despair, Jesus—as the incarnate Word
of God, Divinity in the flesh—broke the chains of sin holding
humans captive since the fall of Adam and Eve. In Jesus' death
and resurrection the awesomeness of God's mysterious rescue
plan was revealed. Light came into the hearts of humankind and
gave them Life.

*Indelible Light, guide us to trust and live out
Your message, so that Jesus can fight the
darkness within and give us life anew.*

Overcomers

For everyone born of God overcomes the world.
This is the victory that has overcome the world,
even our faith. Who is it that overcomes the world?
Only the one who believes that Jesus is the Son of God.

1 JOHN 5:4–5 NIV

Earlier in the letter the apostle John writes that there should be no fear among believers. But there is so much brokenness in the world and so much weakness that it is easy to succumb to fear. The hope Christians have, however, is greater than this because the perfect love of Christ casts out fear. When Christians follow Jesus with their whole being they are new people who have become children of God. He works in and through His children to bring an end to the things that are distorted and perverted. It is faith, belief, and trust in God and His Word, which God builds up in His children that gives Christians the ability to overcome. Only by faith in Jesus as God in the flesh, come to save humanity, can people overcome the darkness in the world. Whenever problems seem unbearable, daughters of the King of kings should always remember that God has planned a way out and that Christians are more than conquerors because of the sacrifice of Jesus who loves us. Jesus Himself said that the world would hate His followers but that they should take heart because He has overcome the world.

Master of the Universe, thank You that in
Your victory You overcame the world and
that by faith in You we also can overcome
the power of sin in and around us.

A Little Suffering for a Whole Lot of Faith

Resist him, standing firm in the faith, because you know that the family of believers throughout the world is undergoing the same kind of sufferings. And the God of all grace, who called you to his eternal glory in Christ, after you have suffered a little while, will himself restore you and make you strong, firm and steadfast.

1 PETER 5:9–10 NIV

Why does God allow suffering? It is the question asked by both believers and non-Christians. God doesn't want His children to suffer. Enmity toward God produces suffering. And resisting Satan means going through lots of pain because we are fighting against the sinful nature around and in us. Gold is only refined through fire, and so Christians can only grow to be more like Jesus if they die to themselves increasingly each day. That is painful. However, the outcome is stronger, bolder, and kinder women who shine like gold because they radiate the light of Christ. God brings about this restoration and renewal. The follower of Jesus is also encouraged that she is never alone in her suffering. Jesus experienced the ultimate suffering by bearing the sins of humankind, and His followers throughout the ages suffer for teaching a rebellious world to return to God. He knows how hard it is, and He is right there beside His daughter giving her greater hope and peace.

God of all grace, help Your daughters stand firm in their love of You. Enable us to remain strong and steadfast so that we can have faith as great as a mustard seed, which can move mountains.

God Is Sovereign

I will praise your mighty deeds, O Sovereign LORD.
I will tell everyone that you alone are just.
PSALM 71:16 NLT

God is sovereign. Think about those words for a minute. This means He has the ultimate authority. Supreme power. The highest rank. There is no one else we can run to whose opinion is higher—or holier—than the Lord's. He, alone, has the answers to what we face, and His sovereignty assures us that we can trust Him, even when everything around us is whirling out of control. Sure, it's not always easy, but it's always the right choice.

Have you acknowledged God's sovereignty in your life? If so, it might be time to take your hands off of the situations you're dealing with and trust that He—out of His great love for you—will offer the best solution. No trying to fix things on your end! Relax. Your sovereign Lord has everything under control in His time, and His way.

Dear Lord, I have to admit, I don't always trust Your sovereignty. I trust my own instincts first. Help me to let go and trust You in every situation, trusting You with Your timing and Your answers. Today I choose to let go, releasing my troubles into Your capable hands.

Mondays

*May the God of hope fill you with all joy and peace
as you trust in him, so that you may overflow
with hope by the power of the Holy Spirit.*
ROMANS 15:13 NIV

Ah, Monday! How we love it! (Not!) Most of us dread Mondays because they represent "getting back to work." We live for the weekends, but the Lord doesn't want us to dread our work week. We need to be excited, hopeful, as each new week approaches. After all, each new day provides an opportunity to love others and share the Gospel message.

Think about that for a moment. You are an ambassador of Christ, spreading His love to those you come in contact with. Whether you're headed to the classroom or the workplace or you're homeschooling your kiddos, Monday can be a fun day, a fresh new start, a chance to pray for God-encounters. When you spend time praying for those fun, divine appointments, God always comes through, surprising you with people in your path. . .usually people who need to see the smile on your face or the song in your heart.

So don't despise Mondays! They are a special gift from your heavenly Father, who happens to believe that every day of the week is pretty awesome, because He created them all!

*Father, I don't always look forward to Mondays.
Sometimes I dread them. Remind me that each
new week is a fresh chance to share Your love.*

Spring

*There is a time for everything,
and everything on earth has its special season.*
ECCLESIASTES 3:1 NCV

Don't you love the four seasons? They represent change, and change can be a good thing. Springtime is delightful because it's filled with images of new life. Rebirth. Joy. All you have to do is look around you and your heart can come alive. Flowers budding. Trees blossoming. Dry, brown grass morphing to green. This season is a true do-over, isn't it!

The Bible teaches us that God ordained the seasons. He set them in place and wants us to enjoy them. In the same way, we go through different "seasons" in our spiritual lives, too. Think about it. Our hearts can get frozen over (winter). Then God breathes new life into us and a thawing begins (springtime). From there, we move into full blossom, a season of productivity (summer). Then, as with all things, we slow down, preparing for change (autumn).

Yes, God surely ordained the seasons, but springtime is one with a remarkable sense of expectation, so enjoy it!

Father, I love springtime! Everything feels so new, so fresh. I'm ready to put yesterday behind me. The heaviness of the "winter" seasons in my life evaporates on a warm breeze. I appreciate the lessons learned over the past several months, but I'm so happy it's spring!

Second Chances

But if we confess our sins to him, he is faithful and just to
forgive us our sins and to cleanse us from all wickedness.
1 JOHN 1:9 NLT

Ever had a really bad day, one where you wished you could
crawl back in bed, pull the covers over your head, and start over?
Sure, we've all had days—or weeks—like that. Maybe we've said
something, or done something, we regret. Perhaps we've been
wounded by the words or actions of someone we thought we
could trust, and returned injury for injury. We've slipped up. . .in
a big way. Oops!

If you're in an "Oops!" season, don't give up. God can
redeem any situation you're going through by offering a second
chance. There's no mistake you've made that's too big, too
bad for Him to handle. Just confess your mess-up to Him and
watch what happens next. Today's scripture assures us that He
is faithful (won't leave you) and just (sure) to forgive us our sins.
He offers a do-over. Not only that, He cleanses us from the
inside out of all our wickedness. Whew! Talk about a fresh start!

So, what's stopping you? Your do-over awaits!

Lord, I'm so grateful for second chances. I've messed
up so many times and in so many ways. Sometimes
I want to hide in the corner. But You're a God
of do-overs. Thank You for redeeming even the
worst situation and offering me new chances.

Others Focused

Do to others as you would like them to do to you.
LUKE 6:31 NLT

We live in a "me, myself, and I" time, don't we? Turn on the television and you see commercials focused on improving self with makeup, perfume, or health products. Check out the latest, greatest books and you'll find a zillion self-help titles, guaranteed to bring you great success and happiness. Not that focusing on self brings happiness. Not at all. Glance in the mirror and you'll see a dozen reasons to complain about how you look or to wish you could trade lives with someone else. Such are the woes of hyper-focusing on yourself, after all!

It's time to turn our gaze off of "self" to those around us. When we're "others" focused, there's very little to complain about. Our own needs and wants take a backseat. Oh, it's hard at first. Turning your eyes from self to others is never easy. But the rewards? They're out of this world!

Dear Lord, I'm so glad that You are turning my focus. I don't want to be self-absorbed. When my gaze is turned to those around me, I see Your heart for mankind, not my wants and wishes for myself. Thank You for offering me this God-focused perspective.

Perfect Peace

*You will keep in perfect peace
those whose minds are steadfast,
because they trust in you.*
ISAIAH 26:3 NIV

Peace is an elusive thing. We allow our emotions to control us and then wonder why peace rarely follows. Strangely, peace has nothing to do with emotions. Ponder that for a moment. Your peace—or lack thereof—isn't controlled by an emotional puppeteer. You can choose peace in the middle of the storms of life.

What's robbing you of your peace today? Take that "thing" (situation, person, etc.) and write it down on a piece of paper, and then pray over it and shred it. Release it to God. Keep your mind steadfast on God, not what was written on the paper. It's no longer the driving force in your life. Your trust is in God, and He cares even more about your situation (or that person) than you do, anyway.

Letting go. . .taking your hand off. . .will bring peace. It's never easy to release something that's had a hold on you, but you will be blessed with supernatural peace once you do.

*Oh, Lord! I've been holding on to things I should have
let go of ages ago. Please forgive me, Father! Today
I release those things into Your hands. As I let go,
flood me with Your peace from on high!*

Sabbath Rest

Now, since God has left us the promise that we may enter his rest, let us be very careful so none of you will fail to enter.
HEBREWS 4:1 NCV

We move at such a rapid pace. Life tugs and pulls at us and we respond, sprinting toward goal after goal. What overachievers we are!

The Lord never intended for us to go around the clock. He didn't design our bodies to run in "energizer bunny" mode 24-7. We can live like this for a little while, sure, but eventually something's gotta give, and it's usually our health. Or our emotions. Or our relationships. Or—worst of all—our times of intimacy with God.

We are created in the image of God, and He is always on the move! Still, He instigated the Sabbath for a reason, because He knows mankind's tendency to go, go, go. Sure, we have work to do. Yes, we have people to care for and souls to reach. But if we're broken down from lack of sleep or from over-extending ourselves, there won't be anything to offer others. So, slow down! Take a breather. For that matter, take a nap. And don't apologize for it! Moments of respite are precious.

Lord, thank You for the reminder that You want me to rest. It's not always easy. I'm such a go-getter, but I have to confess that taking a break feels really, really good. Draw me away to Your side for a special time of rest, I pray.

Corporate Worship

Praise the LORD!
Sing to the LORD a new song.
Sing his praises in the assembly of the faithful.
PSALM 149:1 NLT

Worship is so powerful in a private, intimate setting, but there's something equally as powerful in corporate worship. There, side-by-side with other Christians, we lift our hearts, our voices, our words of praise in a mighty, thunderous chorus. What bliss! And, what a wonderful way to prepare for heaven, where we will gather around the throne of God and sing, "Holy, holy, holy!" together with all His people.

When we come into the house of God, like-minded and ready to focus on Him, we are a force to be reckoned with! The gates of hell cannot prevail against us. Two or more (in this case, often hundreds) are gathered together in unity. And unity is the key. Likeminded. Together.

When we enter into corporate worship, we aren't focused on self. The problems of the day wash away. We aren't focused on others, though they are surrounding us on every side. We are solely focused on God, the one we adore. Our eyes, our hearts, our thoughts, are on Him, alone.

Father, I love worshiping with fellow believers.
What a blast to stand alongside my brothers
and sisters in Christ to lift my voice in song and
to hear Your Word preached. Whether we're
singing, praying, or hearing a life-changing
message, we do it all for You.

Joy for the Journey

The LORD is my strength and my shield;
my heart trusts in him, and he helps me.
My heart leaps for joy, and with my song I praise him.
PSALM 28:7 NIV

There are times when joy seems impossible. When you're going through a rough season, for instance, or when you're face to face with a proverbial Goliath. The enemy of your soul would like nothing more than to rob you of your joy. He's skilled at tripping you up, creating havoc.

But guess what? It's possible to praise—to be joyful—even in the middle of the battle. There's a great story in the Old Testament about a man named Jehoshaphat who was facing a mighty opposition—an army, no less! He sent the Levites (the praise and worshipers) to the front lines. In other words, he led the way into the battle with praise on the lips of his warriors. And guess what? They prevailed!

The same is true in our lives. We must lead the way with praise. If we will maintain the joy in our hearts, even in the midst of our battles, we will be triumphant in the end. So, don't let the enemy steal your joy, even if you're walking through a difficult season. There are plenty of victories ahead if you don't give up.

Lord, I must confess, I don't always feel like singing a song of
praise when I'm facing a huge battle. In fact, I
usually just want to curl up in a ball and give up.
Thank You for this reminder that I can be joyful,
even when I'm in the middle of a struggle.

A Healthy Body

*My dear friend, I know your soul is doing fine, and I pray that
you are doing well in every way and that your health is good.*

3 JOHN 1:2 NCV

If you've ever faced a health crisis or watched a loved one go
through a catastrophic illness, you realize the value of good
health. There's nothing like almost losing it to realize what
you've had all along! In spite of modern technology, great
doctors, and the advance of research, health issues persist.

We face seasons where our bodies refuse to cooperate with
us. During those times we have to remember who our healer
really is. Doctors are great, but ultimately, God is our healer. He
longs for us to turn to Him—to trust Him—during our seasons
of physical and emotional weakness. He also longs for us to
take care of the bodies He's given us. How can we do this? By
watching what we put in it and by getting the proper amount
of rest and exercise. Our vessels are precious gifts, and we can't
afford to wreck them with excessive food or poor nutrition.

If you're in a rough place health-wise, pour out your heart
to the Lord. Ask Him to show you the foods that you should
be eating and the ones you should avoid. Visit your doctor and
get his input, as well. Working as a team, focus on turning your
health issues around.

*Father, I don't want to abuse this precious vessel
You've entrusted to me. I need to take better care of
my body. Show me Your plan for my health, Lord,
then guide me as I take steps toward better health.*

Mid-Week Attitude

You must have the same attitude that Christ Jesus had.
PHILIPPIANS 2:5 NLT

If someone hollered, "Attitude check!" what would come to mind? Years ago, church folks were taught to respond with, "Praise the Lord!" This is the best way to check your attitude, after all—by lifting words of praise instead of grumbling.

Praising the Lord is easy on Sundays. But, by the middle of the week, we're often facing work-related stresses, school woes with the kids, exhaustion, and more. It's not always so easy to keep our attitude in check, is it?

If we follow the mandate in today's scripture—if we really have the same attitude that Christ Jesus had—we will keep our focus on the goal. What's your goal? Your calling? Jesus kept His eye on the cross. You must keep your eye on the goal you've been called to during this season of your life. Perhaps it's raising children. Or participating in ministry. Or a particular job. Maybe you're called to start a Bible study or write a book. You can trust God to help you as you maintain forward motion. When you're looking ahead with expectation in your heart, the midweek attitude won't be so difficult. After all, you're not focused on today. . .your eye is on the prize.

Thank You, Lord, for the reminder that You've got big plans for me! How could I be discouraged when You're guiding me toward my destiny? I thank You in advance for what's ahead and trust You to get me there on Your timetable.

Every Good Work

*And God can give you more blessings than you need.
Then you will always have plenty of everything—
enough to give to every good work.*

2 CORINTHIANS 9:8 NCV

Maybe you cringe every time you hear that God wants to bless you. Perhaps you think that message is overblown by television evangelists or positive thinkers. Here's a biblical truth: We serve a God who owns the cattle on a thousand hills. He has more than enough for every situation. Does that mean He's going to shower down excessive heavenly blessings on you every day? Maybe not, but there will definitely be days—and seasons—when the blessings flow.

Whether you're in a season of plenty or lack, remember that God hasn't forgotten you. Today's scripture is a promise you can take to the bank. He can give you more than you need. When He does, you will have plenty of everything. Specifically, you will have enough to do the work that He has called you to.

So, brace yourself! Maybe those TV preachers are on to something. God loves you so much and wants to give you what you need, not so that you can gloat in your possessions, but so that you are equipped to do His work.

*Lord, I get it. You don't want to bless me just for the
sake of spoiling me. You long to give me the things
I'm lacking so that I'm well-equipped to carry forth
Your message to my friends and loved ones.
Thank You, Father!*

Emptiness

*You have made known to me the paths of life;
you will fill me with joy in your presence.*
ACTS 2:28 NIV

Imagine you're looking at a full-to-the-brim rain barrel. You've been in a season of abundant rain. It never occurs to you that a dry season might be around the corner.

Now picture yourself, weeks later, staring down into the barrel, noticing that it's bone dry. Drought has taken its toll. Now you have a picture of what it's like when you go through a season of spiritual wholeness and spiritual drought. Your rain barrel—your heart—is only as full as what's poured into it.

Did you realize that God can refill your heart with just one word? When He sees that your well is running dry it breaks His heart. The only solution is to run to His arms and ask for a fresh outpouring of His holy water, the kind that will replenish your soul and give you the nourishment you need to move forward in Him.

It's up to you. God is waiting to meet with you. His everlasting water is prepped and ready to be poured out on you. All you need to do. . .is run to Him.

*Father, I've been blaming my dry spell on so many different
things: Exhaustion. Frustration. You name it,
I've pointed the finger at it. Lord, I need the kind
of water that You provide—the kind that will
never run dry. Today, Lord, I run into Your arms,
ready to be refreshed!*

Spring Break

*You are the giver of life.
Your light lets us enjoy life.*
PSALM 36:9 NCV

Don't you love spring break? It's a great opportunity to celebrate the season. Kids romping and playing in the sunshine. A trip to the park. Catching up on sleep. Pausing to enjoy the celebration of life around you. Making plans for the summer. These are the little things, but they mean oh, so much!

Doesn't matter how you choose to enjoy your break, it can be lovely. Even if you can't take the time off. Even if you're not surrounded by everyone you'd hoped to spend time with. Even if nothing is as you wish. You can choose to set aside this special time, just you and God.

Make the most of it. Sit outside on the porch swing. Take a walk in the springtime sunshine. Praise Him for the change of seasons. Pay attention—really pay attention—to the budding of the flowers and the greening of the leaves and grass. Before long, a true celebration will erupt in your heart, one you won't soon forget. So, what are you waiting for? Make this a "break" to remember!

*Father, things don't always turn out like I'd hoped.
I make plans and they don't pan out. This year,
regardless of my situation, I choose to take a "spring
break" with You. Let's spend extra-special time
together, Lord! I'll meet You in the sunshine,
and we'll take a long walk together.*

Carrying the Cross

*Then Jesus said to his disciples, "If any of you wants
to be my follower, you must turn from your selfish
ways, take up your cross, and follow me."*
MATTHEW 16:24 NLT

The Easter season is the perfect time to focus on Jesus and
the work He did on the cross. He bore the sins of mankind,
the burden of our transgressions upon Him as He hung dying.
The weight of our sin started taking its toll from the moment
the heavy wooden cross was placed upon our Savior's back. He
carried it up the Via Dolorosa, the Way of Sorrows, with only
one thing on His mind: us. No matter how painful, no matter
how agonizing, Jesus didn't stop walking. He carried, carried,
carried the cross. . .all the way to Calvary.

There are many instances in life when we feel as if we are
carrying a cross—a heavy burden. We have God's assurance
that He won't ever let us face temptation too strong to bear. But
that doesn't mean we won't feel weighted down at times. This
is especially true when we're living for the Lord. He asks us to
lay our selfishness down and to focus on others. This can seem
burdensome at times, but it's actually God's way of giving us
freedom. And there's nothing less weighty than freedom in Him!

*Father, life is hard at times. Heavy. Things
don't always go my way, and I have to put
my selfishness aside. It's not easy, but thank You
for the reminder that You were willing to carry
the cross all the way to Calvary for me.
I can carry whatever crosses come my
way. . .with Your Help.*

A Small Deal

Each one should test their own actions.
Then they can take pride in themselves alone,
without comparing themselves to someone else.
GALATIANS 6:4 NIV

Do you have a tendency to overreact to life's challenges? Do you make a big deal out of things? If so, it's time to accept a challenge. For a full week, make up your mind to "make a small deal" out of your challenges. When you're tempted to panic, take a deep breath, count to ten, and make the smallest possible scenario out of it that you can. Will this be difficult? Absolutely. Is it possible? Definitely.

When you decide to create "big deals" out of everyday situations, you find yourself facing relationship strains, high blood pressure, and other woes. These things morph and grow to crazy proportions when you overreact. When you choose "small deals" you will experience forgiveness, peace, and the ability to bounce back without holding bitterness. It's your choice!

When you opt to make a "small deal" out of things, you will also have the satisfaction of knowing that you are pleasing your heavenly Father's heart. Now, that's a very big deal!

Lord, I don't want to be seen as someone who
overreacts to things. I acknowledge that I've
done this at times. Please remove this tendency
from me so that I can live at peace with others.
I want to please Your heart, Father.

St. Patrick's Day: Leaving a Legacy

But the LORD's love for those who respect him continues forever and ever, and his goodness continues to their grandchildren.
PSALM 103:17 NCV

Have you given any thought to the legacy you will leave behind after you're gone? If you're a mom or a grandma, you surely have pondered the generations coming up behind you. Maybe you've wondered what, specifically, they will remember about you. If you're not yet married or don't have children of your own, perhaps you could give thought to the legacy you will leave behind to your friends, coworkers, and/or neighbors.

It's an amazing thing to think about God's goodness carrying on from one generation to another, and then another. If you really pause to think it through, the original twelve disciples left a legacy for the early church. Those dedicated believers—in spite of persecution and pain—left a legacy for the next generation, and so on. Without the seeds they planted, the church would surely not have survived.

It's so important to press through. Be a seed planter, no matter how difficult your life. Others are watching and gleaning from your example.

Father, I can see how important my seed-planting is! I want to leave a legacy, Lord. Above all else, I want people to remember me for my walk with You.

A Creative God

In the beginning God created the heavens and the earth.
GENESIS 1:1 NIV

Did you realize that you are made (designed, created) in the image of a very creative God? It's true! He breathed life into you, after all. It stands to reason that some of His creativity would have spilled over into you, His daughter.

The same God who created the heavens and the earth—who decided a giraffe's neck should be several feet long and a penguin should waddle around in tuxedo-like attire—designed you, inside and out! And He gifted you with a variety of gifts and abilities, all of which can be used to His glory.

So, what creative gifts reside inside of you? Have you given them a stir lately? Maybe it's time to ask God which gifts are most useable for this season of your life. He's creative enough to stir the ones that can be used to reach others. He will bring them to the surface and prepare you to use them—much like He did during Creation—to bring beauty out of dark places.

So, brace yourself! Your very creative God has big things planned for you!

Lord, thank You for creating me in Your image. I get so excited when I think about the fact that Your creativity lives inside of me. Just as Your Spirit moved across creation in the book of Genesis, I ask You to move across the creative gifts in my life and stir them to life!

G.R.A.C.E.

Because he was full of grace and truth,
from him we all received one gift after another.
JOHN 1:16 NCV

Perhaps you've seen the acronym for G.R.A.C.E. (God's Riches at Christ's Expense). What does that mean to us, His daughters? We face all sorts of challenges and sometimes feel depleted. Dry. In those moments, all of God's riches (peace, joy, longsuffering, favor, help) are ours. What did we do to deserve them? Nothing. That's the point of grace: someone else paid the price so that we could receive God's gifts for free.

Take a good look at today's scripture. God promises not only to give grace and truth, but one gift after another. Picture yourself as a little girl at your daddy's knee. Now picture him giving you not one gift. . .not two. . .but one on top of the other, on top of the other. He overwhelms you with his beautifully wrapped gifts, topped off with ribbons and bows. Talk about blowing your socks off!

God does the same thing when He "gifts" us with things we don't deserve: forgiveness, comfort, satisfaction, provision. What a generous God we serve!

Father, I know that I haven't done anything
to deserve Your grace. . .Your gifts. And yet, You
continue to pour these things out on my life anyway.
Thank You for Your grace, Lord. You give, and
give, and then give some more.

Responsibility

*From the Israelites' half, Moses selected one out of every
fifty people and animals, as the Lord commanded him,
and gave them to the Levites, who were responsible
for the care of the Lord's tabernacle.*

NUMBERS 31:47 NIV

As women, we face the word *responsibility* at every turn. We're
responsible, not only for ourselves, but often for our families,
as well. Sometimes responsibility can get old. Carpool. Work.
Exercise. Healthy eating. It gets old. We just want to be
irresponsible for a while, forget about being "big girls" and resort
to childish behavior.

God is all over the idea that we should rest. Step back. But
He's not a fan of irresponsibility. It's okay to break from your
work for a designated season, but don't opt out for long. To be
responsible is to be disciplined, and we please God's heart when
we remain disciplined. Especially when it's hard.

You have a job to do. For that matter, you have many jobs
to do. And God will strengthen you for the tasks in front of you.
You're not alone. Start each morning in prayer and thank Him
for entrusting these things to you, then dive in. He will meet you
there!

*Father, sometimes I want to hang up my
"responsible" hat and put on my "irresponsible"
one for a while. Thank You for working through
me, Lord. I need Your energy, Your strength,
Your version of discipline!*

A Princess Mindset

For God is the King over all the earth.
Praise him with a psalm.
PSALM 47:7 NLT

You are a daughter of the King of kings, true royalty! In spite of that fact, it's often difficult to see yourself that way, isn't it? When you're feeling bedraggled and tired, when you're facing mounting bills, when your enemies rise up against you, it's easier to feel like a little peasant girl.

It's time for a princess mindset! You've got to remember several things: First, the King welcomes you into His presence. In fact, He bids you to come as often as possible. Second, you're going to live forever with the King! You'll walk on streets of gold and live in a mansion. Third, the Prince of Peace lives in your heart. Accepting Jesus as Savior assures you of a personal, day-in, day-out conversation with the One who spun the heavens and the earth into existence.

You. Are. Royalty. Of course, that also means you have to live like a daughter of the King! You're representing Him, after all. So, chin up. Put all whining and complaining aside. People are watching you so that they can know how a daughter of the King lives. Lead by example, Princess!

Father, You are the King of kings! How often I forget that being Your child makes me a princess in Your sight. I want to live in such a way that others are drawn to my Daddy, God, by my actions.

A Joyful Noise

Sing aloud unto God our strength:
make a joyful noise unto the God of Jacob.
PSALM 81:1 KJV

Aren't you glad the Bible commands us to "make a joyful noise unto the Lord" instead of saying something like "Sing like an angel"? Many are born with amazing vocal abilities. They wow us with their choir productions and their amazing solo performances. But some of the rest of us are lucky to croak out a word or two in the right key.

God doesn't care about your vocal abilities. He longs to hear a song of praise rise up out of your heart, even if it's sung in three or four keys. Think about that for a moment. He's listening as millions of believers sing out—in every language, every key, every pitch. And it doesn't bother Him one bit because He's not listening to the technique, He's listening to the heart.

Still not convinced? Read the book of Psalms from start to finish. It will stir up a song in your heart, and before long your toes will be tapping and your heart bursting. Why? Because you were created to praise Him. So, don't worry about what others will think. Make a joyful noise!

Lord, my heart wants to sing happy songs today!
I'm not going to worry anymore about my voice,
whether I'm singing in church or in the car or in
the shower. I was made to praise You, Father,
so I choose to make a joyful noise!

Whiter than Snow

Take away my sin, and I will be clean.
Wash me, and I will be whiter than snow.
PSALM 51:7 NCV

If you've ever looked out over a pristine, white field covered
in glistening mounds of white snow, you know what purity
looks like. Everything underneath those mounds of snow has
disappeared from view, to be seen no more. The white snow
covers it all, making it irrelevant.

That's how forgiveness works. When we come to God
and confess our sins, He is faithful and just to forgive us. His
forgiveness washes over us in exactly the same way that the
snow covers the ground below. All traces of yesterday—the
awful things we've done, the pain we've caused, the heartache
we've gone through—are gone. In place of the bad memories,
glistening white forgiveness, sparkling with the hope of better
days to come.

If you haven't yet asked Jesus to be the Lord of your life,
if you haven't accepted His forgiveness for the sins you've
committed, this is the perfect day—the perfect season—to do so.
He can wash your sins away and leave you whiter than snow.

Father, even though it's springtime, I love the image of snow
that I find in this scripture. It's a reminder that my
past really can be in the past. I want to live for
today, Lord, so that I can have the courage to
step into tomorrow without worrying about
what happened yesterday. Cleanse me, Lord!

Clear Vision

*In the same way, wisdom is pleasing to you.
If you find it, you have hope for the future,
and your wishes will come true.*

PROVERBS 24:14 NCV

If you've ever worn glasses, you know what it's like to try to go without them. Talk about a fuzzy world! You take tentative steps, cautiously moving forward, knowing that, at any minute, you might trip over something or knock something down.

Clarity of vision is a wonderful gift. Once you put those glasses on, you can clearly see the road ahead and take bold, big steps. Confidence rises up inside of you as you focus on the path set before you.

In this same way, God can bring clarity/vision to your path when you ask for His wisdom. Picture yourself in a rough situation. You don't know which way to go. You ask for the Lord's wisdom. He offers it, and the road ahead of you is suddenly clear. It's as if you've put on spiritual glasses! That's what His wisdom does—gives definition. Boldness. Confidence. Makes clear the path.

What are you waiting for? No need for a fuzzy road ahead. Put on those glasses, girl, then take a bold step forward!

*Father, I'm so excited that I don't have to walk around
confused and blinded. No fuzzy roads for me, Lord!
Today I pause to ask for Your wisdom so that the
road ahead will be clear. Thank You for great
vision and the confidence to move forward.*

Knowing Who You Are in Christ

*We are made right with God by placing our
faith in Jesus Christ. And this is true for
everyone who believes, no matter who we are.*

ROMANS 3:22 NLT

Sometimes we measure our value by "what we do" (our work or
our talents), but this should never be. Who you are is more than
a name. More than a face. More than the job/work you do. You
are uniquely created, a true one of a kind. You are God's kid. His.
Loved. Cherished. Blessed.

What does the Bible say about you? You are: a new creation.
A royal priesthood. A holy nation. The righteousness of God. A
holy temple. A member of the body. A citizen of heaven. Saved
by faith. Raised up by Him. The aroma of Christ. Filled with
heavenly gifts. Delivered from the domain of darkness. Capable
of doing all things through Him who strengthens you. On and
on the descriptions go.

Wow! When you read all of those things, you begin to see
yourself as God sees you. You're not "just" another person. You're
a child of the One True King, and He delights in you! Today, take
a close look in the mirror. Don't stare at your reflection in the usual
way. Get God's perspective. Then begin to see yourself the way He
does.

*Lord, I needed this reminder that I'm all of
the things you say I am. First and foremost,
I'm yours! So, no putting myself down,
Father! Give me Your eyes to see myself
the way You see me.*

Trust and Obey

*So they would all trust God
and would not forget what he had done
but would obey his commands.*

PSALM 78:7 NCV

From the time we were children, we knew the song: "Trust and obey, for there's no other way to be happy in Jesus than to trust and obey."

It's one thing to talk about trust, another to live it. And here's the problem: if you don't trust God, you probably won't obey His commands. So, these two things go hand in hand. Don't believe it? Here's an example: imagine the Lord asked you to take a huge step of faith, something completely outside of your comfort zone. You would likely hesitate. But, would you eventually take the step, even if it made no sense to you? If you trusted God—if you had seen Him work time and time again in your life—you would eventually take the step of faith, even if it made no sense. Why? Because you trust that He's got your best interest at heart. (And you've probably figured out that He has something pretty remarkable up His sleeve!)

God is trustworthy. He won't let you down. Once you settle that issue in your heart once and for all, obedience is a natural response.

*Father, I know I can trust You. Sure, there
will be faith-journeys ahead. I know that.
But Lord, I want to obey, to step out boldly.
When I do, You take me to new, exciting places
I've never been before. Thank You for
leading and guiding, Father!*

Offense

*"Isn't this the carpenter? Isn't this Mary's son and the
brother of James, Joseph, Judas and Simon? Aren't his
sisters here with us?" And they took offense at him.*

MARK 6:3 NIV

"I'm so offended!" How many times have you felt like crying out
these words? Probably more times than you could count. We all
go through periods of offense, especially when we feel like there's
a target on our backs. Some people wear offense like an out-of-
season garment. It's always with them, but it's not terribly pretty
or appropriate.

Jesus certainly knew what it felt like to be rejected, but
He wasn't one for offense. The same couldn't be said about the
religious zealots who had it out for Him, though. They took
offense at everything! If Jesus healed someone on the Sabbath,
they got offended. If He spoke the truth about His deity, they
got offended about that, too!

You know, there are some people who are just going to be
offended. You can tip-toe around all day trying to protect their
feelings, but it's a waste of time. Instead of worrying about
hyper-sensitive people, try turning your focus to God. Make
sure your life, your words, and your actions aren't offensive to
Him. As long as you can answer in good conscience to your
heavenly Father, He can take care of the feelings of others. And
while you're at it, lay aside any feelings of offense you might be
carrying. They will only weigh you down.

*Father, I choose to lay down my offenses today.
Help me forgive those who have offended.
And Lord, help me not to tip-toe around those
who are easily offended. Deal with their
hearts in Your own way and time, Father.
They are not mine to fix.*

Preparing for the Journey Ahead

*The LORD your God has blessed you in all the work of
your hands. He has watched over your journey through
this vast wilderness. These forty years the LORD your
God has been with you, and you have not lacked anything.*

DEUTERONOMY 2:7 NIV

If you've ever packed for a vacation, you know what it's like—you
stare at mounds of clothes in your suitcase and wonder, "How
much of this am I really going to need?"

The truth is, some women overprepare. We pack too many
shoes, too many blouses, too many pieces of jewelry. We're so over
burdened with stuff that the journey gets off to a rocky start.

Now think about this from a spiritual perspective. Picture
the Israelites in the wilderness. They could only take with them
what they could carry for the journey. Too much baggage and the
journey would be slow-going.

If you knew the Lord was about to lead you into a new
experience with Him, what would you take with you? Maybe it's
time to scale back. Ask God what's important to keep—and what
to get rid of. Shake off the nonessentials (things like bitterness,
unforgiveness, and anger) and move forward into a new place
with the Lord. He will replace those missing items with things
like peace, joy, and love. Ah, now that's traveling light!

*Lord, I don't want to make my journey harder
than it already is. I don't want to drag around
weighty things like bitterness, jealousy, pain, and
frustration. Today I lay those things down.
Please refill my spiritual luggage with peace.
Joy. Hope. Gentleness.*

Hosanna! Lifting Praise!

*And they that went before, and they that followed,
cried, saying, Hosanna; Blessed is he that
cometh in the name of the Lord.*

MARK 11:9 KJV

There's something about the word *Hosanna* that stirs excitement within us. "Hosanna!" Pure adoration. Praise. Worship. When Jesus rode into Jerusalem the week before His crucifixion, His followers had no clue what was coming. With joy-filled hearts, they worshipped. One week later, with Jesus' body in the tomb, their adoration turned to pain.

Here's the wonderful thing about our worship: God expects it from us, whether you're facing a joyous moment or a pain-filled one. Why? Because He realizes that the "Hosannas" we usher forth are battle cries. When we cry out to Him with praise, especially during tough seasons, His heart is stirred.

Jesus rose from the grave! The "Hosannas" from the week prior were still very much on His mind. And, as His followers witnessed the resurrection for themselves, they surely realized that their praises could carry on, not just for the Passion Week, but for all eternity.

*Lord, I see now that You want me to praise You,
to sing "Hosanna" every day of my life. Whether
things are going well or crumbling around me,
I choose to offer praise and adoration.
You are worthy, Father!*

Difficult Weeks

The LORD hears his people when they call to him for help.
He rescues them from all their troubles.
PSALM 34:17 NLT

We all go through difficult seasons. Sometimes they stretch over many days, filling up a whole week. Health challenges. Financial woes. Relationship struggles. They can be so frustrating and interrupt the daily flow of things. Nothing seems—or feels—right.

Today, as you think about the rough weeks you've faced in your life, pause for a moment to remember the week before Jesus' crucifixion. He rode into Jerusalem with "Hosannas!" ringing out all around Him, but things took a turn for the worse pretty quickly. In just a matter of days He went from "local hero" to persecuted, beaten, bruised, betrayed, and crucified.

We could stop right there and be filled with a sense of desperation, but thank goodness, the story goes on. A new week began the following Sunday—a week of resurrection and glory as Jesus came forth from the grave! In much the same way, our bad seasons will turn around. New life will come. Hope will be restored. The key lies in not giving up. Trust Him. Even when it doesn't make sense. The grave clothes are coming off! He's breathing new life into your family, your situations, your finances, and your very soul.

Father, I know You understand! What a terrible week
Your Son faced in Jerusalem. I can't even imagine
all He went through, but it must have broken Your
heart. Thank You for the reminder that the next
week was filled with resurrection power!
This brings me such hope!

Commune with Me

*The cup of blessing which we bless, is it not the communion
of the blood of Christ? The bread which we break,
is it not the communion of the body of Christ?*

1 CORINTHIANS 10:16 KJV

Oh, what a blessed privilege, to commune with the Lord. To spend time with Him. To break bread together. To remember the work that Jesus did on the cross. Yet how often do we do this without really "remembering" the depth of its meaning?

The night that Jesus was betrayed—the very night before some of His closest followers turned on Him—He sat down for a special meal with them. He took the bread and broke it, then explained that it, symbolically, provided the perfect picture of what was about to happen to His very body on the cross. Then He took the cup of wine and explained that it, too, had pertinent symbolism, for it represented His blood, which was about to be spilled on Calvary.

The disciples surely couldn't comprehend fully what Jesus was talking about, but less than twenty-four hours later, it was abundantly clear. And now, two thousand years later, it's clearer still. And Jesus still bids us to come and commune with Him. He longs for us to remember—to never forget—the price that He paid on the cross that day.

Commune with me. Such simple words from God to mankind. Run to Him today. Spend time in holy, sweet communion.

*Father, I get it! It's not just about breaking
bread together. It's all about spending time
with You. Being with You. Remembering
all You did for me. I long to curl up next to
You and hear Your heartbeat today, Lord.
I choose to commune with You.*

Talking to the Father

*The prayer of a righteous person
is powerful and effective.*
JAMES 5:16 NIV

We have all had those inevitable days when we are exhausted or discouraged and it seems too hard to carry on. We might feel as dry as the desert sand, with nothing left to give. This is a time when we could use nourishment for our souls.

The prophet Zechariah said, "Ask the Lord for rain in the springtime, and he will answer with lightning and showers." Matthew Henry explained this scripture: "Spiritual blessings had been promised. . .We must in our prayers ask for mercies in their proper time. The Lord would make bright clouds and give showers of rain. . .when we seek the influences of the Holy Spirit in faith and by prayer, through which the blessing held forth in the promises are obtained."

When these times hit, use "knee mail." Don't just "tweet" a short sigh to the Lord, but carve out some time to pray, to praise, and petition our heavenly Father for strength to carry on. He is faithful to answer our pleas and send refreshment to our hearts. It could be in the form of a restful night's sleep, a friend or relative to exhort and encourage, or a stranger's greeting. We never know how the Lord will answer our petitions, but answer He will. God's inbox is never too full.

*Dear Lord, how we long for Your presence.
Father, hear our prayers this day;
extend Your hand of mercy to me. Amen.*

It's Really Mine?

*And if we are [His] children, then we are [His]
heirs also: heirs of God and fellow heirs with
Christ [sharing His inheritance with Him].*
ROMANS 8:17 AMP

An inheritance is a bequest, a birthright, a legacy. And as
children of God we can be given that inheritance. It's hard to
believe, but the Word tells us it is true. To attain that inheritance,
however, we must know the correct password.

Christians have but one password: Jesus. Once we acquire
this password through salvation and set our hope in Him, we
become heirs of Christ. Children of the King. Precious saints.
Names given to us by the Father so that we can inherit His
kingdom.

Unlike the security passwords for a business, this password
cannot be hacked or compromised. We are safe and secure in the
Father's arms and able to access the gifts He has promised.

Gain your password to swing open the gates of heaven
by professing your belief in the resurrected Christ Jesus. Jesus
period. No other name is needed. Choose this day to accept your
inheritance. Then read the fine print in His Word. So many
scriptures tell all that is available to you as a believer. Eternal life,
provision, blessing upon blessing. What amazing gifts He has for us.

*Dear heavenly Father, today I choose to follow
You. I give You my life, my all. Teach me
Your ways and guard my heart that I
might gain my inheritance. Amen.*

Do Not Lose Heart

And they crucified Him.
MARK 15:24 NIV

How can it be called Good Friday? It seems incongruous when we know what took place. A video that is entitled "It's Friday... But Sunday's Coming" has made the rounds of many churches. A deep voice rumbles and tells of the death of Christ. But the words in the title—Sunday's coming—reveal the hope and joy for Christians to live in expectation. Jesus was crucified, died, and paid for our sins. They buried Him. Yes. And it was indeed a dark time.

Then on Sunday, He arose! Hallelujah.

As we walk our Christian pathway, let's not forget that despite any dark times in our lives, our "Sunday" is coming. When we realize all Jesus has done for us, how can we not have hope? Circumstances might be bleak, but we continue to trust in the Lord our God, for scripture states He is in control. Scripture states He has a plan for us. It might not be what we anticipated, but when we are in an attitude of surrender, His ideas outshine any we might have.

If you are in difficulty, don't give in to despair. Look forward to the future. Lift your voice of praise to Him who died on the cross. Shed your tears for today, then allow the Holy Spirit to minister to your aching heart. Put aside your mourning, for Sunday's coming.

Dear Jesus, it is difficult to comprehend that Your death on the cross was to pay for my sins. Thank You, Jesus, for Your sacrificial gift. Amen.

Who Are You?

*He came into the world, and though the world
was made through Him, the world did not
recognize Him [did not know Him].*
JOHN 1:10 AMP

Have you ever seen someone, spoken to them, and the whole
time your brain is running through your database—who is
this person? You can't place him or her in context. One of life's
frustrating moments, until the aha moment, and a sigh of relief
trickles in. Yes, you do know who it is. Certainly a trusted friend
wouldn't require you to frantically scroll through a list because
you have a relationship with that person.

Does your database recognize the One who created you?
Do you have a passing acquaintance with God or do you have
a relationship with Jesus? Are you certain or filled with doubts?
This unease can be fixed with an open heart and a sincere prayer
for salvation.

A footnote in the Amplified Bible states, "It is not enough
that one knows God is God, for only a fool would deny that, but
God demands of every person who is to be recognized by Him
that he accept Him as Lord of his life, his Sovereign Ruler, to
Whom he yields implicit obedience. When Thomas was able to
say of Jesus, 'My Lord and my God!' his doubts ceased to exist."

*Dear Jesus, I look to You this day in full surrender.
I choose to have a relationship with You. Please
come into my heart and be my Lord. Amen.*

Having It All

*I came that they may have and enjoy life, and have it in
abundance (to the full, till it overflows).*
JOHN 10:10 AMP

Today is the day we mark the risen Christ. Does He live in your
heart? Is He the very light of your life? An abundant life follows
when we ask Him to be our Savior, for the Holy Spirit to reign
supreme.

We can get everything we want with our birthdays,
Christmas, the malls, dot com websites. The ever-looming
question becomes "Oh but is it what we need?" Scripture tells
us to keep our eyes fixed on Him. John spoke of Jesus and
how a spiritual life can and will fulfill us beyond our wildest
expectations.

God does not promise us abundance. He promises that we
might have life and have it more abundantly if we accept His
grace, His blessings, and His Son. When we commit our hearts
and our days to Him we experience spiritual abundance. But
when our focus is on the world, we will inevitably forfeit the
spiritual abundance that might be ours.

Think today and choose this abundant life by accepting
Jesus. Scripture tells us to acknowledge Jesus by confessing that
He is Lord and believing God raised Him from the dead,
for that is the way to inherit eternal—abundant—life.

*Dear Lord, I do accept that Jesus was Your Son, that
He died, was buried, and rose again to save us from
our sin. Come to live in my heart this day. Amen.*

Growing Up

*And now, just as you accepted Christ Jesus as your Lord,
you must continue to follow him. Let your roots grow
down into him, and let your lives be built on him.
Then your faith will grow strong in the truth you were
taught, and you will overflow with thankfulness.*

COLOSSIANS 2:6–7 NLT

When we reach out to the heavenly Father and choose to accept
Him into our hearts, our journey has just begun. We want to
walk on the pathways He has chosen for us, and to do that, we
must learn to follow the map: His Word. The foundation of our
faith must be built on Christ's presence in our lives. Building
a strong foundation takes time, so don't become fainthearted
when you walk forward a few steps only to slide back. Our God
understands our struggles.

In Him we are planted so that our roots grow strong. In
Him we are built up, by studying and hearing the Word and
fellowshipping with other believers. In Him we are established,
as the foundation is dug deeper and cemented firmly.

This is not a quick process; it is a journey, and we cannot say
one day we will arrive. For these are lifelong lessons and we are
guided by the Holy Spirit. Each time we open His Word and
hear His voice, we experience something new. He is an awesome
God. Let us give thanks to the great Teacher.

*Dear Jesus, we love You and are so grateful You
sacrificed Your life for us. Teach us what we
should know to become close followers of You.*

An Extravagant God

Return to the LORD your God,
for he is merciful and compassionate,
slow to get angry and filled with unfailing love.
JOEL 2:13 NLT

There are often times when we are exhausted and discouraged and we allow our minds to roam to dark places. Despair and disappointment set in. A woe-is-me attitude prevails within us. How is it possible to rise from the doldrums? How do we continue? We turn our faces toward the Lord God and know He is in control.

Scripture tells of God's mercy and loving-kindness. It speaks out and urges us to come back to God. This doesn't necessarily mean a change of circumstances, but a change of heart. This change is a choice we intentionally make. It's not necessary to be in a church building or a revival when we make this choice. While many changes happen there, ours can be in our closet, our car, or our office. We reach inwardly to the Highest and ask for His mercy. And scripture says He is merciful and full of grace. He hears our prayers.

Focusing on the negative, choosing despair, doesn't bring life. Voluntarily focusing on Jesus will. Praise Him for all your blessings: they are there, look for them. Some might be tiny, others magnificent. But they're all because of our Lord Jesus Christ. He is a most patient God and extravagant in His love.

O heavenly Father, I praise Your name.
You are extravagant in Your love, and I
am grateful for all You've done. Amen.

I Can Count on You

Because of the LORD's great love we are not consumed,
for his compassions never fail. They are new
every morning; great is your faithfulness.

LAMENTATIONS 3:22–23 NIV

Thomas Chisholm penned words to a hymn which often resounds throughout churches: "Great is Thy Faithfulness." These words proclaim an eternal truth: God is with us always, through everything. "Pardon for sin and a peace that endureth. . . strength for today and bright hope for tomorrow." Despite any circumstance we can reach for the hand of our Father and know He is present.

God is faithful to us even when we are not faithful to Him. God keeps His promises even when we stray far from His will. He continues to love us even when we disobey. But God does not force His blessings upon us. To experience His love and grace, we must claim them for ourselves. With a conscious choice, we must ask Him to be present in our lives and then tune our hearts to listen to what He says. As His children we show our loyalty and devotion when we walk close to Him, committing our lives to the study of His Word. And as we learn of His promises, we realize we can count on Him.

Whatever our condition, we know for certain our God is faithful and loves us eternally. Be comforted. For God is here.

Dear Lord, how we praise Your name for
Your faithfulness. Forgive us when we
fall short of Your will for our lives.
Help us to hear Your whisper. Amen.

Hear Me Now?

*Don't worry about anything; instead, pray about everything.
Tell God what you need, and thank him for all he has done.*
PHILIPPIANS 4:6 NLT

Today we live in an anxious and worried world. As protection against this onslaught of fretfulness we need to absorb the truth of Scripture and the faithfulness of God. The Interpreter's Bible states: "Man has been trying. . .to substitute faith in the future for faith in God, but the result is not making sense. When prospects are rosy, man is hopeful; but when things are black, man is in despair. . . We have worshipped a future which is precarious instead of a God who is the same yesterday, today, and forever."

Not worrying is not easy. Living in communion with the Father doesn't remove the frustrations of our daily lives, but it should put them in perspective and in second place. Our shifted focus can make the problems seem smaller. When we heed His call and stay close to Him, our lives take on more peace. God's possibilities are not limited.

Yes, the Lord does know our needs, but He wants to hear from His children, so talk to Him. Voice your desires, whatever they may be, with a thankful heart. Expect to hear from Him when You listen. Rely on the promises in His Word.

*Dear Lord, I need more of You in my life. I want to
voice my concerns and desires to Your listening ear.
Thank You for loving me. Amen.*

I Surrender

I will rejoice in the Lord!
I will be joyful in the God of my salvation!
The Sovereign Lord is my strength!
He makes me as surefooted as a deer,
able to tread upon the heights.

HABAKKUK 3:18–19 NLT

Sometimes life seems like an uphill battle and we certainly don't feel like celebrating. We find ourselves frustrated by the demands of the day and worried about the future. It's just too difficult to stay the course—keep on keeping on. We're tempted to throw up our hands in frustration and quit. That's when we must realize we're in the perfect position: hands raised in surrender.

Learn that God's promises are true. When we relax in His care and focus on Him, He will be with us in all our difficulties. He didn't promise a life with no problems. He did promise to carry us through. In Proverbs 3:4 in the Amplified Bible, the word *trust* is extrapolated: lean on, trust in, and be confident in the Lord. Are we leaning on the Lord? Do we trust Him with our future and the future of those in our care? Have we become confident in His Word?

Surrender and trust. Two words that lead to life and joy. Choose to surrender and trust this day. He'll then bring you safely over the mountains.

Dear Lord, surrendering and trusting doesn't
come naturally. Gently guide me so I might
learn of You and become confident in Your care.
Enable me to live life to the fullest. Amen.

Ups and Downs

*[Inasmuch as we] refute arguments and theories and
reasonings and every proud and lofty thing that sets itself
up against the [true] knowledge of God; and we lead
every thought and purpose away captive into the
obedience of Christ (the Messiah, the Anointed One).*

2 CORINTHIANS 10:5 AMP

Living according to our fickle feelings is like riding a roller-coaster: one day up, one day down. It's easy to fall into the trap of believing those thoughts more than what God says in His Word. Don't let every emotion that surfaces dictate the direction of the day. Capture loose thoughts with a Christ-centered net.

To begin this process, we should latch on to God's promises and steady our course. We need to line up our feelings with what we know the Bible says. The apostle Paul said, "We walk by faith and not by sight." Sometimes we won't sense God's presence, but because He's promised He'll never leave us, we must believe He's there. Jesus said, "My peace I leave you." Accept that peace. Let it rule in your heart. Concerned about having enough? "My God shall supply all your needs." Proven promises to stand on. Promises we can live by. Search the Scriptures for promises. They are there.

God is a God of faithfulness, and He works in ways that faith, not feelings, can discern. Trust Him. We must—even when we don't feel like it.

*Dear heavenly Father, I choose to accept Your
promises as a child of the King. Thank You
for all You've done for me. Amen.*

Music to His Ears

*Speaking to one another with psalms, hymns, and songs from
the Spirit. Sing and make music from your heart to the Lord.*
EPHESIANS 5:19 NIV

One of the most powerful moments in the Christian life
may turn out to be at a supper table with fellow believers or
conversations around a fire. Uplifting and encouraging one
another can also happen when we sing. Today many churches
resound with praise music that fills the congregation with
enthusiasm. These songs should not be directed to those around
us but in our hearts to the Lord. Spiritual fullness comes to
expression in joyful fellowship, in song and thanksgiving.

King David crawled in caves and crevasses hiding from his
enemies, yet he found time to pen many praise songs to the King
of kings. Despite his circumstances, he knew God was in control.
Paul sang in the dank darkness of a dungeon cell, praising his
Creator even though life looked bleak. God's grace was extended
to these men as they praised in their suffering.

How much more should we make a melody to the Lord
when we are free to move about, to worship, to sing. God wants
to hear music from our hearts, not arias with perfect notes. So
we will lift up our voices and join in the praise to our Creator
and Lord. Harmonious, harsh, or hoarse, He's filtering
our melodies with His love.

*Dear heavenly Father, I worship You.
I adore You. Thank You for Your
goodness and mercy. Amen.*

Look to the Promise

*Let us hold unswervingly to the hope we profess,
for he who promised is faithful.*
HEBREWS 10:23 NIV

"I promise to pick up the dry cleaning." "The check is in the
mail, I promise." How lightly we use the word promise. We
toss it around with very little meaning attached. The definition
of promise is a statement telling someone you will definitely
do something, or that something will definitely happen in the
future. The use of the word means you can hang your hat on
it! This some thing is coming. Oh how often we fail to carry
through with our word. It's wonderful we can know for sure—
definitely—that God's promise is eternal.

God's Word contains promises upon which we can and must
depend. The Bible is a priceless gift, a tool God intends for us to
use in our lives. Too often we look away from "The Manual."

Are you tired and discouraged? Fearful? Be comforted in the
promises God has made to you through His Word. Experiencing
worry or anxiety? Be courageous and call on God. He will
protect you and then use you according to His purposes. Are you
confused? Listen to the whisper of the Holy Spirit, for our God
is not a God of confusion.

Talk to Him, listen to Him, trust Him. Trust His promises.
He is steadfast, and He will be by your side. Always.

*Father, how we thank You for Your promises.
You are steadfast, loving, and caring.
We cannot praise You enough. Amen.*

Much Love

*Therefore, I tell you, her many sins have
been forgiven, as her great love has shown.*
LUKE 7:47 NIV

Scripture records the story of Jesus dining with Simon the
Pharisee. At the dinner, a woman of loose morals came forth,
kissed Jesus' feet, and washed them with her tears. Simon was
incensed. He felt Jesus should reprimand the woman; after all,
she had sinned greatly. Jesus didn't condemn her but He forgave
her. Her faith saved her because she poured out everything
at His feet. The Interpreter's Bible states, "The significant
difference between the woman and Simon is not that she had
been a worse sinner than he. . .but that she has realized more
truly and deeply the reality of her sin."

Often we feel we fall short in our walk with God. We
plunge into the trap of measuring ourselves by another's
yardstick. This isn't what God wants for us. He desires that
we fall at His feet and worship Him—loving Him with an
extravagant love. When sin enters our lives, as it will, we confess
that sin and turn to His face. He's there in the darkest hours.

Others may know what you've done, but Jesus knows what
you can become. Simon the Pharisee saw this woman as a weed,
but Jesus saw her as a potential rose and watered it. When you
fall in love with Christ, the first thing He opens is
your heart. Be transformed by the Father's grace.
Love extravagantly.

*Dear heavenly Father, I love You.
Pour Your love into my heart this day. Amen.*

Choose Happy

*A happy heart is good medicine and a cheerful mind
works healing, but a broken spirit dries up the bones.*
PROVERBS 17:22 AMP

Feeling gloomy, blue, out of sorts? Do you have an Eeyore
personality, always "down in the dumps"? Scripture exhorts us to
choose joy, to choose happy. And it's not always an easy task.

When a person is ill, a gloomy spirit can make it difficult
for God's healing power to work. William J. Parker, a theologian,
stated, "Let the patient experience an inward awareness of
[God's] healing force and let him overcome his heaviness of heart
and he will find his new outlook to be like medicine." Despite
the sickness, we look to our heavenly Father for encouragement
and strength, a heavenly tonic. A smile and a glad heart heals us
from within and also helps those who come into the circle of its
influence.

At times it might seem impossible to cultivate a cheerful
outlook on life, but in our Christian walk it should become an
intentional act as much as learning to control our temper or be
kind. This new spirit within grows from a faith that all things
can work together for good when we walk in God's light and
look to Him for everything.

*Dear Lord, today my spirit is heavy, my heart
downtrodden. Help me lift my eyes to You and
choose to believe You are at work in my life. Create
in me a happy, clean heart, O Lord. Amen.*

Mapquest

Show me your ways, Lord, teach me your paths. Guide me in your truth and teach me, for you are God my Savior, and my hope is in you all day long.

PSALM 25:4–5 NIV

Stopping to ask directions is almost a thing of the past. Today we have GPS systems and Mapquest: plug in the info we need and we're off—choosing our own paths. But are they always the right ones? Scripture calls for the Lord to teach us. To guide us. When we use the Bible as our manual, we can trust that the Lord will direct us on the right roadway.

"Guide me in your truth" lets us be assured that God is faithful and the paths in which we are led are the correct paths, ultimately leading us home. The Interpreter's Bible states, "We all want to walk by sight occasionally; forever walking by faith is a strain; wherefore, seeing that God is gracious, this is a prayer that is often answered positively, especially in retrospect. Sometimes we can say 'Yes this is best for me;' more frequently, we look back and see it was the best for me."

To have God show us our ways, to guide us, means we must have teachable spirits. We must be willing to listen and follow. We must plug in to His power and grace, before we begin our journeys.

Father God, help me hear Your voice. Let me know Your heart and guide me always. Amen.

I Am

God said to Moses, "I am who I am. This is what you
are to say to the Israelites: 'I am has sent me to you.'"
EXODUS 3:14 NIV

The words "I am" ring out in the present tense. These words are
used some seven hundred times in the Bible to describe God
and Jesus. When Moses was on the mount and asked God who
He was, a voice thundered, "I Am." In the New Testament,
Jesus said of Himself, "I am the bread of life; I am the light of
the world; I am the Good Shepherd; I am the way; I am the
resurrection." Present tense. Words of hope and life. I Am.

Who is God to you today? Is He in the present tense?
Living, loving, presiding over your life? Is the Lord of Lords "I
Was" or "I've Never Been" to you? Have you experienced the
hope which comes from an everlasting "I Am" Father? One who
walks by you daily and will never let go? "I Am with you always."

We are surprised when we struggle in the world, yet hesitate
to turn to our very Creator. He has the answers, and He will fill
you with hope. Reach for Him today. Don't be uncertain. Know
Him. For He is, after all, I Am.

Father, we surrender our lives to You this day.
We choose to turn from our sins, reach for Your hand,
and ask for Your guidance. Thank You for
Your loving kindness. Amen.

Thank You

*As for me, I will always have hope; I will praise you more and
more. My mouth will tell of your righteous deeds, of your saving
acts all day long—though I know not how to relate them all.*
PSALM 71:14–15 NIV

Those in the workplace, be it an office or at home, really
appreciate a "thanks—well done" every now and then. Kudos can
make the day go smoother. And when others brag on us a tad, it
perks up the attitude. Think then how our heavenly Father loves
to hear a hearty "thank You" from His kids.

Our lives should be filled with praise to the Living Lord and
King of Kings. He is a mighty God who created us and watches
over us. We ought to tell others of the deeds He has done in our
lives. For the power of our testimony is great. Tell how He is our
Savior and our hope. The psalmist exhorts us to hope continually
because we know even in the darkest days, He has given us a
promise to never leave our sides.

Synonyms for praise include: admire, extol, honor, glorify,
honor, and worship. This day take one or two of these words
and use them to thank your heavenly Father. Don't take Him for
granted. Give Him the praise He deserves.

*Father God, how good You are. You have blessed us
immeasurably, and for that we choose to glorify
Your name. Let us shout it from the mountain:
Our God is good, forever and ever. Amen.*

Bill of Rights

But to as many as did receive and welcome Him,
He gave the authority (power, privilege, right)
to become the children of God, that is, to those who
believe in (adhere to, trust in, and rely on) His name.
JOHN 1:12 AMP

The United States has a bill of rights that lays out guarantees of personal freedoms and limits the government's power. As US citizens, we observe these amendments to maintain an orderly and acceptable society. As Christians we also have rights.

Scripture states we have been given "rights" as children of God. We have the "right" to receive direction from the Holy Spirit (Romans 8:14–17). We have the "right" to make our requests known to God (Matthew 6: 9–15). We have the "right" to personal freedom from sin (Galatians 5:1). And we have the "right" to rule in our sphere of authority on the word of our testimony (Revelation 12:11).

Are you a child of the King? Are you an heir to the throne who can lay claim to these rights? Lift up your eyes to the heavens and declare your desire to become one of the family of God. He hears you. The Word says you can trust in His goodness and mercy, His loving kindness. Reach out this day and receive your gift of salvation.

Father God, I want to be one of Your children, not
just to attain the "rights" but to undo wrongs and
sin in my life. Open my eyes that I may see. Amen.

Free at Last

*For the Lord is the Spirit, and wherever
the Spirit of the Lord is, there is freedom.*
2 CORINTHIANS 3:17 NLT

Rules exist to keep order in our lives and to establish boundaries.
Parents have rules for their children; the police have rules for
drivers. All are necessary for men to get along with each other, to
cooperate. And when people operate completely outside of the
rules, chaos can ensue. So when we begin life as a Christian we
learn that Jesus did not come to bring chaos—He came to bring
each of us a new life.

In Scripture, Paul was speaking to the church in Corinth,
but he certainly wasn't telling them to throw caution to the
wind and live completely outside the box. What he was saying
was once the Spirit of the Living God lives inside you, there
is freedom, an emancipation from bondage, a release from sin.
What a cause for rejoicing! Free indeed.

But we cannot live this way in our own power. When we
form this covenant with God, and are saved, then with Jesus and
the Holy Spirit, we can defeat the enemy who is trying to steal
and destroy. Put on this armor to face the world. Be ready for the
fight. Look to the Word to provide you with the needed tools to
walk through each day.

*Father God, thank You for the Holy Spirit
You have placed inside my heart.
Quicken me to hear Your voice. Amen.*

Reach Out

*Now faith is the assurance (the confirmation, the title deed)
of the things [we] hope for, being the proof of things [we]
do not see and the conviction of their reality [faith perceiving
as real fact what is not revealed to the senses].*
HEBREWS 11:1 AMP

Driving through the fog is scary and a cause of many accidents.
Isn't it wonderful that we don't have to worry about steering our
lives through a fog? The God of the universe is our director, and
we can have faith that He will steer us clear. Problems may arise,
hazards might jump in our pathway, but when we reach our hand
to the Lord, He reaches down to us.

Scripture teaches that we are to hope in Him. To have
Christ at the center of our lives and to recognize His mighty
power is to rely on the tried and true. Generations before us tell
of His wondrous care. David was pursued by enemies; he cried
unto the Lord. Paul was beaten and imprisoned; he cried unto
the Lord. The willingness to wait for God, the eager expectation,
was the faith of the men of old.

The word assurance literally means "a thing put under. . .a
foundation." With this solid foundation we can hope for the
future—those unseen things. A believer looking forward to a
union with God is assured that He will be there, waiting to
receive him.

Lean into Him. Reach for the heavens, knowing full well
He will grasp your hand.

*Lord, how I long to feel Your presence.
Teach me to hold Your hand and
be led by Your Spirit. Amen.*

His Delight

"The Lord your God is with you, the Mighty Warrior who saves. He will take great delight in you; in his love he will no longer rebuke you, but will rejoice over you with singing. "

ZEPHANIAH 3:17 NIV

Delight. What a wonderful word! The connotations of enjoyment and pleasure, joy and gladness. You are usually delighted when something has pleased you. Maybe it's the song of a bird; the chatter of your child; or simply a quiet, starry night which soothes your senses and fills your heart with satisfaction.

Scripture tells us the Lord will take delight in us and will rejoice over us with singing. Imagine that! The very Mighty Warrior of the Universe relishing His creation. And that creation is you. It's hard to imagine when we have our dirty faces or are out of sorts that He could care for us at all. But it's true. Our God saves and loves. Our God is truth and mercy. He loves His children.

Take a deep breath and carve out some time to appreciate and bask in the truth of the Bible. God loves you, and He delights in you. You are the apple of His eye. Reach out a hand to Him this day, knowing full well He will interlace His fingers with yours and never let go. Selah. Pause and reflect.

Father God, how we love You. We do not understand the depth and breadth of Your love for us, but we are ever so grateful. Amen.

Cleaning Up

*Come close to God and He will come close to you.
[Recognize that you are] sinners, get your soiled
hands clean; . . .and purify your hearts.*
James 4:8 AMP

Picture a muddy, unshorn sheep. A shepherd would have a job
before him to clean up that animal because the fleece is quite
deep. He must dig down with the shears layer by layer, tugging
at the wool as he goes. In order to shear the sheep, he has to
have hold of it, a firm grasp on a wiggling, uncooperative animal.
Whatever it takes, the shepherd cleans the sheep.

Now picture us. Uncooperative, squirming, with insides
that need to be cleaned. Our thoughts and actions have not
been pure. Maybe we have lost our temper, taken advantage of
another, or gossiped. Actions that are not what God wants of us.
Actions that are called sin. Sin that blackens the heart. Like the
sheep, we must be gathered in and cleaned.

Our most glorious God has promised He will do that for us
when we ask. If we draw near to God and ask for His forgiveness,
He will cleanse our hearts and make us part of His fold. Hallelujah.
What a magnificent and overwhelming plan He has for us!

*Dear Lord, is gaining a new life truly as simple as
that? I reach out my hand in surrender and
ask You to become the King of my life. Thank
You for all You have done for me. Amen.*

From the Roots Up

Blessed is the one. . . . whose delight is in the law of the Lord, and who meditates on his law day and night. That person is like a tree planted by streams of water, which yields its fruit in season and whose leaf does not wither—whatever they do prospers.

PSALM 1:1–3 NIV

Picture the tree outside your dwelling. It began as a seed, grew into a sapling, and eventually reached to the sky. The roots grow deep into the ground, finding nourishment. When a tree is deeply planted, it will stand against most elements thrown its way because of the strong roots holding it into the soil.

So should we become. Deeply planted in God's Word. Fixed on Him. Then will we grow in wisdom and truth. To grow is to become fruitful and spread the Gospel to others. To grow is to be healthy, withstanding problems as they come, knowing full well our strength is from Him.

This day find a section of scripture. Read it out loud. Meditate on the words and let them nourish your soul. Let the Holy Spirit minister to you. For He has promised when we do we will not wither and we shall prosper. Seek out worthy mentors and listen carefully to their advice. Act in accordance with the beliefs you have learned. Grow!

Lord, how we long to know more of You.
To bask in the radiance of Your glory.
Help us this day to hear the words spoken
to our hearts from You. Amen.

Seriously?

*I urge you to live a life worthy of the calling you have
received. Be completely humble and gentle; be patient,
bearing with one another in love. Make every effort to
keep the unity of the Spirit through the bond of peace.*
EPHESIANS 4:1–3 NIV

Do you have a friend, relative, or coworker who you feel is trying
to drive you crazy? At times, do you think you need to throw your
hands in the air and walk away; or maybe get in that person's face
and tell it like it is? While there are times for confrontation and
discussion of conflicts, often at the center of the problem is "me."
I am my problem. Perhaps we need to look in the mirror and
evaluate the situation to see where we can improve.

Scripture encourages us to be humble, gentle, and patient.
Then to bear one another in love. Wow! Huge directions.
Doesn't the Lord get it? Doesn't He see how. . . Wait. Yes, He
does. He understands full well we cannot accomplish these tasks
in our own strength. That's why He has given us the Holy Spirit.
So we can lean on Him to guide us to peace.

As we walk through the days ahead, let us keep our eyes
lifted, which removes the problems from our sight. Maybe not
from our lives, but the focus isn't necessarily on the difficulty—
be it human or otherwise. Our focus is on Jesus. And with His
help, we can conquer all.

*Father God, refresh the Holy Spirit within me.
Let me feel His presence. Amen.*

The Comparison Trap

*Make a careful exploration of who you are and the work
you have been given, and then sink yourself into that.
Don't be impressed with yourself. Don't compare yourself
with others. Each of you must take responsibility for doing
the creative best you can with your own life.*

GALATIANS 6:4–5 MSG

In John 21, the apostle John records a conversation Jesus had with
Peter shortly after His resurrection. Jesus prepared a breakfast for
His disciples after a night of fishing. Then Jesus invited Peter to
go for a walk. Just days before Peter had denied knowing Jesus.
Now, three times Jesus asked Peter if the fisherman-turned-
disciple loved Him. By asking this question, Jesus not only let
Peter know that he was forgiven for his lapse of faith, but also He
let Peter know that God still had a purpose and plan for Peter. He
also spoke of how Peter would eventually die for His gospel.

Peter, maybe a little embarrassed by all the attention he was
getting, looked over his shoulder and saw John following them.
Peter asked the Lord, "What about him? How will he die?" Peter
fell into the comparison trap.

Jesus answered, "What does it matter to you what I have
planned for another? Live your life according to My plan. That's
all you need to be concerned about."

And that's all Jesus still requires of His followers. God has
a unique plan and purpose for each one, equipping them as they
keep their eyes on Him and follow Him daily.

*Father, show me Your plan for
today and help me not to compare
my path with others. Amen.*

A Pattern of Forgiveness

*Therefore, my friends, I want you to know that through Jesus
the forgiveness of sins is proclaimed to you. Through him
everyone who believes is set free from every sin.*
ACTS 13:38–39 NIV

Forgiveness means to pardon another who has wronged you.
Forgiveness needs to be extended without and released from
within so bitterness will not grow and consume you. And
there is no doubt that this can be difficult. As Christians we
are commanded to do so by scripture. We often show pity and
compassion to others and let a situation go, get over it, apologize.
However, all too often we look in the mirror and anger surfaces
at ourselves.

Forgiving ourselves is the hardest step in the Forgive
Pattern. Popular Christian speaker Joyce Meyer stated, "Forgive
yourself for past sins and hurts you have caused others. You can't
pay people back, so ask God to." It's a choice. When tempted to
dredge up the wrongs, the sins, which you have asked the Lord
to forgive, make a concerted effort to erase those thoughts. Lay
aside all that "stuff." When you are embittered against yourself,
forgive! If Jesus doesn't remember it, why should you?

Scripture tells us you are forgiven from every sin when you
ask! So once you've prayed for forgiveness, face yourself in the
mirror and say, "I'm free!"

*Father God, I choose this day to ask for
Your forgiveness for specific sins. And when
I've confessed, I ask You to help me forgive
myself. Holy Spirit abide within. Amen.*

Just the Pits

But as for you, ye thought evil against me;
but God meant it unto good.
GENESIS 50:20 KJV

We can speak of ourselves as "being in the pits," which is symbolic of deep difficult experiences in life. Many times we are in the pits because of our mistakes, our wrongdoings. But sometimes there's no explanation. Sometimes it's an emotional pit, we are discouraged or depressed. And while in that pit, we can become comfortable. The pit makes us bitter, or we can let it make us better.

In Genesis, Joseph's brothers threw him into a pit to end his life. Instead, he was rescued and that life experience transformed him into a godly man. He experienced extremes in life: literally from rags to riches. Yet his character shined through because whether in the pits or the palace, his faithfulness to God never wavered. He defined his success as doing God's will. Then he was able to see the evil turned into good.

It might take some time to get to a mountaintop when we're in the valley, but we can struggle out of the murky depths with God's help. The Holy Spirit within can enable us to turn things around so we are at least on level ground.

Dear Lord, help me. I'm so down I don't know
which way is up. Please, Father, take me by
the hand and pull me from this pit. Amen.

Thunder Roars

*But everyone who calls on the
name of the LORD will be saved.*
JOEL 2:32 NLT

Do you ever tremble with fear? Whether it be from dangers
without or emotional distress within, fear can paralyze people. It
is as though a hand grips us by the throat and we are pinned in
place with nowhere to go. Yet the Lord our God has said do not
be afraid, He will save us.

The book of Psalms reveals a man who quivers and hides in
caves to escape his enemies. Time and again David calls out to
the Lord, because he has been taught God will calm his fears.
The circumstances do not always change, the thunder may still
roar, but just like David we can know our lives are secure in the
hand of the Almighty Creator of the Universe. He will save us.
It's a promise.

Today make a list of those things that cause you to quake in
your boots. Read the list out loud to the Lord and ask Him to
provide the necessary bravery to overcome each one. Ask Him to
see you through the deep waters and to hold you tightly over the
mountaintops. For when you call on His Name, He hears and
answers. Listen closely and remember He saves.

*Father, I'm scared. Please hold me close and
calm my anxious heart. Tune my ears to hear
Your Word and know what to do. Amen.*

Are You Sure?

No unbelief or distrust made him waver (doubtingly question)
concerning the promise of God, but he [Abraham] grew strong
and was empowered by faith as he gave praise and glory to God.
ROMANS 4:20 AMP

Doubt and uncertainty can upend us if we let them. When we
are unsure of something, our steps falter, our words stutter, and
our hearts rattle in our chests. Fear can set in. We must guard
against this anxious spirit and trust the word God has spoken. To
protect against an onslaught of concern, we must learn to lean on
Him and allow the Holy Spirit to flow within us.

Paul wrote about doubting God's promises and said that
feeling can only be combated by rejoicing. He who was chained,
in prison, shipwrecked, and often in danger speaks of singing
praises and being full of joy! But how, in our world, are we able
to overcome our moods and rejoice? It is difficult, most certainly,
and has to be a conscious choice. Steeping your heart in the
Word of God, knowing verses which will comfort you, is a great
beginning.

A doubting spirit is not of God, for He is not the author of
confusion. Theologian Matthew Henry stated, "God honours
faith; and great faith honours God." To truly give Him the glory,
we must trust. Of this we are sure.

Lord, help us in our unbelief. Our very
human nature causes us to look to the right
and to the left. Help us to keep our focus
on You and to trust implicitly. Amen.

The May Pole

Even the wilderness and desert will be glad in those days.
The wasteland will rejoice and blossom with spring crocuses.
Yes, there will be an abundance of flowers and singing and joy!
The deserts will become as green as the mountains of Lebanon,
as lovely as Mount Carmel or the plain of Sharon. There the
Lord will display his glory, the splendor of our God.
ISAIAH 35:1–2 NLT

Mingled with the sweet laughter of children, crepe paper streamers floated around the May pole in Marie's kindergarten classroom. The teacher instructed them to hold gently onto the end of their streamer as they circled together around the metal support pole that tethered the whole scene together. Streamers twisted and twirled between them as they concentrated on their paper connection to it all, some arms held high, some lower, as requested. Then reverse, pay attention, twirl the other direction. Open windows blew in the hope of spring.

Recalling the scene, the colors floated somehow in her mind, blending perfectly with the aroma of drying finger paintings and cookies that someone's mother had baked. That day would stick in Marie's mind as one of joy and hope for years to come. She thanked God for moments like this one that pointed her to the great hope of Christ and now reminded her of the unfading hope that awaits her in eternity.

Lord God, thank You for continuing to provide
times of beauty and joy that point to the
promise of eternal splendor with You. Amen.

Springtime Rescue

*He reached down from heaven and rescued me; he drew
me out of deep waters. He rescued me from my powerful
enemies, from those who hated me and were too strong for me.
They attacked me at a moment when I was in distress,
but the Lord supported me. He led me to a place of safety;
he rescued me because he delights in me.*

PSALM 18:16–19 NLT

For so many around her, spring was a lovely time of hope. For
Jenn it was a time of heavy despair this year. The memories
had overcome her. How her family could have done such awful
things to her was incomprehensible. Flashbacks flooded her
whole being. It was a breakdown that landed her in the hospital
for two weeks.

Good counseling and medical care helped her to begin the
long road to healing and forgiveness. Weak, afraid, and unsure
of so much, she returned home where flowers bloomed at her
front door and sunshine warmed her entirely. Things everywhere
looked brighter. She thanked God for bringing her closer to
wholeness in the loving rescue He had orchestrated for her. She
was beginning to see the great love the almighty God had for her.

*Lord, whatever despair I may find myself in, big or small,
thank You for Your great love for me. Thank You
for the spectacular rescue mission You completed at
the cross, and for the ways You regularly rescue
me that I may never even see. Amen.*

Lasting

*The life of mortals is like grass, they flourish like a flower
of the field; the wind blows over it and it is gone, and its
place remembers it no more. But from everlasting to
everlasting the Lord's love is with those who fear him,
and his righteousness with their children's children.*

PSALM 103:15–17 NIV

Surrounded by ornate scrolling, an old building downtown had
a name engraved on it that Sarah had never heard of. Intrigued,
she asked her mother, who had grown up in this town. Her
mother didn't know who this person was either. Sarah asked her
grandmother, also born and raised there, and she also didn't have
a clue who this person was.

Apparently a person of wealth to afford such a building, this
mysterious figure had incredibly good architectural design taste.
Sarah marveled at the intricate marble work atop pillars that had
stood the test of time. She wondered about the life of this person,
who according to the date on the building would have lived just
four generations ago. This person's influence had to count for
something in the community, his contributions certainly notable,
and yet he was already forgotten.

Sarah thought about the kind of impact her days on this
earth might have. It was a stark reminder that the things that last
are eternal things, the faith and love that we share with others.
The things that point to Christ, and hopefully eternity with
Him for those who see the light of Christ shining
through us in a dark world.

*Lord, strengthen me to shine for You today,
to make an eternal difference for Your glory. Amen.*

Steps

*[With] unfailing courage, now as always heretofore,
Christ (the Messiah) will be magnified and get glory and
praise in this body of mine and be boldly exalted in my
person, whether through (by) life or through (by) death.*
PHILIPPIANS 1:20 AMP

Clair and her husband, with their adventurous son, were
climbing the south face of Half Dome in Yosemite, California.
The eight mile hike up used far more energy than anticipated.
The steep set of big steps carved into the face of granite was
behind them. Now they faced an eight hundred foot ascent to
the famous mile-high summit.

Clair was exhausted, and now stunned. Her husband, son,
and his friend were going ahead. As some hikers turned back she
contemplated what to do. She would regret not finishing. Yet she
looked with concern at the two cables that would hold their lives.
"What if the cable breaks?" she asked her son's friend. He smiled
confidently. "It won't break."

One step and grip at a time, she pulled herself up the forty
five degree grade that grew steeper toward the top. This was the
most mentally and physically challenging thing she had done in
her life. Looking down the face of rock she realized that she took
the regular steps of life for granted. She thanked God for the
exhilaration of this experience, and for the strength to do it.

She passed a frightened woman resting at a cable
support and encouraged her. "You're doing great.
One step at a time."

*God, give me strength and courage for
every step I take today, and thank You
for being with me in each one. Amen.*

Growing Hope

"For I know the plans I have for you," declares the LORD,
"plans to prosper you and not to harm you,
plans to give you hope and a future."
JEREMIAH 29:11 NIV

Tulips of every color lined the streets in Holland, Michigan. It was Tulip Time. A sea of bright yellow blooms smiled from their beds in the park, with a couple hundred red ones cheering on next to them. The seemingly endless varieties and arrangements left visitors and locals alike in awe. Even black tulips were bright after the long winter they had endured.

The flower beds had been properly cared for during the summer and fall, so the tulips could winter well and put on their stunner of a show come spring. Every burst of color redeemed the cold, dark winter days. It renewed their hope every spring. They were reminded once again that the dreary, often bitter days that seemed so unnecessary, indeed had a purpose. Without dormancy these beautiful blooms cannot go from one stage to the next. Spring growth is dependent on a winter season.

The glorious hope that spring represents is a beautiful picture of how God works, how He grows us through the seasons of life.

Lord, thank You for the eternal hope and love
You give me every day. Help me, God, to grow
in each season You have given me. Amen.

Cans

*He is the Maker of heaven and earth, the sea,
and everything in them—he remains faithful forever.
He upholds the cause of the oppressed and gives food
to the hungry. The Lord sets prisoners free.*

PSALM 146:6–7 NIV

Shelley held on to him as they bobbled on and off the roadside on a moped. They needed groceries, and aluminum cans brought ten cents each. She held the bag as he bent down to grab the cans. At the end of the evening they went home with twenty dollars' worth. A dear friend was watching their infant son, who they soon packed into the car. The three of them were off to the grocery store to get food to last until payday.

Years later, she would think back to this time and thank God for the provision, even though it seemed so hard. It was such a humbling season in their lives.

Following it though, God brought them to a good job and community where they would stay for decades and raise four sons. They grew in their faith and their freedom in Christ. Yes, God had been faithful, and continued to be.

*Lord God, thank You for the way You provide for me,
even when I am not grateful at the time. You see
what I need, and You provide. Thank You. Amen.*

Interceding for Us

*For he that is mighty hath done to me
great things; and holy is his name.*
LUKE 1:49 KJV

Troubling issues in our nation are complex and too numerous to count. Sometimes it is difficult to know what to pray for, how to pray, or even where to begin. There are many Christians who have given up on praying for our nation's leadership, leaders who do not observe this designated day of prayer. It can feel hopeless at times, and actually it is. Without God it is hopeless.

Thank God that He does hear, for we have an intercessor in Christ, by the power of the Holy Spirit, who is always there interceding on our behalf. He is our Hope. Hope for a nation grounded in His principles, but fallen like the rest of the earthly world.

Let us pray, and thank Him for what He is already doing. Then, look expectantly to what God will do through a people who love Him and seek to shine for Him in truth and love.

Lord God, thank You for seeing our every need, and for the ability to come to You anytime, all the time, in prayer. Amen.

Dark Skies

*The angel of the Lord encamps around those who fear him,
and he delivers them. Taste and see that the Lord is good;
blessed is the man who takes refuge in him.*

PSALM 34:7–8 KJV

Sheets of rain poured from the dark skies. The car shuddered and jumped as they sped home in flash flood conditions hoping their home wasn't flooded, too. The headlights reflecting off the forceful puddle sprays brought blinding flashes of light that impaired their vision. The news was predicting the river to rise sixteen feet above flood level with continued rain the next day.

Sally couldn't help but think back to just yesterday. She had planted flowers and sat on the porch enjoying the warm spring sunshine.

Today they were working to protect their home and keep one another safe in the storm. The contrast was already a bit stunning, then the lights in the neighborhood went black. That's when Sally saw a tornado warning alert on her phone. As soon as they pulled into the garage they went straight to the basement by the light of their cell phones.

Sally found herself thanking God for a safe place in this violent weather, and she prayed for her community. A tornado did pass through just a couple miles away, knocking buildings off their foundations and leaving people without their possessions, but there was no loss of life. Some neighbors met for the first time cleaning up together, and bringing meals and clothing to those in need.

*Lord, thank You for being my refuge in
every storm, and for the people You
provide to help me through. Amen.*

It's Weddin' Time!

*"There will be heard once more the sounds of joy and laughter.
The joyful voices of bridegrooms and brides will be heard
again, along with the joyous songs of people bringing
thanksgiving offerings to the Lord. They will sing,
Give thanks to the Lord of Heaven's Armies, for the
Lord is good. His faithful love endures forever!"*
JEREMIAH 33:10–11 NLT

White orchids and warm breezes graced the newlyweds smiling
broadly as they descended the church steps surrounded by cheers
of joy. A gleaming white limo awaited them beyond the blowing
bubbles, as light as their spirits this day.

This was wedding number three of the ten that Shelby had
been invited to this year. 'Tis the season! It was a privilege to
experience so many celebrations with dear friends and family.
Yet, for Shelby it was bittersweet. One thing that never failed to
pierce her heart was the bride and father dance. For Shelby and
her husband it was a regular reminder that their daughter who
died twenty-five years ago would be in the marrying stage of
life now. With each wedding this dance brought contemplative
emotion for them.

Thankfully as the years wear on they anticipate the dance in
eternity that will far exceed anything in this life. Furthermore,
the dance of Christ with His bride, us— and it's impossible for
us to imagine how glorious this will be.

*Lord God, thank You for the hope and promise
of eternity with You, and for the great love
You have for us, Your bride. Amen.*

My Broken Yellow Flower

I remember your genuine faith, for you share the faith that first
filled your grandmother Lois and your mother, Eunice. And I
know that same faith continues strong in you. This is why I
remind you to fan into flames the spiritual gift God gave you
when I laid my hands on you. For God has not given us a spirit
of fear and timidity, but of power, love, and self-discipline.
2 TIMOTHY 1:5–7 NLT

Joey giggled with James as their brother ran up the aisle.
"Mommy, look!" Johnny said, smiling widely with one of the
flowers given to mothers at the door after church. "I picked
yellow, your favorite color!" He shoved it toward her, breaking
the stem.

It still warmed her heart, and somehow strengthened her
weary body. Baby Justin started to fuss in her arms. She juggled
her overstuffed bag, adjusting to get his bottle.

"Here, let me help you," her dear friend Sharon said, taking
the baby for a bit. "It makes me tired just watching you." Sharon's
children were all grown and doing well. She was a tremendous
encouragement to young mothers, especially to Sally. Each week
at church Sally sought her out for a few moments of sanity.

Now, years later with her sons all in their twenties, she
enjoys encouraging the young mothers in her circles. "You're
going to make it," she says, hearing Sharon's voice in her head.
It makes her smile.

Lord, thank You for the blessing of mothers
and motherhood. Whether as a mother or
to a mother, strengthen me in my role
that I may shine for You. Amen.

Mother's Dance

*The Spirit of the Sovereign Lord is upon me, for the
Lord has anointed me to bring good news to the poor.
He has sent me to comfort the brokenhearted.*

Isaiah 61:1 nlt

Adam's mother passed away two years before his wedding, a
wedding that came just a year or so after he declared to his
brothers that he would be the last to marry. This was the sort
of thing he didn't mind being wrong about. But then, God had
brought some pretty amazing changes to his life, so why was he
surprised?

The wedding was a wonderful day for everyone present, but
Adam and Kayla's families were especially blessed. His brothers
toasted to a woman their mother would be proud that Adam had
chosen. When it came time for the traditional groom's dance
with his mother, guests watched as Kayla's mother, Deb, stepped
out onto the floor and danced with her new son-in-law.

This alone would seem sweet enough, but add to it the loss
of the bride's sister and only sibling years ago—Linette would be
in her early twenties now. Guests who didn't know their stories
wondered why some eyes welled up and spilled over. Why some
looked away and swallowed hard, and yet others smiled broadly
with joy.

This mother's dance with the groom was a beautiful picture
of God's love for us, how He provides comfort and joy in this life
until we are joined with loved ones in eternity.

*Lord, thank You for the blessings You
bring through others whom You put in
my life. Help me to be a blessing
where You have placed me. Amen.*

Awry

*For My thoughts are not your thoughts, neither are
your ways My ways, says the Lord. For as the heavens
are higher than the earth, so are My ways higher than
your ways and My thoughts higher than your thoughts.*

Isaiah 55:8–9 amp

There was so much Mary did not understand. The more she
grew in her faith, the less she realized she knew. She had dear
friends going through the terrible tragedy of losing their college
daughter. A neighbor was dying of cancer just two doors down.
Just waiting to die. A friend's rental home was bought by the
city, citing eminent domain. His political views didn't line up
with the city leader, and he was given a fraction of what the
house was worth in the sale.

The list of injustices and things impossible to understand
just kept growing.

One clear spring evening Mary looked up at the stars. The
vastness is always striking on a clear night. She thought how
small she was in the scope of it all, and how God cares about it
all. He not only cares, He intervenes in ways that she could not.
Somehow, He knows what is best even when it all seems awry. He
would take care of her and her friends, somehow, through it all.

*Lord, thank You for being the Sovereign Almighty!
Help me to trust Your ways, even when. . .
mostly when, I don't understand. Amen.*

Up and Away

Then, because so many people were coming and going that they did not even have a chance to eat, he said to them, "Come with me by yourselves to a quiet place and get some rest." So they went away by themselves in a boat to a solitary place.

MARK 6:31–32 NIV

Dexter had been playing in the woods near the house for some time now. His mother looked out the window scanning the boyhood terrain with tree forts, a fire ring, and scrap wood. It was hard not to worry when she thought back to the times she had to run out in a hurry to help her injured sons.

Just then she spotted him about twenty feet up in one of the trees, just sitting there. A bit panicked she ran outside. "What are you doing?"

"I'm just reading and relaxing," Dexter said calmly from his comfortable perch.

He had always been an agile climber, and she knew it wouldn't be right to steer him away from the strength and courage that would grow him to manhood, but this was a bit rattling. "I'm okay, Mom," he reassured her, seeing her conflicted face.

Afterward in the house he agreed that he would let her know in the future when he was reading in a tree, and she resolved to do two things. She thanked God that he desired time alone to think and read, even though it was so high up; and she would pray more!

God, help me to take the time away that I need in solitude, wherever that may be. Strengthen me in wisdom and grace. Amen.

Message in a Bottle

*This is the confidence we have in approaching God:
that if we ask anything according to his will, he hears us.
And if we know that he hears us—whatever we ask—
we know that we have what we asked of him.*

1 JOHN 5:14–15 NIV

"Look what I found, Daddy!" Dave and his boys were walking along the river and found what seemed a bit surreal. It was an actual message in a bottle. Albeit a plastic soda bottle, still, the note was a child's cry for help. She wrote of her parents using drugs. She was clearly frightened, feeling helpless and alone.

The note was found just downstream from a small-town neighborhood, and there was enough information in the note to deduce a few things. Dave told a trusted sheriff deputy, who ended up knowing the family. He planned to keep an eye out for the children. At the same time Dave and his family began praying for the girl who wrote the message and for her family.

That little girl wrote a note crying out for help. Who would have believed that it would actually work? God knew, and thankfully He sees and hears it all whether there is a desperate plea or not. But isn't it great that He loves to respond to requests?

*Lord, thank You for caring intimately about
me and every facet of my life. Help me to
remember to come to You with my needs,
and the needs of others. Amen.*

Finding God Real

*The fool says in his heart, "There is no God." They are corrupt,
and their ways are vile; there is no one who does good.
God looks down from heaven on all mankind to see if
there are any who understand, any who seek God.*

PSALM 53:1–2 NIV

"I used to be an atheist. Now, I'm not." The congregation
clapped and cheered this young man's story at a baptismal service
celebrating several new believers in Christ. One lady shared how
lost and empty she had become and how her friends' faith walks
drew her to church, and then to Christ Himself. Story after story
brought hope to life.

One woman and her husband shared how hopeless they had
each come to feel. Their marriage was falling apart. Some costly
decisions caused him to lose his job. For some time she had been
considering divorce, just like those in her family had chosen. She
thought she had made up her mind to leave him. That was, until
some neighbor friends from church came alongside them.

They sought God. He answered. It was a process, of course,
this journey of faith, but trusting God with their struggles was
life changing. He has been a very real presence in helping them
work through things.

*Lord, thank You for being not only alive
and well, but active in my life. Show me
what You have for me today. Amen.*

Drenched in Light

*The people walking in darkness have seen a
great light; on those living in the land of
deep darkness a light has dawned.*
ISAIAH 9:2 NIV

With already two hours more of daylight than the short, dark
winter days, Clair felt revived returning from an evening walk.
Her front steps, always in the shadows during the winter solstice,
were now warm with sunshine. Newly planted petunias reached
for the sunlight from their pots, basking in the drench of warmth
along with Clair.

Birds chirped from all around as they found building
materials for nests and food for their young. A robin fluttered
near her as if looking to see if she had anything useful. The
fragrance of a blooming tree was brought over by a gentle breeze
that made her sigh with happiness.

These were the days she longed for in the thick of waiting
for winter to end. She let it melt her for a moment as she sat on
the porch step and savored the moment, thanking God for the
simple things in this spring day.

*Lord, thank You for the promise of better days no
matter what season it is where I am in this life.
Bless this day, right where I am. Amen.*

The Feeder

*Are not five sparrows sold for two pennies? Yet not
one of them is forgotten by God. Indeed, the very
hairs of your head are all numbered. Don't be afraid;
you are worth more than many sparrows.*
LUKE 12:6–7 NIV

Susan started filling the bird feeder again, something that she
didn't do during the winter. In just minutes birds began stopping
by to grab a few seeds and kernels. Black birds, cardinals, and
sparrows were soon regulars, with a pair of blue jays making
an appearance from time to time. Of course the squirrels were
pretty interested, too, if they could just figure out how to get to it
without falling. Sometimes the blue jays chased the whole crowd
away. All of this activity brought nearby cats to the scene trying
to catch a bird, most times unsuccessfully.

Watching some of these moments from the kitchen window
provided Susan with a lot of sweet, quiet stretches and plenty of
smiles. It was entertaining, but even more than that it reminded
her of how God provides for the smallest things. Whether
straight from the stem or out of a feeder the tiny sparrows would
not go hungry. She marveled at God's creation and how He must
smile, too, taking care of and watching all that He made.

*Lord God, thank You for all that You have
created and how You care for our every need. Amen.*

Safe and Secure

*In thee, O LORD, do I put my trust: let me never
be put to confusion. Deliver me in thy righteousness,
and cause me to escape: incline thine ear unto me,
and save me. Be thou my strong habitation, whereunto
I may continually resort: thou hast given commandment
to save me; for thou art my rock and my fortress.*
PSALM 71:1–3 KJV

Rae had gone with her young sons for a couple days to visit
her brother. He was a brave single man to have her crazy crew
stay the night. After they all ate macaroni and cheese dinner
together, the boys settled in with a movie while Rae and her
brother sat in the kitchen with dessert and caught up.

Lost in good conversation she suddenly realized that three-
year-old Dexter was nowhere to be seen. She quickly walked the
short hall of the three-bedroom apartment scanning each room
until she found the sweetest scene she had ever found him in. In
her brother's room there lay Dexter snuggled in the center of the
large fluffy bed, tucked under the down comforter, surrounded
by a little cloud of pillows. When he saw her he giggled and
cuddled in with the toys in his hands.

Rae felt so good to see her child so happy, safe, and secure.
It made her think how much God must love protecting and
blessing her, too.

*God, thank You for being a strong and
secure place of rest for me, in this world
and in my heart and soul. Amen.*

Fortress and Fierce Winds

Fear not, nor be afraid [in the coming violent upheavals];
have I not told it to you from of old and declared it?
And you are My witnesses! Is there a God besides Me?
There is no [other] Rock; I know not any.
ISAIAH 44:8 AMP

Just as Gael looked out the window to assess the strong winds
whipping up outside, her neighbor's heavy trash can blew down
the street. A bike in her driveway on its kickstand crashed onto
its side. The dog was whining.

Gael quickly went down to the basement while she looked
at the weather on her phone for emergency alerts. It turned out
to be just very strong winds that day, gusts of over sixty miles per
hour. They lost a few shingles from the roof, and everything that
wasn't nailed down outside fell over.

It was a real blessing to have a safe place to go even though
she wasn't in real danger that day. It was encouraging to think
how this paralleled God, by analogy only, of course—the way
He was always a Rock for her no matter what came her way.
Whether weather or a storm of life, He is truly our stronghold.

Lord God, thank You for being a fortress
for me every day. Give me the protection
and strength I need for today. Amen.

Always For Me

*If God is for us, who can ever be against us? Since he
did not spare even his own Son but gave him up for us all,
won't he also give us everything else? Who dares accuse us
whom God has chosen for his own? No one—for God
himself has given us right standing with himself.*

ROMANS 8:31–33 NLT

Sheri's students adored her. She taught physical education and
managed a good balance of learning, physical fitness, and fun.
Beyond that she enjoyed encouraging her students as individuals.
She took an interest in their aspirations, and they would often
talk about what they were thinking about for the future. Sheri's
faith shone through in her work without having to mention a
word of it. Her students took notice and several of them began
attending the youth group that she and her husband led. Young
people were coming to Christ; many of their parents became
Sheri's friends and began to think about a faith walk themselves.

An administrator at her school strongly opposed the
influence she was having and found a reason to take her out of
her position and move her elsewhere in the system. The injustice
was disheartening for many months. That was until she realized
that her new position was becoming a great fit for her, something
she didn't think was possible. God was using her here, too, just in
a different way.

*God, thank You for being for me, always!
Even when it all seems wrong, continue to
make a way for me to shine for You. Amen.*

A Little Lost and Hungry

" 'Never again will they hunger; never again will they thirst.
The sun will not beat down on them, nor any scorching heat.
For the Lamb at the center of the throne will be their shepherd;
he will lead them to springs of living water.
And God will wipe away every tear from their eyes.'"
REVELATION 7:16–17 NIV

Sunshine warmed their faces through the trees at the trailhead.
It was the longest hike Mike and Sue had ventured out on and
would take them the day to traverse the nine miles to the summit
and back. Their layers of clothing kept them warm through the
shady passes, still quite cool in the Smoky Mountains. They
enjoyed a magnificent view to the east, with shade under the
bright green trees. Every breathtaking scene encouraged them
to the top where the journey was worth every step. They were
careful not to stay too long so they could make the return before
nightfall. The descent proved a bit easier than the climb up, but
the trail splits looked unfamiliar. After a while they realized they
had taken a wrong turn. Sue was getting tired, discouraged, and
very hungry. By the time they made it back on course they were
an hour behind and out of food and water. "It's probably about
four more miles; we'll be fine," Mike encouraged.

Water from a drinking fountain never tasted so good than
that day when they made it back just after dark. Dinner at the
nearest restaurant was pretty spectacular, too.

Lord, thank You for providing for me.
Bless this day, too, with all that I need. Amen.

Longing to Belong

*You are citizens along with all of God's holy people. You are
members of God's family. Together, we are his house, built
on the foundation of the apostles and the prophets. And the
cornerstone is Christ Jesus himself. We are carefully joined
together in him, becoming a holy temple for the Lord.*

<small>EPHESIANS 2:19–21 NLT</small>

Clad in orange and navy blue, Danny and Kim made their way
to their seats at the Detroit Tigers game with their three young
sons. As they made it up the last two flights of stairs two young
men with blue face paint ran happily by.

Finally at their seats, the national anthem was just
beginning. They remained standing and reminded the boys to
remove their ball caps, which they did proudly. Kim noticed a
whole group of painted-faced people directly across the stadium
from them, cheering and having a great time together. With
each runner advancement and run scored during the game they
ran the aisles cheering. Other fans had cow bells and pom-poms.
They stood exuberantly with each successful play, celebrating.
Some started a crowd wave, getting most everybody to their feet.
It was a great experience to be part of something much bigger
than themselves. There was a feeling of belonging for each one
pulling for the team.

Kim thought about how we all long to belong, and our
culture provides a lot of places to do that. Thankfully God
provides a place for us to belong that doesn't
depend on this world's circumstances, and
our admission has already been paid.

*Lord, thank You for a place of belonging,
here, now, and forever. Amen.*

Yackity Yak

*Understand [this], my beloved brethren. Let every
man be quick to hear [a ready listener], slow to speak,
slow to take offense and to get angry.*

JAMES 1:19 AMP

The family had gathered for a Memorial Day weekend celebration at Aunt Sally's big place on the lake. There were people there that Susan hadn't seen in years and others she hadn't even met yet. She greeted her sweet aunt until other guests arrived and needed her aunt's attention. Then she began working her way through the group to catch up with a few people.

In the great room several men were talking intensely about baseball players and statistics while a game aired on the projection screen behind them. Down in the family room overlooking the lake a group of mothers talked oh so confidently about the best and latest child-rearing practices they were employing, and how their neighbors were not. Susan kept walking. Out on the patio a group of college-age relatives were talking about heated political issues. She stood for a few moments, listening, and considered joining the conversation, but a couple of them were doing nothing but putting down whoever didn't agree with them.

She wandered toward the water's edge where children were playing corn hole on the beach and Uncle Rich sat relaxing in one of the Adirondack chairs. "How are you, Susan?"

She sat down and thanked God for people who listen more than they talk. She realized that day that she wanted to be more like that.

*Lord, help me to be a good listener and think
carefully about the words I use today. Amen.*

Constant and Shifting

When I look at the night sky and see the work of your fingers—
the moon and the stars you set in place —
what are mere mortals that you should think about them,
human beings that you should care for them?
Yet you made them only a little lower than God
and crowned them with glory and honor.
PSALM 8:3–5 NLT

Rachel's brother sent her a postcard from his international business travels. He was somewhere in Italy this time and wrote, "It's amazing that I can look up at the stars wherever I am and know that the people I love can see them, too." It warmed her heart, and she never looked at the night skies the same way again.

She thought about how steady the stars were for people, a sure guide to stay on course or to find their way when they are lost. Constant as they are, they still shift all year long, and yet even that is predictable. Stars die and are formed continually, too, yet the ever-changing line-up doesn't change the order that God has placed in the universe. What comfort Rachel felt thinking on how God had it all in His hands. Furthermore, He had given her a place in it all, a place where she was loved and cared for by the God of the Universe Himself.

Lord God, thank You for the predictability
and order You have given me in this world
You created. Guide me today. Amen.

Sacrifice

*My command is this: Love each other
as I have loved you. Greater love has no one
than this: to lay down one's life for one's friends.*
JOHN 15:12–13 NIV

When Julian Arechaga enlisted post 9/11 with the Marine
Corps he was still a teenager. After his second seven-month
deployment to Kandahar, Afghanistan, he was free to request
transfer to a non-deployable unit. But his sense of duty brought
him to a third deployment, to Fallujah, Iraq. Still not willing
to leave his unit, his fourth deployment was to Ramadi, Iraq,
a rough place. Now a sergeant and squad leader for a quick
reaction force, he and his men were responding to a firefight
that another squad was involved in, but Al-Qaeda fighters were
targeting the reaction force this time, rather than the initial
squad that received fire. Sergeant Arechaga was driving the
Humvee that hit a buried IED (explosives) in the road. The
vehicle was split in two. Sergeant Arechaga and two other
marines died that day. Their loyal sergeant, then twenty-three
years old, left behind his bride of only a few months, and many
who loved and respected him.

Sergeant Julian Arechaga gave his life that others might
live in freedom. He, and thousands upon thousands more, have
sacrificed their lives for a greater purpose.

In a similar way Christ died for us. Willingly, eagerly, with
loyalty to His mission, He gave His life that we would have a
way to be free from sin and separation from God.

*Lord, today I thank You for Your sacrifice
for me, and for those who have sacrificed
for my country. Amen.*

A Place of Peace

May God give you more and more mercy, peace, and love.
JUDE 1:2 NLT

Semi-trucks boxed Mary in slow mode on the interstate en route to the city. Tight on time, she sipped her coffee and nibbled on a breakfast bar trying to keep her building road rage contained. The car behind her started tailgating. The daily commute for a week-long work class made her thankful she didn't do this every day.

Parking quickly in the garage she made it up to the top floor of the library just in time. She found her way to the only empty seat in the very front. The instructor was very interactive with the people nearest her. Mary sighed silently and settled in. It was going to be a long day.

During class she was getting texts from one of her children with a tuition crisis, and as the break was beginning her husband called. Mary stepped out the doors where there was a peaceful roof garden she had never known existed. The phone conversation about student loans and their son's college tuition was a stark contrast to her surroundings. Flowers in raised beds boasted bright colors and reached toward the sun. A gentle breeze blew through petite trees and tall grasses. Mary sat down on a wooden bench and began to feel unexpectedly calm. She and her husband figured out what to do to help their son out of his crisis. After the call she enjoyed this surprising place of peace.

*Lord, thank You for providing peaceful places
on crazy days, and most of all for being my
peace any time I come to You. Amen.*

Wisdom in Our Walk

The fear of the Lord is the beginning of wisdom;
all who follow his precepts have good understanding.
To him belongs eternal praise.
Psalm 111:10 niv

Dexter wanted to keep hiking higher up the mountain where they were blazing their own trail over and around boulders. His brothers loved the adventure as much as him but insisted it was getting too late in the day and the temperature was dropping. They all turned back, much to Dexter's disappointment; he had really wanted to get to the top.

At the base of the mountain sat Mom and Dad waiting at the meet-up point, and thankful for the wisdom of Dexter's older brothers. Had the boys continued it would have gotten dark and they may not have found their way back down safely.

They had a healthy fear of putting themselves in danger, and knowing the sheer consequences of their decisions gave them wisdom. It is a beautiful picture of how it works with God. He gives us clear commands and guidelines to protect us, and if we listen and apply them, we grow in wisdom.

Father God, thank You for Your Word and the
wisdom we can gain by listening to You. Amen.

Simple Joy

Yet I am confident I will see the LORD'S GOODNESS
while I am here in the land of the living.
PSALM 27:13 NLT

Marie's husband was out of work and unmotivated to find another job. The overdue bills were mounting along with the stressfulness of the situation. For many weeks she had trouble sleeping and needed rest so desperately to make it through her long days at work.

Nearly exasperated, finally one night she got a good night's sleep. She awoke to birds singing just outside her slightly open window where a gentle breeze blew the curtain open enough to let in sunshine and the smell of lavender just now in bloom.

There was much that Marie could not control about the situations in her life, it was a difficult season to be sure, but she decided to enjoy the blessings. She spent a few moments just savoring the simply joys of sleep and morning sunshine.

Lord God, in the midst of many circumstances outside of my control, thank You for the simple things today. Amen.

Panicking to Peace

Let them continually say, "Great is the LORD,
who delights in blessing his servant with peace!"
PSALM 35:27 NLT

On an unseasonably hot day, Rachel and Dave entered Cedar
Point, their favorite amusement park, with their four teenage
sons and four of the boys' friends. The first screaming roller
coaster was a group activity. They all had a great time even
waiting in line talking and laughing. When the group decided to
go different ways and meet up later Rachel turned to get water.
When she turned around they were all gone, including Dave.

She walked around looking, thinking surely they wouldn't
leave her behind, but they were nowhere to be seen in the
crowds. She walked aimlessly for a while, trying to call a few
of them on their phones, and no one was picking up. She was
surprised by how panicked she felt being all alone even though
she was totally safe, and so were they. She realized that they had
inconsistent reception at the edge of Lake Erie. Still, she was
very upset. What would she do on her own? She started feeling
sorry for herself.

Then she started thinking about all the times she longed for
time alone when the boys were young. As she walked around she
began thanking God for how wonderfully the boys had grown
and for this beautiful day. She bought some ice cream for
herself and enjoyed a peaceful walk on the beach.

God, thank You for unexpected blessings,
even when they seem like inconveniences
at first. You are so good to me. Amen.

Fade

> *"Shout that people are like the grass. Their beauty fades*
> *as quickly as the flowers in a field. The grass withers*
> *and the flowers fade beneath the breath of the* LORD.
> *And so it is with people. The grass withers and the*
> *flowers fade, but the word of our God stands forever."*
>
> ISAIAH 40:6–8 NLT

Her four children were young when she made that T-shirt with the puff-painted flowers and Isaiah verse on it. She wore it a lot longer than she thought she might, seeing it frequently in the two and three loads of laundry each day. She had so much energy those years, volunteering at Vacation Bible School and keeping up with the kids, house, and all of her other work. The elder ladies in the church would marvel, remembering their own younger motherhood days and how fast they grew older, but somehow she felt like it would never come.

Now, what seemed so far away was suddenly upon her. She looked at her hands now folding only a load of laundry every day or two, and she had to look twice. Those were her grandmother's hands! Her children were all in their twenties now and independent. Her elders were so right, and thankfully she was enjoying this stage of life. Now she could hold the young mothers' babies and encourage those who felt time would never go fast enough.

> *Lord, give me the grace and wisdom for the*
> *stage of life I am in right now, and help*
> *me to encourage others in Your Word,*
> *with eternal perspective. Amen.*

Sitting and Secure

*My salvation and my honor depend on God; he is my
mighty rock, my refuge. Trust in him at all times, you people;
pour out your hearts to him, for God is our refuge.*
PSALM 62:7–8 NIV

Heavy rains blew in under the overhang at a sharp angle. Rae
checked the cover over her infant daughter in the carrier on her
lap. She peeked in at her cute little face and took in deeply the
sweet aroma of her baby's breath. They had just been on their
first shopping trip together. Sitting on that red bench outside
Hill's Department store she savored the moments as they waited
for her husband to pick them up.

Rae could not have known that this was their only shopping
trip and that her daughter would stop breathing during that very
night. There was no way she could be prepared for the pain that
came from losing her, and then waiting until eternity to see her
again. Rae returned many times to that blessed moment on the
red bench and thanked God for it.

Later, for a long time, she didn't want to count her blessings,
for fear of losing them. After years of wrestling with God she
came to sit securely on life's benches of blessing—never knowing
what would come of tomorrow, but trusting God with all of it.

*Lord God, no matter what tomorrow brings, help
me to trust You with that and with today. Amen.*

A New Month

*Because of the Lord's great love we are not consumed,
for his compassions never fail. They are new
every morning; great is your faithfulness.*
LAMENTATIONS 3:22–23 NIV

There is something nice about the first day of the month. It is the day we turn our calendars to a clean page with no engagements scribbled through for cancellation or rescheduling just yet. It is new and fresh and inviting! Or. . . is today just the day the rent or other bills are due? It all depends on how you see the world. As a believer in Christ, it is much easier to see the glass as half full rather than half empty. God's Word tells us that His mercies are new every morning. He is faithful to His people. His compassion never fails. Regardless of our circumstances, we know that God is in control and that He will never leave us. Perhaps the new month ahead will be packed with activity and you will wish things could slow down or maybe you will find yourself bored and wishing for plans. Either way, your heavenly Father is ready to work in your life this month. Will you welcome June today? Will you commit to being open to God's blessings and all that He desires to teach you in the next thirty days?

*Lord, thank You for a new month and a fresh start.
Help me to welcome it with great anticipation
of what You have in store for me. Amen.*

A Time for Sadness and a Time for Joy

A time to weep and a time to laugh,
a time to mourn and a time to dance.
ECCLESIASTES 3:4 NIV

Solomon has been declared the wisest man who ever lived. The third chapter of Ecclesiastes, which Solomon authored, tells us that there is a time for everything. Do you find yourself in a time of weeping or a joyful time today? You may be mourning a deep loss in your life. You may ache to your very core with disappointment and sorrow. There is a time to be sad. You don't have to put on a show or an artificial happy face. It is okay to grieve. It is appropriate even. There are times in our lives when we must rely on God's grace just to see us through another day. We may need to lean on other believers and let them carry us for a time. But the good news is that there are also joyful occasions. Psalm 30:5 says that weeping may last for a night but that joy comes in the morning. If you are in a sorrowful period, know that joy is just around the corner. You may not be able to imagine it today, but you will smile and even laugh again. If you are joyful today, know that even when you face sad days, the Lord will be there walking with you. He never leaves us alone.

Thank You, God, for the knowledge that sadness does not last forever. There are highs and lows in life, and as Your Word declares, there is a time for everything. Amen.

Praise Him

*But Jesus answered, "I tell you, if my followers
didn't say these things, then the stones would cry out."*
LUKE 19:40 NCV

Jesus says that if His people do not praise Him, the rocks will
cry out. We serve a God who must be praised. He is worthy of
honor and praise. We serve a God who created the universe and
everything in it. He is not a small g god. He is a capital G God.
He is a great big God, and He deserves great big praise. How do
we praise Him? We praise Him by telling Him of His greatness.
When you pray, before you begin asking the Lord for things,
try telling Him how wonderful you think He is. Speak scripture
back to Him. Tell Him that He is the Great I Am and your
provider. He is the Prince of Peace and the King of Kings. He
is the Lord of Lords, the Savior, your Abba Father. Praise Him
for you are wonderfully made. Praise Him for His presence that
is always near. Then your heart will be filled with thankfulness
and you can move into a time of thanksgiving in your prayers.
Certainly it is appropriate to ask God for things that others need
or that you yourself desire, but God is honored when you begin
with praise.

*Lord, I praise You for who You are. You are the
Creator of this beautiful world. You are the King of
Kings and yet, You became a man and lived on
earth. You died for me. I praise You for these
things and so much more. Amen.*

A Place in Heaven

*"My Father's house has many rooms; if that were
not so, would I have told you that I am going
there to prepare a place for you?"*
JOHN 14:2 NIV

At times, heaven seems far, far away. You gaze into the sky and
try to imagine it—God on His throne, angels singing, no more
tears, only joy, only praise for the Father. But you can't see it. It is
not visible to the human eye.

Other times, heaven seems ever so close. Have you said
good-bye to a loved one who was a Christian? You simply let
them slip away, out of your grasp, from one world to the next,
from earth to heaven. Heaven seems close in those moments,
just beyond a thin veil, almost reachable, almost visible. If
someone you love dearly and who recently talked and laughed
with you has gone there suddenly, heaven feels a little closer.

There is much we do not know about heaven, but we know
that our Jesus is there preparing a place for us. We are not aware
of the exact date or time that we will leave this earth, but God
is. The Bible says there is an appointed time for each of us to
be born and to die. There is no question for the Christian about
what happens after death. We will go instantly into the presence
of the Lord. If you know Jesus as your Savior, He is preparing a
place in heaven—just for you.

*Thank You, Jesus, for preparing a place
for me in heaven . . . with You . . .
where I will live eternally. Amen.*

Put on Love

And over all these virtues put on love,
which binds them all together in perfect unity.
COLOSSIANS 3:14 NIV

Paul wrote a letter to the Colossians, a church he loved and had spent time with, a group of people whom he knew needed this advice. We need the same advice today. He told the Colossians that as God's people they were dearly loved. He admonished them to exhibit compassion, kindness, and humility. As if this was not enough, Paul also told them to show gentleness and to have patience with one another. He told them to bear with one another and to forgive one another as the Lord had forgiven them. Then Paul said a peculiar thing, but it really makes a lot of sense. He told them to put on love.

But how does one "wear" love? Imagine a winter morning. You put on long underwear, then a shirt, followed by a sweater, and on top of all that, you wear a coat. It binds it all together. Like the buns on a burger! Like the chocolate wafers of an ice cream sandwich! What enables you to forgive, to show compassion, to be gentle? What can cause even the most type-A personality to be patient with another believer? Love. Only love. It binds it all together. It causes the Christian to look and act and even feel different from the non-Christian. It is the greatest of all the virtues. Don't start your day without putting on love!

Father, let Your love show in all that
I do today. Help me to be quick to forgive
others as You have forgiven me. Amen.

Seek Peace

Turn away from evil and do good.
Search for peace, and work to maintain it.
The eyes of the Lord watch over those who do right;
his ears are open to their cries for help.
PSALM 34:14–15 NLT

If something is worth searching for, it is often very valuable. Pirates search for treasure. A lady may search for just the right dress for a party or the perfect pair of shoes to match an outfit. Children playing hide and seek search for the participant who is hiding. To find this hidden person and capture him is to win the game!

God's Word, in the Psalms, tells us to search for peace. Peace is more valuable than all of the wealth on earth. To lay your head on your pillow at night and know that you are at peace with God and with those around you is a tremendous blessing. True peace is known only by the Christian. The world offers counterfeit versions, but only God can give true and lasting peace that passes all understanding. Seek peace. Search for it. Protect its presence in your life at all costs. If you are on a path that does not bring you peace, you are on the wrong path. Ask God to give you the strength to say no to the things that curtail peace in your life. Peace is essential.

Father, help me to find peace. Reveal to me any
area of my life that is not pleasing to You that I
might rid myself of it. I want to be at peace
with You and with those around me. Amen.

God Is in the Details

Give all your worries and cares to God,
for he cares about you.
1 PETER 5:7 NLT

Do you ever wonder if God cares about the details of your life?

Take a look at nature. God is definitely a God of details. Notice the various patterns, shapes, and sizes of animals. Their life cycles. The noises they make. Their natural defenses. Details!

Have you wandered through the woods? Towering trees. Their scents. The cool refreshment their shade provides. The different types of leaves, and the tiny, life-bearing veins that run through them. How intricate!

What about the weather? It is filled with details from the hand of your God. The Creator sends raindrops—sometimes gentle and kind, other times harsh and pelting. He warms us with the sun, cools us with breezes, and yes—it is true—He fashions each snowflake, each unique, no two alike! The same way He designs His children!

Do you wonder if God cares about that struggle you are facing at work or the argument you had with a loved one? Is He aware of your desire to find that special someone or the difficulty you find in loving your spouse? He cares. Tell Him your concerns. He is not too busy to listen to the details. He wants to show Himself real and alive to you in such a way that you know it must be Him. The details of your life are not little to God. If they matter to you, they matter to God.

Thank You, Lord, for caring about
the details of my life. It means so
much to know You care. Amen.

Laziness vs. Rest

*Come unto me, all ye that labour and
are heavy laden, and I will give you rest.*
MATTHEW 11:28 KJV

In our society, we are so very busy. Many people work seven days a week. Even children's schedules are packed with lessons and tutoring, special classes, and clubs. They dance and play sports. They go, go, go . . . just like the adults in their lives. Why are we all so busy? Are we running from the quiet? Are we afraid to rest? We complain about the busyness but continue to pack our calendars and to-do lists. Do we think we might appear lazy or strange if we simply choose to stay home, to have quality time with God and with our families?

Certainly, the Bible warns against laziness with such verses as Ecclesiastes 10:18, which says: "Laziness leads to a sagging roof; idleness leads to a leaky house" (NLT). But Jesus Himself rested. He often went away from the crowds to rest and to pray, to rejuvenate. We are commanded to remember the Sabbath and keep it holy. This involves rest. We are encouraged to be still and know that He is God. Don't confuse laziness with rest. Just because you are not busy one day or one evening does not mean you should experience unnecessary guilt. Find a balance between work and play, busyness and rest. You will be better off for it in the long run.

*God, help me to avoid laziness but to seek
out rest when it is needed in my life. Amen.*

Count Your Blessings

Every good action and every perfect gift is from God. These good gifts come down from the Creator of the sun, moon, and stars, who does not change like their shifting shadows.

JAMES 1:17 NCV

There is a popular contemporary Christian song that says it well.

> For all Your goodness I will keep on singing
> Ten thousand reasons for my heart to find
> Bless the Lord
> O my soul
> O my soul
> Worship His holy name!

There is an old hymn that drives the same point home: "Blessings all mine and ten thousand beside."

Whether you stand with hands raised or kneel beside your bed in silent prayer, moved to tears of gratitude, does not matter. Whether your lips utter the words of a hymn or a contemporary chorus is not of any consequence. What matters is that you praise Him. What matters is that you thank Him. Every good and perfect gift that you find in your life has come straight from the hands of God. He withholds nothing good from His children. Even earthly parents know how to love, and they desire to give good gifts to their children. How much more does your heavenly Father love you! How much more does He want to lavish blessings upon you! Thank the Lord today for the blessings in your life.

Father, I am so blessed. Why do I grumble and complain? Look at all that You have done in my life! Look at all that You have freely given me! Thank You, Lord, for Your many blessings. Amen.

God Cares about Your Disappointments

You number and record my wanderings; put my
tears into Your bottle—are they not in Your book?
PSALM 56:8 AMP

There are disappointments in the Christian life. God has not
promised us otherwise. When sin entered the world in the
garden that day through a bite of fruit, disappointment was
instantly included in the consequences. This is a fallen world.
We live and move and have our being in a place that truly is not
our home. One day and for all eternity, in heaven, everything
will be perfect as it is supposed to be. We will spend our days
praising God. There will be no more tears or loss. We will not
be let down or hurt in any way. But here, and for now, there
is disappointment. We must learn to live with it. We should
embrace it even.

It is in the sorrows of life that God shows Himself so real
and loving. He is near to the brokenhearted. The Bible says He
"collects our tears." Have you gone through a divorce that you
never dreamed would take place? Are you heartbroken over a
child's decisions? Has someone hurt you or abandoned you at the
time you needed him or her most? God is there in the midst of the
hurt. He may not always take the storm away but He will always
ride it out with you. Take refuge in the Lord. He cares for you.

Thank You, heavenly Father, for caring when I hurt.
Even in my disappointments, I can see You at
work in my life. I love You, Lord. Amen.

Joy vs. Happiness

*And the disciples were filled with joy,
and with the Holy Ghost.*
ACTS 13:52 KJV

There is a popular children's song about joy often sung in Sunday school or church. It goes like this: "I've got the joy, joy, joy, joy down in my heart to stay!" While it was written for children, it bears a wonderful message for all of us.

The difference between happiness and joy is that joy stays. If you are a believer in Christ, He resides in your heart. No matter what your circumstances, you can maintain a joy that is deep in your heart. You are a child of God and He will never leave you. You know you have the promise of eternal life. Happiness, on the other hand, is an emotion that comes and goes within minutes. Ever heard a baby crying loudly but when he or she gets what she wants—a bottle, the mother, or a toy—the crying ceases immediately? Sadness has turned to contentedness. Temporary! Take the object of the baby's affection away and the tears return. As adults, we are not that different from these young ones. The break-up of a dating relationship or news that we are going to have to move due to a job transfer can zap us of our happiness. Not so with joy! Joy remains. Peace and joy go hand in hand.

The Christian never has to lack either.

*Lord, thank You that even when I am not
particularly happy, I have joy in Jesus. I have
joy deep down in my heart because You have
saved me and made me Your child. Amen.*

When You Are Tempted

*No temptation has overtaken you except what is common to
mankind. And God is faithful; he will not let you be tempted
beyond what you can bear. But when you are tempted,
he will also provide a way out so that you can endure it.*

1 CORINTHIANS 10:13 NIV

Have you ever felt that temptation was just too great? Have
you given in to it? You are not alone. It is not easy to resist
temptation. Satan, the prince of darkness, is always seeking to
devour God's children. He knows your personal weaknesses and
uses them against you. The good news is that there is always a
way out when you are tempted to sin. Every temptation that you
have ever faced or will face in the future has been experienced by
others. No temptation is new. Satan just recycles the same juicy
bait and uses it again and again, generation after generation.
Staying in God's Word and praying daily will help you to resist
temptation. Being part of a Christian community will help
with this also. As you bring down your walls and allow other
believers to get close to you, they can pray for you and hold you
accountable. Remember that no matter what temptations you are
facing today, the pay-off will be far greater if you resist than if
you give in. Jesus stands ready to help you escape if only you will
reach out and take His hand.

*Lord, help me in this area today: (fill in this blank
with your area of greatest temptation to sin). I need
to see the way out. Thank You, Father. Amen.*

Laugh Today!

*A happy heart makes the face cheerful,
but heartache crushes the spirit.*
PROVERBS 15:13 NIV

Some researchers say that a positive attitude can actually help
you to live longer! Isn't that amazing? Did you know that
laughter can do the same thing? Find something to laugh about
today. Abraham's wife, Sarah, laughed when she discovered
she was pregnant at an old age after longing for a baby for so
many years. God surprised her when she had given up! Perhaps
God has granted you an unexpected blessing. If so, laugh with
joy today! If you have trouble with this, read the comics in the
newspaper. Watch a humorous YouTube video of a dog or cat.
Rent a movie that has some good, clean comedy. Read a few
entries in a joke book. Do whatever it takes to find some humor
in this day. Often, the greatest laughs come when we are free
enough to laugh at ourselves. Have you done something really
silly lately? Have you made a mistake that left you chuckling?
Laughter is good for the soul. The book of Proverbs says that if
your heart is happy, your face will show it. Are you going around
with a long face? Do people look forward to seeing you or are
you a "Debbie Downer"? If you find yourself complaining today,
try replacing negative words with cheerful ones. Everyone
enjoys being around someone who wears a smile.

*Father, grant me a happy heart today.
Where there is depression or bitterness within
me, replace the negativity with joy!
Thank You, Father. Amen.*

Freedom in Christ

*"And you will know the truth,
and the truth will set you free."*
JOHN 8:32 NLT

Today is Flag Day, a day on which Americans around the nation commemorate the American flag. There will be parades and speeches. Flags will fly with national pride in all fifty states. The red stands for bravery. The white, purity. The blue, liberty. As the symbolism of the American flag brings to mind your freedom as an American, think upon your freedom in Christ as well. Grace has been given to us as a free gift. We could never earn it or deserve it, but Jesus died for our sins on the cross. Knowing the truth of the Gospel sets you free! You are free to live an abundant life in Christ, and you have been granted eternal life. Certainly God has set before us commandments and statutes that we should follow. They are laws that will keep us healthy and at peace. They are for our best interest, for the Bible promises that God does not withhold any good and perfect gift from His own. But there is so much freedom in Jesus. Exercise your freedoms as an American, and neglect not your freedom in Christ. Express your love and appreciation to Him today for saving you.

*Lord, I am thankful for America and that You have placed
me in this country where I have so many freedoms as
a citizen. I also am a citizen of Your kingdom.
Thank You for my freedom in Christ! Amen.*

Forgiving Others

*As far as the east is from the west, so far
has he removed our transgressions from us.*
PSALM 103:12 NIV

Forgiveness. The word rolls off the tongue much more easily
than it penetrates the heart. When someone has wronged you,
it is natural to feel hurt. It is not easy to forgive a person who
has wounded you. Forgiveness is no small thing. It is a tall order.
The greater the offense, the harder you may find it to forgive.
The model prayer that Jesus taught His followers includes this
line: "Forgive us our trespasses as we forgive those who trespass
against us." What was Jesus saying here? He was reminding us
to emulate our Father's ability to forgive. Have we not all sinned
and fallen short of the glory of God? Certainly! But our heavenly
Father forgives us. He removes the dark stain of sin and says He
will speak of it no more. It is gone. As far as the east is from the
west. That is a long way! God does not keep bringing up your
past sins. If you have asked Him to forgive you, He has. Pray for
your heavenly Father to reveal to you just how much He loves
you. As you experience His love and forgiveness, you will want
to forgive others—regardless of the depth of the hurt they have
caused in your life.

*God, forgiveness is not always easy. Help me to
sense Your deep love for me. Remind me of all
that You have forgiven me of so that I might
be able to forgive others. Amen.*

Finding and Sharing Comfort

*Praise be to the God and Father of our Lord Jesus Christ,
the Father of compassion and the God of all comfort, who
comforts us in all our troubles, so that we can comfort those in
any trouble with the comfort we ourselves receive from God.
For just as we share abundantly in the sufferings of Christ,
so also our comfort abounds through Christ.*

2 Corinthians 1: 3–5 niv

Young children find comfort in a pacifier or a stuffed animal.
Perhaps the most common comfort to them is a special blanket.
As we grow older, comfort is harder to find. Certainly, a warm
blanket or a hot bubble bath will bring temporary comfort when
we are cold. A talk with a friend may soothe your worried heart a
bit. But real comfort is found in a relationship with the Lord. No
matter what trial or trouble you are facing today, He is there to
comfort you. You can rest in Jesus. You can come to Him and lay
down your concerns. You can talk with Him, listen to Him, or
even just speak His name. There is power and peace to be found
in the name of your Savior. One extra benefit to finding comfort
in the Lord is that you are then better equipped to comfort
others. You can offer a word of compassion to another who is
experiencing a similar hurt to that which you have known. You
are ready to comfort because you have been comforted.

*Father, please comfort me in that area of my life
that troubles me. Equip me to comfort those
around me. Amen.*

Times of Trouble

You turned my wailing into dancing;
you removed my sackcloth and clothed me with joy,
that my heart may sing your praises and not be silent.
Lord my God, I will praise you forever.
PSALM 30:11–12 NIV

David knew times of trouble, and he also knew what it meant to be relieved of trouble. He experienced want, and he experienced abundance. He hid in fear of losing his life to a king that he knew hated him . . . and later, he danced with joy, praising God, amazed at God's provision and protection. Can you relate? You probably have never been chased by a king and his armies. But every life is full of ups and downs. There will be times when all you can hope to do is survive in the shelter of the Lord's wing. You know He is there but you cannot sense His presence. You trust Him, but you don't know how in the world He will turn things around. Just keep trusting. Just keep believing. Just keep praying. David cried out to the Lord for mercy. Not just this psalm but many others are filled with David's pleas to the Lord. God is faithful to hear our prayers. Just as He turned David's sorrow into joy, He can do the same for you.

Father, I ask You to turn my weeping
into laughter. Teach me to praise You
no matter my circumstances. Amen.

Waiting

*Wait for the LORD;
be strong and take heart
and wait for the LORD.*
PSALM 27:14 NIV

In our society, we wait in line to buy groceries, to make bank deposits, and to pick up our kids from school. We wait in classrooms, exam rooms, and even in rooms called "waiting rooms." Waiting is part of life. Because we dislike it, we seek to make things faster. With the invention of drive-through windows, we don't have to get out of the car. The meal is handed to us from a window as we drive by and pay. Microwaves have shortened cook times. We can even sign in online at an after-hours medical clinic to avoid waiting with all the other sick people. We can wait at home instead, where we are able to multitask!

Some things are worth waiting for. Would you agree? The right spouse is definitely worth the wait. Some people drive around for a few minutes waiting for that front-row parking spot to open up. Sometimes we wait for just the perfect moment to share some news, whether good or bad, with family members or friends.

Waiting for God to answer our prayers is easier said than done. God does not hurry. Nor is He ever late. He is always right on time to bless us, and He has our best interests at heart. Seek God's answers for your questions, and be patient. Waiting on the Lord will always pay off.

*Help me, Lord, to be more patient. I know that
when You ask me to wait, You have a reason.
Thank You, Lord, for Your provision. Amen.*

God Will Rescue You

He brought me out into a spacious place;
he rescued me because he delighted in me.
PSALM 18:19 NIV

God miraculously delivered the Israelites from the waters of the Red Sea. He took them to the Promised Land of Canaan, which was rich and flowing with milk and honey. But He did not do this immediately. The Israelites had been in bondage for forty years in Egypt. God heard their cry. He saw their oppression. The Bible tells us that the Lord came down and rescued them. He does the same for us today. It may be that you have been in a hard place for a long time, so long that you have nearly given up on God. You may not believe that He will come for you, that He even wants to rescue you. The Israelites felt this way also. God is still in the business of rescuing His own today. When He saves you out of a depressed and sorrowful situation, He will take you to a new place. From Egypt to Canaan, so to speak. Have you sought God's deliverance? Be diligent in prayer. In His timing, God will answer your plea, just as He did for the Israelites. You are His child. Even while you remain in the desert, He can refresh your soul. Seek Him. He delights in you.

Father, help me to have faith that You know
what is best for me. Hear my cry from my own
personal "Egypt" today. I need to know
that You delight in me. Amen.

A Matter of Life or Death

For if you live according to the flesh, you will die; but if by the Spirit you put to death the misdeeds of the body, you will live.
ROMANS 8:13 NIV

A diabetic is dependent upon insulin. A cancer diagnosis demands medical treatment. For the blind, a cane or a seeing-eye dog is essential. These are matters of life or death.

The Bible teaches of another such matter. It is an ongoing war within the believer that simply must be won by the right side! It is spiritual life versus spiritual death.

The Holy Spirit indwells believers in Christ. Jesus Himself taught His followers about this third part of the Trinity before He ascended into heaven. He promised that a Helper would come. This Helper, the Holy Spirit, came when Jesus went away. The Spirit convicts us of sin. The Spirit, sometimes referred to as our Counselor, also guides us in truth.

If you are a Christian, the Holy Spirit is your personal power source. The strength to do what is right is within you if you choose to live by the Spirit and not by the flesh. You will be tempted to follow voices that tell you to do as you please or that "it's okay if it feels right." You will experience anger and other emotions that can lead you astray in life. But if you pay attention, your Helper, the Holy Spirit, will reveal the Father's ways. It is a matter of life or death. Which will you choose?

*Father, today I choose life. May Your
Holy Spirit lead me in truth. Amen.*

Your Heavenly Father

*If ye then, being evil, know how to give good gifts unto
your children: how much more shall your heavenly
Father give the Holy Spirit to them that ask him?*
LUKE 11:13 KJV

Today is the day set aside for honoring fathers. It may be a joyful
or a painful day. Depending on the relationship you have had
with your earthly father, you may look forward to this holiday
or you may dread it. The good news is that whether or not your
earthly father has played a positive role in your life (or any role
at all), you have a heavenly Father who loves you with a deep,
unconditional love! Perhaps you grew up in a home without a
father's presence due to death or divorce. Maybe your father
led your family well in many ways but fell short when it came
to spiritual matters. If you have a good relationship with your
father, celebrate him today by telling him just how much he
means to you! You may wish to write him a letter or make a
phone call. If you have had conflicts with your father, perhaps
today is a day that you can set those feelings aside and find a
way to forgive. Every father–child relationship is different. You
may not even know who your earthly father is, but you know the
Father of all fathers. You are God's child now.

*Lord, thank You for earthly fathers and the great
impact they can have on our lives. Thank You
most of all for being our heavenly Father who
loves us beyond our human comprehension. Amen.*

Running the Race

*Wherefore seeing we also are compassed about with
so great a cloud of witnesses, let us lay aside every weight,
and the sin which doth so easily beset us, and let us run
with patience the race that is set before us, Looking
unto Jesus the author and finisher of our faith.*
HEBREWS 12:1– 2 KJV

The Christian life is a race. It must be run with endurance. It
requires training and discipline. It is about putting one foot in
front of the other, sometimes quickly, sometimes slowly, but
always, always moving forward. When a runner stumbles in a 5K
or marathon, what does he do? Does he just sit down right then
and there and call it quits? If the race is not run with perfection,
does he just throw in the towel? Of course not! Likewise, as you
are running the race, when you get sidetracked or distracted,
when you fall to temptation or take your eyes off the goal, ask
Jesus to get you back on track. An old hymn puts it like this:
"Turn your eyes upon Jesus. Look full in His wonderful face.
And the things of earth will grow strangely dim, in the light of
His glory and grace!" Look to Christ, the author and finisher
of your faith. He will run right alongside you, encouraging you
every step of the way.

*Jesus, help me to keep my focus on You as I
journey through this life. It is not always easy,
but You are always with me. Amen.*

Hold God's Hand

*"I am the LORD YOUR GOD, who holds your right hand,
and I tell you, 'Don't be afraid. I will help you.'"*
ISAIAH 41:13 NCV

It is a typical Saturday in a suburban neighborhood. The sun is shining brightly. A daddy runs alongside his six-year-old daughter's bicycle, holding on to the back to reassure her she won't topple. Cheering on the bike rider from the porch, the little girl's mother holds the hands of a toddler son and helps him climb up and down the porch steps. He does it again and again. It is a new accomplishment for him, and it is fun! A couple of doors down, a grandfather holds the hands of one of his twin grandsons. The boys are taking turns being swung around in the air. They laugh and grow dizzy, falling over in the soft green grass, but they always come back for more. Children reach out for a hand many, many times each day. It is good for them to have a hand to hold as streets are crossed or steep steps are climbed. Often, a child wants to hold a trusted adult's hand simply for comfort or companionship. God offers you a hand in much the same manner. You are His child. Take His hand today. He will walk with you wherever you go. If you let Him, He will even lead the way.

*Lord, thank You for holding my hand as
I face challenges in my life. It helps to know
You are with me. I will not be afraid for
my God goes with me. Amen.*

Praying for Forgiveness

*Who can discern his lapses and errors? Clear me from
hidden [and unconscious] faults. Keep back Your servant
also from presumptuous sins; let them not have dominion
over me! Then shall I be blameless, and I shall be
innocent and clear of great transgression.*

PSALM 19:12–13 AMP

Sin is part of our lives in a fallen world. It would be impossible
to know all of our errors. The psalmist's prayer here is one worth
emulating. He asks for forgiveness for his known sins and also
for those committed unconsciously. Who knows how many
times per day we offend God without even being aware of the
offense? We have sinned in the past. We will sin in the future.
And we have sinned even this very day, if only in our thought
lives. And so we come before a Holy God, through Christ, who
makes a way for us to enter into His presence. We come and
we lay it down. We ask to be forgiven for that which we did
on purpose and that which we did not. The psalmist prays that
presumptuous sins would not have dominion over him. The
Message calls them "stupid sins." The New International Version
refers to these sins as "willful." The apostle Paul warned against
taking advantage of grace. The Christian should be constantly on
guard against sin because sin breaks God's heart.

*Father, keep me from sin. Forgive me for
offenses I've committed of which I was not
even aware. Make me more sensitive to Your
Word that I might be aware of sin and
avoid it in Your strength. Amen.*

"Doing Life" Together

*Iron sharpeneth iron; so a man
sharpeneth the countenance of his friend.*

Proverbs 27:17 KJV

Many churches encourage members to become part of a home group or community group. These groups are known by different names. One church refers to them (appropriately!) as life groups. While certainly there is nothing new about Bible study classes, which have been around for centuries, this idea of doing life together throughout the week is new to some believers. For some, studying the Bible, prayer, and worship have long been isolated to Sundays. Setting aside the Sabbath is a start, but God desires that Christians live and grow in community with one another throughout the week, not just when they enter the church building. Believers grow and challenge one another when they meet together regularly. We become closer to God when we open up and allow other believers to pray for us. Home groups in some churches have bonded so deeply that when a member is sick, other members will provide meals or care for the person's children if needed. As relationships are formed, it becomes possible to speak into one another's lives in love. Christians need one another. As iron sharpens iron, so one believer sharpens another. When you have been with brothers and sisters in Christ, it will show in your countenance and it will alter your interactions with those around you who don't know the Lord.

*Father, help me to find a community
of believers within my church with
whom to connect and "do life." Amen.*

Pride vs. Humility

A man's pride shall bring him low:
but honour shall uphold the humble in spirit.
PROVERBS 29:23 KJV

A great leader is known by his or her character. It is perhaps the
things that one doesn't take part in that sets him or her apart.
Great leaders are not prideful or boastful. They don't consider
their accomplishments to be things they have done "in and of
themselves," but they recognize the hand of God on their lives.
Great leaders know that it takes a team to reach a goal. A great
CEO treats the lowest man on the totem pole with as much
dignity as he treats an equal. A great school principal knows that
the teachers, assistants, bus drivers, and cafeteria workers make
a huge impact on the students and the climate of the school.
No one likes a bragger. It gets old hearing anyone go on and
on about themselves. The Bible is filled with the teaching that
the low shall be made higher and the proud will be brought to
destruction. A paraphrase of this verse as found in The Message
goes like this: "Pride lands you flat on your face; humility
prepares you for honors." Take note of the areas of your own
life where pride may sneak in and destroy. Replace pride with
humility. Others will notice. You will not go unrewarded when
you seek to be humble in spirit.

Father, root out any pride that You find in my
heart and replace it with humility, I ask. Amen.

Work as unto God

*Work willingly at whatever you do, as though you
were working for the Lord rather than for people.*
COLOSSIANS 3:23 NLT

Whatever you do today, work as if you are working for the Lord
rather than for man. What does that mean? For the employee,
it means work as if God is your supervisor. He does see and
hear everything you do. When you are tempted to slack off,
remember that the Bible warns against idleness. When you are
tempted to grumble about your boss, remember that God has
put you under this person's authority— at least for this time. For
the stay-at-home wife or mother, it means that even changing
a diaper or washing dishes can be done for the glory of God.
This verse has to do with attitude. Are you working in the
right spirit? Work is not a bad thing. God created work. God
Himself worked in order to create the earth in six days. And on
the seventh, He looked at the work of His hands and He rested.
Consider your work a blessing. If you are employed, remember
today that many are without jobs. If you are able to stay at home
with your children and keep your house, keep in mind that many
are not able to do so for one reason or another. Whatever you do,
work as if you are working for God.

*Lord, help me to remember that I am working
for You and not for man. You are my eternal
reward. I want to please You in all that
I set out to accomplish. Amen.*

In the Image of God

*Then God looked over all he had made,
and he saw that it was very good!*
GENESIS 1:31 NLT

God started with light, and His finishing touch was mankind.
He created the heavens and the earth and everything in them.
God was pleased with His creation. After He created the ocean
and dry land, the plants and animals, He said that it was all
good. But then He created man, and He said this was very good.
Mankind is different from all of the rest of God's creation. We
have intellect beyond that of animals. We have souls. We are
made in the image of God. He is creative. We have a bit of
creativity within us. Each of us is unique, and our creativity is
displayed in a variety of ways. He is loving. We are capable of
love. We are His children, and we are to reflect who He is. Just
as a child looks somewhat like their earthly parents, we bear
God's image. We are to look like our heavenly Father. When
others listen to you, do they know that you are a child of the
King of kings? When they look at how you carry yourself, do
they see humility and yet, confidence? You are a child of the
Creator of the universe. Made in His image, you represent Him
on this earth.

*Father, I am created in Your image. I am Your child.
Help me to live like it today. Help me to reflect
Your light in a dark world. Amen.*

Pleasing God

*Let the words of my mouth and the meditation
of my heart be acceptable in Your sight, O Lord,
my [firm, impenetrable] Rock and my Redeemer.*
PSALM 19:14 AMP

The Christian's life should be a prayer and a walking testimony
to Christ's redemption. The way that others around you know
that you are a Christian is through your words and your actions.
God sees even beyond these to your heart. He knows your
thoughts, your motives, and the secret feelings that no one else
is able to discern. He hears the words that come from your
mouth, but if they do not match what's in your heart, He knows.
Both should be pleasing to the Father. As you walk and talk,
consider Jesus. The popular slogan "What Would Jesus Do?" has
come and gone. At one time it was on bracelets and billboards.
Imagine that it still is. Would you desire that every interaction
you have with another, each decision you make at work or
school, and every thought that crosses your mind be pleasing to
the Lord? You can only accomplish this through being in close
fellowship with Christ, reading the Word, and allowing the Holy
Spirit to enable you where you are weak. Ask God today to help
your words and actions be pleasing to Him.

*Father, I want to please You with my speech, actions,
and thoughts. Strengthen me through Your Holy
Spirit whom You have sent to be my Helper. Help
me to honor You in all I do and say. Amen.*

Encouraging Those around You

Pleasant words are as a honeycomb,
sweet to the mind and healing to the body.
PROVERBS 16:24 AMP

Are you an encourager? Are your words pleasant and cheerful when you enter a room? Do you find yourself talking mostly about yourself, or do you focus on the other person in the conversation? The tongue is a powerful thing. Words can encourage or discourage, build up or tear down. As you go throughout your day today, seek to be one whose words are healing to the body and sweet to the mind as the writer of Proverbs describes. If you are in the workplace, take time to greet your coworkers with a genuine, "Good morning." Be sure to truly listen for an answer when you use the phrase "How are you?" rather than moving on as if your question were rhetorical. You will find that while kind words encourage the person who receives them, speaking them to others will also bless you. You will feel good knowing that you have lifted someone's spirits or shared in their sorrow. You will begin to focus on others rather than going on and on about your own problems or plans. It has been said that conversation is an art. Hone your conversation skills this week. Speak words of encouragement, words of life that remind the hearer he or she is special to you, and more importantly, to God.

Father, help me to speak life today.
May my words be pleasant, sweet, and healing.
May my conversations be pleasing to You. Amen.

What Next?

If any of you lacks wisdom, you should ask God, who gives
generously to all without finding fault, and it will be given to you.
JAMES 1:5 NIV

Ever been lost in an unfamiliar place? Trees block street signs,
and other streets aren't marked at all; construction causes
confusing, squiggly detours. Embarrassment or even panic grows
as the minutes pass.

In life, we hit unexpected detours that make us unsure of
where to turn next. They might be difficult decisions involving
family, healthcare, jobs, or relationships at church. Maybe the
weight is migrating from the tension in your shoulders to settle
in your heart.

The good news is that our heavenly Father knows the way out
of our confusion and will help us when we are at our most frantic.
James tells us that God promises to give wisdom to those who ask
for it in faith; He gives wisdom "generously" and "without fault."
Sometimes it's intimidating to ask for advice from others, but God
doesn't look down on us for admitting our weakness. He chooses
to lavish His love and His gifts on error-prone people because
they are a part of His family in Christ. We can entrust ourselves
and our lives to our heavenly Father, knowing that through Christ,
we have access to "all the treasures of wisdom and knowledge" that
our Savior possesses (Colossians 2:3 NIV).

Dear heavenly Father, thank You that You have
my days planned out for me and I am safe in
Your hands. Please grant me wisdom when
I am at a loss and help my spirit be sensitive
to Your Spirit's leading. Amen.

So-Called Wisdom

*Such "wisdom" does not come down from heaven but is earthly,
unspiritual, demonic. For where you have envy and selfish
ambition, there you find disorder and every evil practice.*

JAMES 3:15–16 NIV

"Oh, she knows how to get what she wants." That statement
isn't usually meant as a compliment. Unfortunately, women often
have the reputation for being manipulators, passive-aggressive,
and gossipers. Tearing down others is an effective way to gain
status and relational power.

The early Christians who received James's letter were guilty
of the same power-play. In chapter 2, James rebukes them for
showing favoritism to the rich in their meetings and demeaning
their poorer members (2:1–13). In this and other sins, the church
had been following "earthly" wisdom—the wisdom that believes
it has to tear down others to get what it wants, using any "evil
practice" necessary. Disorder resulted—they were harming their
relationships and the church body in the process.

These Christians had forgotten a vital truth. Their worth
did not come from being richer or wiser than anyone else,
but instead it came only through humbly accepting what they
couldn't earn—their salvation through faith in Christ.

Jesus' acceptance of us is what allows us to give up struggling to
maintain our status in comparison to others. What Christ thinks of
us matters most, and He makes us free to walk in God's "heavenly
wisdom" where humility and love reign (James 3:17).

*Father God, forgive me for when I've torn down
others with my words or thoughts to build myself
up. Please fill my heart with confidence that
I am accepted and worthy in You. Amen.*

Emotional

*Record my misery; list my tears on your scroll—
are they not in your record?*
PSALM 56:8 NIV

"Calm down! I can't deal with you when you're like this!"
Countless women have had their ideas, frustrations, and valid
criticisms dismissed because they were presented in a way that
was "too emotional." Her argument may be rock-solid, but given
in the presence of tears? Invalid. Many women feel forced to
swallow their feelings so that others will take them seriously.

Emotions are neither inherently bad nor an unavoidable
inconvenience. They are a gift. Since God created us to reflect
His attributes, we have emotions because He has them. In the
Gospels, Jesus shows a broad range of strong emotion. He cried
with the mourners at a dear friend's death (John 11), celebrated
in a wedding's joy (John 2), flipped over tables in righteous anger
(Matthew 21:12–13), and approached society's outcasts with
compassion (Luke 17:11–19). Because He is the Son of God,
He displayed His emotions without sin. Emotions aren't the
problem; sinful attitudes that twist our emotional responses are.

Sin affects our emotions, but women are not irrational because
they show strong emotion or because they may have difficulty
showing emotion. The Creator does not dismiss our tears or our
anger. He takes us seriously regardless of our emotional state,
inviting us to bring all our burdens to Him. His love is the same,
whether we are at our emotional best or our worst.

*Father God, let Your Spirit bring peace into
my heart, trusting Him to help me sort out
my emotions and react to events in ways
that are pleasing to You. Amen.*

The Victory Is Ours

*The sting of death is sin, and the power of sin is
the law. But thanks be to God! He gives us the
victory through our Lord Jesus Christ.*
1 CORINTHIANS 15:56–57 NIV

With a flourish, the Founding Fathers of the United States of
America signed the Declaration of Independence, demanding
freedom instead of the king's injustice. John Hancock famously
signed his name large enough for King George III "to see
it without his spectacles." Despite Hancock's boldness, the
signers knew their signatures could result in nooses around
their necks for treason. They pledged themselves to the battle
for independence although victory against one of the world's
greatest military powers was more than uncertain.

As Christians, we also have a long battle ahead of us as we
seek to please God while still struggling with our old sin nature.
However, unlike the uncertain future for the signers of the
Declaration, our victory in this spiritual battle is assured. When
Christ rose from the dead, He won over sin and death once for
all and makes all people free who put their trust in Him.

Though we will have to battle against sin during our earthly
lives, our mighty Savior has already won the war. We may feel
weak and prone to mistakes, but our Deliverer will help us say
"no" to ungodliness and to seek His ways. Sin cannot hold sway
while our Savior reigns!

*Father, when I am slipping into sin and feel stuck,
encourage my heart with the truth that Christ
has already accomplished the victory in my heart.
Help me to cling to Him and His strength. Amen.*

Lift Up Our Leaders

This is also why you pay taxes, for the authorities are God's servants, who give their full time to governing. Give to everyone what you owe them: If you owe taxes, pay taxes; if revenue, then revenue; if respect, then respect; if honor, then honor.

ROMANS 13:6–7 NIV

Politics aren't discussed at parties for good reason; even mentioning the government can kill the conversation or, at worst, detonate volatile tempers. The guests bad-mouth and defend politicians in turn, then argue over policy, and poof! The party's fun vanishes. It seems like everyone has a low opinion of authority—at times it's deserved, especially when leaders serve their own interests with their policymaking instead of caring for their people.

Though many governmental systems ignore God, the Bible affirms that He is working in earthly governments. No government rises to power that He doesn't permit (Romans 13:1); also, God uses earthly authorities as His servants to punish and discourage evil (vs. 4). Christians are called to serve their leaders; we pray for wisdom for them so they can carry out their God-given role to rule justly.

Praying for blessing is difficult when the government seems to encourage evil instead of punishing it. Even so, Christians are still called to treat authority with respect and honor, and to behave as peaceably as possible, even during critique. God's people must trust that He will accomplish perfect justice where governments fail.

Dear heavenly Father, thank You that You reign over all. Give me a tender heart toward my leaders so I can pray sincerely for them. Give them wisdom and a hunger for Your justice. Amen.

Daily Reminders

*[Brothers and sisters,]. . . encourage one another daily,
as long as it is called "Today," so that none of
you may be hardened by sin's deceitfulness.*

HEBREWS 3:13 NIV

Everyone needs reminders about their health. Doctors' offices hang posters to draw attention to healthy habits while patients wait for their appointments—how many minutes of exercise to do, how often to schedule check-ups, the right vitamins to take. Though the Bible doesn't have posters, it does remind us how to stay spiritually healthy.

As hard as it is sometimes, sharing our lives with a community of believers is essential to our spiritual health. Hebrews 3 commands us to encourage each other daily, reminding each other of our hope in Christ. Otherwise, we may forget our Savior and turn away from Him in the face of life's difficulties, futilely looking for help elsewhere. Godly encouragement isn't just kind words; its proclamation of truth protects and restores hearts in danger of faltering.

Sometimes it's extremely hard to find the right words to reassure a hurting friend. We all probably recall a time when life was falling to pieces and we weren't eager for a mini-Bible lesson. However, be brave and trust the Spirit; speaking the truth to others as lovingly as we can is a holy duty, a labor of love (Ephesians 4:15). Finally, encouraging others protects us as well—when we share God's goodness and grace with another believer, we remind ourselves of the faithful Lord we love and trust.

*Father God, let my mouth be filled with
encouraging words from You each day. Thank
You that You display Your love through
believers' love for one another. Amen.*

Freedom in Obedience

*I run in the path of your commands,
for you have broadened my understanding.*
PSALM 119:32 NIV

The psalmist has a curious saying here. I'm earnestly following Your rules, because You've set me free. Wait a sec. Rules equal restriction, confinement, and unhappiness, right? A sinful attitude views rules as a nuisance or "necessary evil." Our orderly and perfect God set down His law to show us that first, He is holy and we are not, and second, the rules are there for our benefit and protection so we can lovingly and rightly interact with Him and our fellow human beings.

It may be strange to consider, but God's rules do make us free, but we only view them as life-giving and glorious after we trust in Christ. He changes our hearts to want to do what is right instead of chasing after our selfish, ultimately destructive desires (Jeremiah 17:9). Even with a changed heart, we still have a lot to learn. The Holy Spirit through the Word teaches us how to see the beauty of God's commands, and we grow in our delight in Him.

I'm free to be a rule-follower? We don't lose our individuality when we submit to the Lord. Rather, we become more how humanity was created to be in the beginning—in unbroken fellowship with the Father, loving Him and displaying His marvelous ways to a watching world.

*Dear heavenly Father, thank You for setting me
free from sin. Please forgive me for when I have
belittled Your Word. Help me see the beauty
and love in Your commands and follow
You wholeheartedly. Amen.*

Not Flying Solo

*For we are God's handiwork, created in Christ Jesus to do
good works, which God prepared in advance for us to do.*
EPHESIANS 2:10 NIV

Sometimes when we think about doing "God's work," self-doubt
can get the better of us. We tell ourselves that we aren't smart or
skilled enough; we remember all our skipped prayer times and
say, "The Lord wouldn't want to use me since I've been ignoring
Him. Besides, my work probably isn't worth that much anyway
in the big picture, if I don't completely mess up."

In Ephesians 2, Paul emphasizes that we weren't saved
because of anything we had to offer, but we received God's gift of
salvation through faith. He made us anew in Christ "to do good
works" (vs. 10); we can't brag about deserving salvation, and we
can't brag about our good works being our big idea either! God
planned them for us ahead of time to fit in with His perfect plan.

We may fear that our errors will "ruin" what God has going
on. Consider that the work itself is a gift—the all-powerful
Creator chooses to use us—ordinary believers—to accomplish
mighty things. Throughout the Bible, we read stories of
unremarkable people doing amazing things for the Lord, because
they trusted in His strength to do them. If God has work for
us, we can have confidence that He will equip us for the job, no
matter the challenges ahead.

*Father God, please strengthen me to do the work You
have planned for me. Help me to depend on Your
ability and strength when I doubt myself. Amen.*

Savoring the Word

Jesus answered, "It is written: 'Man shall not live on bread alone, but on every word that comes from the mouth of God.'"
MATTHEW 4:4 NIV

Casseroles are veiled in gently rising steam; jello salads wobble temptingly. Like a net, the smell of fresh rolls draws the guests to the table. Potlucks are meals of chance, roulette for the taste buds. The strategic guest fills her plate with a small bite of everything. There are surprises—what everyone thought was lemon meringue turned out to be a gelatinous banana pudding, while an untouched sauce swelled with savory, meaty flavors.

Studying the Bible's sixty-six books can feel like a potluck, and our reading habits might be picky, too. The Psalms and Proverbs might be sweet and easy to read, but the book of Numbers might have the attraction of week-old dry bread. The "good stuff" gets scooped up, and the other books are overlooked.

As unsavory as they might seem, don't be so quick to pass on challenging sections of the Bible. Jesus said that men and women live by every word that proceeds from the mouth of God, not just some of them. Unlike a hit-or-miss potluck dish, all of Scripture is meant for the Christian's nourishment (Romans 15:4). Seek the Father as you chew on the book of Judges or contemplate the life of the prophet Ezekiel. All His Word is sweet when you can see Him in it.

Father God, thank You for Your entire Word. Please open my eyes to see You and Your goodness in the difficult passages and to spend time with You daily. Amen.

He Gives

*"So do not worry, saying, 'What shall we eat?' or
'What shall we drink?' or 'What shall we wear?'
For the pagans run after all these things, and
your heavenly Father knows that you need them."*
MATTHEW 6:31–32 NIV

What is weighing on your heart? It might be the burgeoning
credit card bill from when the car's transmission failed
unexpectedly last month. It might be a newly discovered lump—
your palms sweaty as you wait for lab results. You might be
wondering if your family is going to stay together or worrying
about family members who don't love God. Worry can tangle a
heart into fearful, anxious knots, cutting off its life.

Jesus tells us that the Creator who cares for the birds and the
wildflowers knows our needs intimately (Matthew 6:28–30). The
same God who keeps the Earth perfectly tilted and spinning so
that the seasons arrive at the right time also cares about medical
bills, missing keys, and difficult family relationships.

The antidote to worry is prayer—telling our Father the
things we lack, the things that hurt, the things that don't seem to
have an answer—because He listens. He opens His hand to bless
and fill us, to calm and heal us, to extend wisdom and peace.
He invites us to seek Him wholly and to lean on His sure and
faithful promise to provide for all our needs (6:33).

*Father God, I want to put You first in my heart.
Help me bring all my worries to You and to leave
them at Your feet. Thank You for how You love
me and promise to provide for me. Amen.*

Loneliness

God sets the lonely in families,
he leads out the prisoners with singing;
but the rebellious live in a sun-scorched land.
PSALM 68:6 NIV

She collapsed into her car, tears stinging her eyes. She had chatted with the neighbors all afternoon at the barbeque, hiding the lump in her throat behind a smile. Did anyone notice her leave? Had anyone cared?

The shame of loneliness often hurts more than being alone. No one wants to sound needy or weak, even as her heart aches for attention. Loneliness can be self-protective—a woman might fear what would happen if she let someone see the real her. Or, pride may lie under the loneliness— "I can go it alone. I don't need anyone."

Both the fearful and the stoic-independent attitudes deny how God designed us. He created us to be in community with Him and with other people. Although only Adam and Eve experienced a perfect earthly community, we still crave community's strength and solace in this sinful world, even if we have been deeply hurt in the past.

The psalmist tells us that God "sets the lonely in families." It is not shameful to ask God to give you a supportive community— He gave you this good desire for a place where you can share your entire self—scars, struggles, joys, and victories. Your God who has promised never to leave you or forsake you can and will provide for your relational needs (Deuteronomy 31:8).

Father God, when I feel lonely, help me
remember that You care about my earthly
relationships. Thank You that You are
near even when I feel alone. Amen.

Entering His Rest

*There remains, then, a Sabbath-rest for the
people of God; for anyone who enters God's rest
also rests from their works, just as God did from his.*
HEBREWS 4:9–10 NIV

What is the ideal way to practice the Sabbath? Christian
brothers and sisters have given as many answers to that question
as there are ways to spend the day. The Bible teaches that the
Sabbath is for resting from the work and cares of the week
just like the Father modeled for us when He created the world
(Genesis 2:2–3).

In Hebrews, however, Sabbath-rest takes on another
meaning. The writer of Hebrews exhorts its readers to "enter
God's rest" and to "rest from their works." In the letter's context,
this rest is a peace that goes heart-deep. Instead of fretting that
we are not right with God, we point to Christ's perfect life and
work, trusting in Him alone to be accepted in God's sight.

Just as God declared that His creation was perfect and
complete ("very good") on the seventh day, Christ pronounced
His saving work to be perfect and complete ("It is finished") on
the cross. We can approach our Creator boldly and without fear
of rejection, resting in the knowledge that we are fully pleasing
in His sight because of His Son. We do not have to work to be
worthy. We can rest in Him.

*Dear heavenly Father, help me rest in the work
Your Son did to save me. Deepen my faith so
that Your peace and Your truth will answer
my worrying heart when I fear I am
unworthy to be Your daughter. Amen.*

Merciful Heavens!

*I love the Lord, for he heard my voice;
he heard my cry for mercy.*

PSALM 116:1 NIV

The days when nothing goes according to plan are frustrating beyond belief. Worst are the unexpected surprises. Summer storms bring down power lines, the computer crashes before important work is saved, a fresh pot of coffee splatters on the floor. No one was planning to spend the day huddled indoors listening to raging winds. The frazzled engineer still has to turn in her report by 5:00 p.m., and Sarah will have to mop the whole kitchen before she can go out for her much-needed cup of joe.

It's a good thing our heavenly Father is compassionate toward His children. Heaven knows we need mercy when even a small thing going wrong can ruin our thankful attitudes for the day, and we definitely need His kindness when we stagger under huge disappointments.

Thankfully, our Father is never surprised at what happens, because all events fit in with His eternal plan (Romans 8:28). He knows His children can't see all the details, but He does know how much they can handle (1 Corinthians 10:13). Best of all, they can call on Him to shower down compassion upon the situation. "Mercy, Father! I can't handle this alone." "Mercy, Lord Jesus! Lift this burden—it's so heavy." The psalmist praises God for hearing and answering his prayer for mercy. He is more generous with His mercy than we suspect—ask Him in faith, and see.

*Father God, I love You because You keep
pouring out mercy upon me when I
need it. Help me continually draw
my strength from You. Amen.*

Reflecting (on) Christ's Beauty

*And we all, who with unveiled faces contemplate the Lord's
glory, are being transformed into his image with ever-
increasing glory, which comes from the Lord, who is the Spirit.*
2 CORINTHIANS 3:18 NIV

What are you thinking about? Careful. The act of contemplation
is powerful. Why else would teachers chide students when their
attention is anywhere but on the lesson? Their daydreams about
recess won't fuel their brains for mathematics. Contemplation
is a moral and transformative action, too. Contemplating the
difficulties of a relationship could sway a person's commitment;
contemplating wealth (or the lack thereof) can create heart-
sinking envy. We pay attention to what we care about; what we
care about shapes and changes us.

Throughout Scripture, Christians are called to "fix their
eyes on Christ" (Hebrews 12:1–2). Here in 2 Corinthians,
Paul writes about contemplating Jesus' glory—the Greek word
translated into English as "contemplate" means both "to meditate
upon" and "to reflect." Dwelling on Christ's life transforms us
into being more like Him.

Thinking on Jesus means to meditate on the truth we
believe about Him. The Word shows us a Savior who gave up
His holy, perfect life to restore the undeserving to Himself, who
rose again victorious over death! The Holy Spirit enables us
to reflect Jesus' loving, sacrificial character in "ever-increasing"
measure as we know and love Him better. As God's children, let
us know our Savior deeply and reflect Him more and more!

*Father God, when my mind wanders, teach me to turn my
attention again to Christ and His beauty. Let me know
Him better so I can show Him better to others. Amen.*

With a Song on His Lips

*The Lord your God is with you, the Mighty
Warrior who saves. He will take great delight
in you. . . [He] will rejoice over you with singing.*
ZEPHANIAH 3:17 NIV

Our relationships with our earthly fathers can greatly affect how
we view our heavenly Father. Whether consciously or not, we
take the earthly father we can see and try to puzzle out what
our heavenly Father is like. Some women had attentive, loving
fathers. If only this were the norm! Some fathers were absent,
never known to their daughters. Other fathers violated the
family's trust through abuse or neglect. Some fathers were caring
but distant—emotional connection difficult or nonexistent.

Where our earthly fathers have fallen short, our heavenly
Father does all perfectly and to the full. He is full of mercy, full
of loving-kindness, absolutely just and right. He brings order
where there is disorder, peace instead of confusion. He heals
bodies and broken hearts, and He keeps all His promises.

Though the Father rules over the whole universe, He is also
close to us. He does not love us at arm's length, His disapproval
looming if we misstep. He sings and rejoices over His children;
He delights in that we belong to Him. The love of our great God
surpasses all earthly love in its perfection, its sacrifice, its provision,
and its salvation. Regardless of our family backgrounds, our
Creator perfectly loves and delights in us.

*Father God, thank You for making me Your
daughter. I am astounded that You delight in me
and sing joyfully over me—show me Your love
and I'll sing back to You in praise! Amen.*

Even the Little Things

*But be sure to fear the LORD and serve him faithfully with all
your heart; consider what great things he has done for you.*
1 SAMUEL 12:24 NIV

No one likes sweeping dust bunnies out from under the fridge,
scrubbing grout, or filing taxes. Sometimes the boss will assign a
grueling task, or worse, an extremely tedious one. It's tempting
to expend the minimum effort required and get on with the
better things in life. This can happen in relationships as well—
we manage the minimum amount of closeness and small talk
without any real depth or connection.

However, as God's children we are called to a higher
standard. Not just to "get things over with," but to do all things
to His glory. Practically, this means doing our best in whatever
task or goal we pursue, knowing that He is the final inspector of
our work, tasks both big and small.

So, should we scurry to scour the oven until the metal
squeaks for mercy? No, we don't work out of fear or out of cold
duty (though sometimes those are the motives that compel us),
but because we desire to please God, knowing how much He
loves us. The way we do the "little things" reveals for whom we
labor—for us? For our employers, family, or friends? We may
benefit from our efforts, but ultimately our work is for our Father.

*Father God, You see all of my work. Please forgive
me for when I have complained, and help me do
my best in everything and do it out of joy in You.*

Love Always

*"My command is this:
Love each other as I have loved you."*
John 15:12 niv

Many women sign cards, yearbooks, and guest books with the closing greeting "Love always." It is a beautiful sentiment to read, knowing that the writer is filled with fondness for the friend whenever she thinks of her.

There are numerous everyday ways to show love always. It could be an encouraging phone call to a friend who is having the worst week ever or helping a neighbor take her car to the mechanic. It could be a well-timed gift of brownies or emergency babysitting or heading out to the movies for some quality time with someone you haven't seen in a while.

Jesus commands His children to show the same love that He demonstrated to us. His death on the cross was the most extravagant expression of love—giving up His holy life to grant eternal life to those who had rejected His ways (Isaiah 53:5). During a regular day, we probably don't usually have the opportunity to snatch a friend out of a life-threatening situation, but we do carry what can save a soul—the truth about Jesus. All the small ways we show love should point to the greatest Love that we've ever been given.

*Father God, thank You for Jesus' perfect love. Help
His love flow from me to the people You've put
in my life, and give me the words and courage
to share about Him with them, too. Amen.*

Forgiveness

"For if you forgive other people when they sin against you, your heavenly Father will also forgive you. But if you do not forgive others their sins, your Father will not forgive your sins."
MATTHEW 6:14–15 NIV

While checking your e-mail, an invitation from a friend pops up in your inbox. Instead of excitement, a horrible, careless remark she once said about you leaps to mind. Your stomach clenches — the comment hurts as much as it did the moment you first heard it. You've tried to forgive her, but anger still needles your heart.

Forgiveness is much more costly than simply saying the words "I forgive you." Forgiveness means letting go of the right to hold a person's wrongs against them. Instead, you absorb the debt the offender owes you. We can give up our right to demand retribution because we are whole in Christ—forgiveness doesn't diminish us. It is out of His grace that we can offer grace to those who've hurt us. As Jesus' followers, we show our gratitude for His forgiveness toward us when we model His actions.

Often, forgiveness looks more like a process than an event. It's okay if forgiving someone takes a long time. Prayer will help that process; asking sincerely for God to bless those you want to forgive will keep your heart soft and free of bitterness. When hurt comes back to haunt you, throw your pain on Christ—He will help you let go.

Father God, I need Your forgiveness every day.
Help me to forgive those who have hurt me,
however long it takes, and give my pain
to You in the meantime. Amen.

Asking for It

*Therefore confess your sins to each other and
pray for each other so that you may be healed.*
JAMES 5:16 NIV

Forgiveness is hard enough to grant, let alone to request. Taking responsibility for your mistakes and asking for mercy from the person you've offended are not easy things to do. It is especially difficult when you didn't know you'd hurt the person in the first place and they had to approach you.

Most people would rather make excuses for their behavior than own up to it. However, asking for forgiveness is one of the most powerful testimonies of your faith that you can demonstrate. When we ask for forgiveness, we acknowledge we have trampled the dignity of another human being. We admit that we have hurt God as well by sinning against a person He deeply loves. In asking for forgiveness, we humble ourselves and throw ourselves on mercy—the mercy of the person we've hurt and our Father's mercy.

It is a gift to be forgiven. Sometimes forgiveness is withheld—a "reasonable" human reaction to sin but painful nonetheless. Even if the person in question refuses to forgive you, you must do all you can to make peace, and then leave it in the Father's hands—He can bring peace where peace seems impossible. Take heart: if you have confessed your sin to the Father, He has forgiven you and will never hold that sin against you.

*Father, help me to be humble and ask for
forgiveness from those whom I sin against.
Thank You for Your forgiveness that frees
me to admit my weakness and foolishness
to others. Amen.*

Wise Like Jesus

*But the wisdom that comes from heaven is first of all pure;
then peace-loving, considerate, submissive,
full of mercy and good fruit, impartial and sincere.*
JAMES 3:17 NIV

Who has wisdom? Look at the fruit of her life. From this verse, we know a wise woman chooses to pursue peace in her community—she forgives someone who hurt her instead of writing him off. She is considerate; she sees others with God's eyes—worthy of her love because they are loved by their Creator, no matter what they have done or left undone. She submits her hurts to her Father, learning from Him how to show mercy as He does. Sincerity blossoms throughout her words and deeds.

If this description of a wise woman leaves you thinking *That's not me!*, don't worry, you certainly aren't alone. Wisdom is a gift from God, born from a desire to follow His Word out of love for Him. Our own efforts can only conjure up an imperfect wisdom and love for others because our natural state is selfish. Humanity lost its capacity to love purely when Adam and Eve disobeyed God in the Garden.

Thankfully, Jesus changes our hearts when we trust in Him so we can be wise as He is wise. With the Holy Spirit's help, we can grow more like Jesus each day. May His wisdom and love deepen in us and spill over to others!

*Father God, thank You for Your promise of wisdom.
Grant me a deeper knowledge of Your Son so
that I may grow wise in Your ways. Amen.*

From Strength to Strength

Blessed are those whose strength is in you,
whose hearts are set on pilgrimage. . . .
They go from strength to strength,
till each appears before God in Zion.
PSALM 84:5, 7 NIV

An old hymn says, "This world is not my home, I'm just a-passin'
through." For the woman who trusts Jesus, her forever home is
in heaven with Him. For now, she remains earth-bound, laboring
in the work He has given her.

For Christians, their stay on Earth is a pilgrimage—a
lifetime's travel toward a sacred destination. The strain of Earth
can be too much—sickness, aging, trials wracking the body and
sapping the soul. Believers cry out with creation for the Savior
to come renew them completely (Romans 8:22–25). He will, but
not yet. For now, they walk on in faith, displaying their love for
Christ in word and deed (Philippians 2:12).

There will be many days where the Christian woman's heart
will falter, but thankfully she doesn't journey alone. When she
stumbles, her Deliverer will lift her up; He will help her rest
through His Word and prayer. She might feel that she is only
plodding along on aching feet, progressing in fits and starts.
But this is the pilgrim's life—persevering, going from "strength
to strength," the strength that God provides for that particular
time. She may not feel strong enough to finish the journey well,
but she should not fear. Her God promises to bring
His children home one step at a time.

Father God, teach me to abide in Your strength
daily, trusting that You will provide all I
need to walk faithfully with You. Amen.

For the Beauty of the Earth

*The Lord loves righteousness and justice;
the earth is full of his unfailing love.*

PSALM 33:5 NIV

Summer. The best citrus fruits are in season, berries ripen, backyard gardens burst with productivity. God has placed such beauty in the spaces where we live, in the smallest leaf and bud, in the intricacies of root systems and the earthworm's travel. The fireflies flicker on night-covered lawns, praising their Creator by doing exactly what He designed them to do.

God shapes His children as well as His creation. He knew us when we were inside our mothers, knows us now in whatever size or shape or situation we find ourselves. The same Creator who lovingly crafted His world's diversity and wonder knows the diversity of His people, the gifts and talents He has bestowed upon us.

He looks and says, "My daughters, I made you, and you are loved." He sees what His hands have knit together and loves us beyond words, regardless of what the magazines say about our bodies' appearances or our own hearts' harsh inner whispers. He built us with inherent dignity, with an eternal soul unlike any other upon the earth.

Believe that He loves you, Daughter of God—all of you, not in spite of you or only parts of you. He loved you so much that He sent His Son for you. You are just as vibrant with His beauty as the most brilliant scene in all creation.

*Father God, help me see myself with
Your eyes and see the beauty You have
put in me and in others. Amen.*

Powerful Prayer

Rejoice always, pray continually, give thanks in all circumstances; for this is God's will for you in Christ Jesus.
1 THESSALONIANS 5:16–18 NIV

Ever fallen asleep during prayer? Or have you ever told a friend you'd pray for her request and then completely forgotten about it until she brought it up again? We've all been there. Squirming inside, you listen to her update, and say, "Oh, yes, I'll keep praying for that." What makes prayer so hard?

We might feel intimidated to talk to a holy God, even though He invites us to tell Him about our lives and ask for what we need. Self-reproach and doubt can get in the way, too; sometimes our prayers sound ridiculous to our ears, or we have been praying for the same request for so long that it doesn't seem like God will answer it. Or, we are worn out simply by the thought of the energy, focus, and humility required for prayer.

However, prayer is a discipline where sweetness and hard work flow together. God commands us to pray continually because prayer is an exercise in trust. We ask the Creator of the Universe to act on our behalf in faith that He will act—it is our faith that makes our prayers effective, not our eloquence.

Whatever your prayer life is or has been, approach God in faith. He is always ready to hear us, and His Spirit will give us the strength to pray (Romans 8:26–27).

Father God, give me strength to pray. I want to be closer to You and to rely fully upon You. Thank You that You always listen. Amen.

Holy, Wholly

But just as he who called you is holy, so be holy in all you do;
for it is written: "Be holy, because I am holy."

1 PETER 1:15–16 NIV

Holiness is one of the most difficult concepts to grasp about God because it is so foreign to us. He is unable to sin, set apart in glorious light. However, we can easily understand why Isaiah fell on his face when he beheld the Lord, feeling his sinfulness weighing heavy upon him (Isaiah 6:5).

Just as the angel cleansed Isaiah's lips, Christ made us His righteous, holy people (1 Peter 2:9). Because Christ has given us His holiness, we don't have to earn it ourselves. For Christians, pursuing holiness isn't fulfilling a set of rules in order to be accepted before God. Instead, it is a heart-deep desire to model our lives after our Savior's perfect example.

Though we are holy in Christ, we still struggle with sin in this life. Where is the Holy Spirit convicting you to practice holiness? Do you have trouble being kind in your words, spoken or unspoken? Are your thoughts filled with peace and thankfulness, or do you struggle with envy? Does the way you treat others honor Christ, especially folks who disagree with you or are different from you?

Don't be discouraged by how you fall short. Our Savior rewards His children who pursue holiness; He will give you grace to learn to practice His ways faithfully.

Father God, thank You that Christ's holiness covers me. Show me the sins I've ignored so that I can be holy in my actions as You are holy. Amen.

Heavenly Vision

*" 'He will wipe every tear from their eyes. There will be no
more death' or mourning or crying or pain, for the old order
of things has passed away." He who was seated on the
throne said, "I am making everything new!"*

REVELATION 21:4–5 NIV

Longing for heaven is a learned longing. How could it be natural
when so much beauty exists on this earth for us to see, taste, and
touch? As wonderful as this short life can be, it will not compare
to what awaits us—seeing the loveliness of the Savior with our
own eyes and hearing His voice with our ears, knowing that we
will never part from Him.

In His presence, all imperfection, pain, and sadness will
vanish, and the earth will be remade. We will be reunited with
our loved ones in Christ who were separated from us on earth by
death or distance. The expectation of that day helps us persevere
through the hurt and brokenness of the present. Knowing that
complete peace and joy lie ahead gives us courage.

Even now, Christ's work isn't on hold—He is making us
new by renewing our hearts and strength; He is teaching us how
to love as He loves in order to draw more people to Himself.
Hold this world loosely, for it will fade in the light of the
Savior's face. He who calls us Beloved is coming again soon!

*Dear heavenly Father, thank You that You gave
us the hope of heaven when You sent Jesus.
Give me a heart that longs for heaven and
longs for Your presence even more. Amen.*

Wholeness

*For in Christ all the fullness of the Deity lives in bodily form,
and in Christ you have been brought to fullness. He is
the head over every power and authority.*

COLOSSIANS 2:9–10 NIV

Self-talk reveals more about a woman than she may realize.
Does she speak to herself with positive words or words of self-
loathing? Truthfully, it is much easier to focus on her broken
parts, whether it is bodily imperfections, struggles with sins, or
circumstances that can't be changed. The mirror and the mind
become battlegrounds, thoughts launching inward like grenades.

When a woman trusts Jesus, she is more than her mistakes
or her victories. She is whole in her Savior. She is whole because
Christ gave her His all—His righteousness, His riches of
wisdom, His perfect life for hers. He called her to follow Him
so that she could share in His abundant life. His love lets her
deflect the cruel words she had aimed at herself.

In Christ, she is no longer condemned because of her
sin—He has wiped it away (Romans 8:1). In Christ, she is never
alone—He has given her His Spirit to comfort her (Romans
8:26–27). In Christ, she can stand bravely, content in whatever
situation she finds herself—His hand is there to sustain her
(Philippians 4:13). Nothing—good or bad—can change His
love or complete acceptance of her. He looks at her and sees His
beloved for whom He died—His Bride, His delight.

*Father God, thank You that Your love
never changes. Help me see myself the
way Christ does and draw strength and
confidence from His love. Amen.*

Eating Worshipfully

*So whether you eat or drink or whatever
you do, do it all for the glory of God.*
1 CORINTHIANS 10:31 NIV

Magazines, advertisements, and television all tell the average
woman that she is too much. Name a body part, and it needs
slimming or toning or something. Culture shames women who
don't match its youthful, slender standard. Women of all types
are pushed to pursue it—for self-improvement, or even simply to
look "acceptable."

As much as it's reviled, food is not wicked. God gave us
food as a good gift that He intended for us to use wisely and to
enjoy, not for it to rule us. Want to eat a brownie? Savor God's
gift and thank Him for it. Rather snack on carrots? Do so for
His glory, not guilt. Our food choices don't make us better or
worse people, but how many of us have judged another woman
for what she ate for lunch?

Our eating can glorify God, especially in contrast to what
the world says about women's bodies. When we eat, how do we
think about ourselves or others? Are we caring for our bodies
with thankfulness to God or slaving after the media's idol? We
are beautiful because our Creator is beautiful. As we battle with
the mirror, we can turn to the One who made us, loves us dearly,
and tells us so in His Word.

*Dear heavenly Father, help me to care for my
body's needs and trust that I am beautiful in
Your sight. Help me to encourage other women
who struggle with this, too. Help me to
love them as You love them. Amen.*

Blessing and Thankfulness

Give thanks in all circumstances;
for this is God's will for you in Christ Jesus.
1 THESSALONIANS 5:18 NIV

"Count your blessings, name them one by one. Count your blessings, see what God has done." As the hymn says, being thankful is a practice. We should take time to contemplate God's blessings to us, especially when there seems to be more trouble than peace in our lives.

No matter how difficult life becomes, God's gifts are still there, abundant and gracious. I knew an artist whose medical conditions caused such terrible pain that she could only stand and walk for a limited time each day. Despite her situation, she made a practice of tracing the threads of God's blessing in her life. If she ate a peach, she would thank God for the peach; the store that sold it; the store's employees; the truck driver; the orchard workers; the farmer who had cared for the trees; and for the soil, air, water, and sunlight. Her spirit radiated thankfulness in the midst of her suffering, even for something as small as a peach.

Our thankfulness is founded on God—He has promised to take care of our needs and to comfort us in our distress. Name what the Father has done for you, blessings big and small, in joyous and in troubled times. All good gifts are from Him (James 1:17). Can you trace the thread of His love in your life?

Dear heavenly Father, open my eyes to Your
many blessings so I may praise Your name!
Teach my heart to focus on Your goodness,
no matter the circumstances. Amen.

Space to Breathe

*Whoever dwells in the shelter of the Most High will rest
in the shadow of the Almighty. I will say of the Lord,
"He is my refuge and my fortress, my God, in whom I trust."*
PSALM 91:1–2 NIV

Summer is one of the busiest seasons of the year. Vacations,
cook-outs with friends, family visits, weddings, and other events
pack the warm days tight as berries in a pie—and that's in
addition to the everyday things that need doing.

Even joyous times can take a toll on us when we don't make
any time for ourselves. It might sound strange to trust God with
the "fun stuff," but because He loves us, He is interested in every
part of our lives, even our overscheduled social calendars.

This season, set aside time to be still before the Father.
Time is His gift to us to spend wisely for His glory. We may
be tempted to invest all of our time in others, but we are called
to rest as well as to serve. God calls us to quiet our souls and
nurture our mental, emotional, and spiritual health. Take a
moment and breathe deeply, go for a long walk, or watch
the sunlight shift from morning to afternoon. Bask in His
presence—wordlessly, in prayer, in His Word, whatever—draw
strength from His presence. The fast-paced life will still be there
when we get back.

*Father God, thank You for being my refuge.
I want to be close to You no matter how busy
my schedule is. Please teach me to take
time to be still before You. Amen.*

Called to Be Storytellers

*I will sing of the LORD's great love forever;
with my mouth I will make your faithfulness
known through all generations.*

PSALM 89:1 NIV

In addition to being prayers and praise songs, some of the psalms also retell portions of Israel's history. The Israelites would sing them together to praise the past deeds of their Deliverer (e.g. Psalm 136). Today's worship songs don't list what He's done for us specifically like the Israelites' songs did, but we should definitely follow their example of remembrance.

Christians often use the word *testimony* to name the story of how they accepted Jesus as their Savior. Salvation is a great proof of God's love, but His work doesn't stop there. He daily fills our lives with His provision, nearness, and loving patience. When we recognize what He has done for us, we can be storytellers of His faithfulness, like the psalmist. We gather strength for the challenges ahead when we recall the victories He granted in the past, and our ongoing testimonies of His faithfulness display His love to those who don't know Him personally.

When you feel troubled, tell yourself your stories of His faithfulness. When did you feel His comfort when you called on Him for help? When has He provided for your needs beyond expectation? Just as He did then, your unchanging God will never stop caring for you.

*Father, thank You that You've never stopped working
in my life. When I am fearful, help me recall Your
goodness and trust You more. Give me opportunity
to tell others what You have done for me, so that
they will come to trust You, too! Amen.*

Fearless

> *God is love. Whoever lives in love lives in God,
> and God in them. . . . There is no fear in love.
> But perfect love drives out fear, because fear has to do with
> punishment. The one who fears is not made perfect in love."*
> 1 JOHN 4:16, 18 NIV

1 John 5:3 says that if we love God, we will do what He commands. It sounds simple enough, but fear can creep in when we consider what it means to show Him complete devotion. Putting Him first in our lives might cost us more than we expect—in our relationships, in our jobs, in how we spend our money or time. We might worry about what others might think of us or fear that we can't accomplish what God calls us to do.

God's unconditional love frees us from fear—the fear of punishment, failure, or harsh judgment from our fellow men and women—because His opinion of us matters most. Through everything, He has promised to be with us and strengthen us. We may feel ashamed of our fear, but God is not angry. Instead, He gives us exactly what we need to strengthen our faith, whether it's the sign of a damp sheepskin (Gideon, Judges 6) or inviting us to touch His wounds (Jesus to Thomas, John 20:24–29).

Do not fear. Christ shows us the vastness of His love to drive out our worries and anxieties. When we rely on Him, we can accomplish anything He asks of us.

> *Father God, I want to step out in faith and
> do what You command. Banish my fears by
> showing me how perfectly You love me.
> Amen.*

Our Idol, Approval

*Then Joshua said, "Now throw away the gods that you have.
Love the LORD, the God of Israel, with all your heart."*
JOSHUA 24:23 NCV

"Anything can be a god, if we put it in a place of priority in our
lives," said the preacher. Misty wrote the quote down in her
journal and underlined the word *anything*. *Lord, is there something
in my life ahead of You?* She prayed silently. *If there is, show me.*
Over the next few days, during work, family time, and rest,
Misty felt that God wanted to reveal something to her. She felt
nervous. What was taking precedence over God? Was it food,
shopping, her kids, or her spouse?

"Lord, I'm ready." she said. "Reveal to me what you want me
to repent of." And in her spirit, she sensed God telling her that
her need for approval from people was taking up far more time
and energy than it should.

She thought about the times she had dressed a certain
way or bought a particular item—even updated her Facebook
status—in order to get a reaction from others. "You're right!" She
prayed, laughing as she talked to God (of course He was right).
"I am way too worried about what other people think. I need to
be concerned only about Your perspective."

*Creator God, forgive me for putting other things on the
throne of my life. Help me to crave Your approval and
perspective much more than the world's. And thank
You for Your gentle conviction and grace. Amen.*

Offering Ourselves to God

Then the people rejoiced, for that they offered willingly,
because with perfect heart they offered willingly to the LORD:
and David the king also rejoiced with great joy.
1 CHRONICLES 29:9 KJV

Diane had felt sad and empty for months, ever since her only child left for college. A single mom with a full-time job, Diane had poured herself into Colton's world with all her non-work time and energy. Soccer games, music concerts, and sleepovers filled her world.

Now, she felt empty, alone. . . and old. She considered getting a dog, but that didn't seem fair to the animal, since she would be gone every day, all day. She took up a hobby, but it didn't satisfy, either. She prayed about what she should do, and tried to be patient. Grief, she knew, took time.

One afternoon, she sat in her office taking a coffee break. As she read the day's paper, a new ad for a volunteer opportunity caught her eye. The local crisis pregnancy center advertised a need for mentors to guide young single moms. Suddenly, her heart leapt. She knew that God had led her to read the paper at that moment.

I could pour myself out again, she thought, *and use what I've learned in parenting to help others.* The prospect filled her with joy, and she picked up the phone to call the center.

Loving Creator, thank You for giving us chances
to share all You've given us. Thank You that our
willingness to sacrifice time and comfort is
always rewarded with joy.

His Presence in Our Panic

*"I have no peace, no quietness;
I have no rest, but only turmoil."*
JOB 3:26 NIV

Felicia's toddler, Noah, lay beside her on the bed. She got up to turn off the light. As soon as she flipped the switch, Felicia got back in bed. Suddenly, he sat up and yelled, "Mommy! Where are you? I can't see you!"

Felicia immediately got up and turned a small light back on. "Mommy's right here," she said soothingly. "I'm not going anywhere." As soon as he could see his mom, Noah quieted down and began to fall asleep.

Similarly, Job cried out to God with questions and confusion after his family, livelihood, and health had been taken from him. God let Job's friends give their (wrong) perspectives on why he was suffering, and then He swept in and silenced all of them with His own questions—and His overwhelming presence.

When we are afraid and anxious, God turns on the light for us, just as Felicia turned on the light for her son. Sometimes the light comes through comforting scriptures. At times, it appears with the touch of a family member. Light often breaks through with a hymn or a worship song that we hear on the radio.

Though we may not understand why we have to suffer, praise God, He never leaves us in the dark for too long. . .and He never, ever leaves us alone.

*Father, thank You that I am never alone, even when
I feel scared and lonely. Help me to open my eyes
and ears to the ways You long to speak peace to me.*

Hoping in Christ

*But if we hope for what is still unseen by us,
we wait for it with patience and composure.*
ROMANS 8:25 AMP

Alyssa grew up crooning into her hairbrush as Shaun Cassidy's album rotated on her record player and the scents of Love's Baby Soft and V05 hairspray wafted around the room. The posters of teen idols on her bedroom walls included Scott Baio, Leif Garrett, and Parker Stevenson. She swooned over their long, feathered hair. . .their shiny, silk jackets. . .and their eyes.

If she could go back in time, she would encourage herself to chill out a bit: Girl, your longings for love and affection are normal. But don't get so wrapped up in the idea of romance that you miss the Person who loves you more than you can ever imagine. Spend more time praying and less time preening. Don't worry so much about having a boyfriend. Concentrate on serving Jesus and making the most of what He's given you. Everything else will come, in His time.

And so it did. Eventually—though it took a lot longer than she would have liked—a cute boy who loved Jesus "caught" Alyssa. They've now been married for fifteen years. However, marriage has taught her that nothing—not your spouse or child or big work promotion or long-awaited retirement—will live up to your expectations. Nothing, that is, except Jesus.

He's the only Person who is perfect. And that's something to croon about.

*Lover of my Soul, grant me the wisdom
to know that others will fail me.
Thank You that You never will.*

Unfailing Love

Let your unfailing love surround us, LORD,
for our hope is in you alone.
PSALM 33: 22 NLT

We hope that our sports team will win the big game and that Starbucks will bring back its hazelnut macchiato. We also hope that our jobs will continue to fulfill us and pay our bills and that God will answer a heartfelt prayer with a long-awaited yes.

Whatever we're hoping for, it's easy to think that God doesn't care about the details of our lives. However, just as a parent cares about everything that happens to her child, so God longs to share every part of our day. Why not talk to Him about all our needs and desires?

As we sip our morning coffee, we can jot down thanks for morning blessings such as flavored creamers and hot water for our shower. While we do our jobs, we can regularly bring our concerns (and coworkers) before God's throne. We could keep scriptures scribbled on Post-it notes in our cubicle—or on our desk—to remind us to think with God's thoughts throughout the day, instead of falling back on worldly patterns. When we lay our head on the pillow at night, we can voice the answered prayers which grace our lives, drifting off to sleep in gratitude at God's unfailing love.

Those small, simple actions add up to a day filled with hope and gratitude. . .and those days add up to a life well-lived.

Father God, thank You for Your unfailing love.
Thinking on that love, which I haven't earned
and can't repay, causes me to fall to my knees
in hope, gratitude, and joy.

Guarding against Gossip

*In the same way, women must be respected by others.
They must not speak evil of others. They must be
self-controlled and trustworthy in everything.*
1 TIMOTHY 3:11 NCV

We women have to be careful when we congregate. Often, good-natured banter turns into chatting about others—both celebrities and real-life acquaintances. Unfortunately, it's a short distance from concern to gossip.

"What was she thinking, posting that picture on Facebook?" we ask, shaking our heads in dismay. Suddenly, we begin tearing another woman down. In 1 Timothy, the apostle Paul warns against those kinds of hurtful habits. He urges Christians to exercise self-control, a fruit of the Holy Spirit.

After all, friendships are based on trust, and if our friends hear us speaking evil of someone else, they might wonder if we ever do the same thing to them.

What's a girl to do? First, remember to respect your fellow women. God created each person with dignity and He sees them through eyes of love. We should, too. Second, try to season your conversations with grace and wisdom. Instead of talking about the newest tabloid tidbit, ask your friend how's she coping with a life challenge—and let your companion know that you can be trusted to keep her answers confidential. Third, pray for your friends and your times together. Not only will these actions please God, but you'll have a better time—and less guilt.

*Lord, thank You for the gift of friendship. Help
me to speak only beautiful, uplifting words
when my sisters and I spend time together.
Remind me to not gossip, and forgive me
when I succumb to that temptation.*

The Shield of Faith

*Above all, taking the shield of faith, wherewith ye
shall be able to quench all the fiery darts of the wicked.*
EPHESIANS 6:16 KJV

When Paul wrote to the church at Ephesus about the shield
of faith, he used the word *thureos* which means "door." Roman
soldiers' shields were large, rectangular, and door-sized. In
other words, they covered every single part of the soldier's body.
It's the same with our faith. The salvation we've been given in
Christ covers us from head to toe. And because He is lavish in
love and steadfast in keeping His promises, we'll always have
enough for every situation we encounter.

The Roman soldiers' shields had one other distinctive
quality: they were made of several hides of leather sewn together.
This meant that every morning, a soldier would have to rub oil
into the shield in order to keep it pliable and to prevent it from
drying out and cracking. This daily renewal was the difference
between life and death. . .literally!

In our own faith-walk, we must daily allow God's Holy Spirit
to refill and re-energize us. The Spirit replenishes our joy, rebuilds
our faith, and redirects our thoughts so that we can live boldly
and courageously for Jesus. This begs the question: what have we
done today to oil our shields? Let's not get complacent and allow
distractions to deter us from our duty! In Christ, we have a true
shield that won't let ever let us down. Praise the Lord!

*Lord, thank You for Your Word and all the
riches I find there. Give me the discipline
to come to You regularly for re-filling.*

Cultivating Contentment

*I wait for the LORD, my soul waits, and in his word I put my
hope. I wait for the Lord more than watchmen wait for the
morning, more than watchmen wait for the morning.*

PSALM 130:5–6 NIV

What are you waiting for—a job, a relationship, physical healing, financial provision? Whatever answer to prayer you are longing for, remember that often it's in the waiting that God performs His perfecting work on our character. Joseph waited for many years, serving in Pharaoh's house (even ending up in jail) before God promoted him. Abraham waited until he was a century old to see the child God had promised to him and Sarah decades before. God was still at work in both men's lives, though His actions and plans were hidden.

Maybe you've waited for God to come through, and so far, He hasn't. The word advent means "arrival or coming, especially one which is awaited." Like the silence the people of Israel endured for four hundred years between the last spoken prophetic word and the arrival of the Christ child, perhaps you've endured silence from God for so long that you think He's not there, not listening—or not inclined to come to your rescue.

No matter what you're going through, please know that God is for you, not against you. He aches with you. And He offers us a choice: be chained in fear or changed by grace.

Which will you choose today?

*Father, forgive me for doubting Your love
and mercy. Thank You that You are
faithful and that You will provide for me.
I believe. . .help my unbelief.*

Waiting on God

Yet true godliness with contentment is itself great wealth.
1 TIMOTHY 6:6 NLT

If you were raised in the 1960s or '70s, you might remember receiving large, heavy catalogs from Montgomery Ward or Sears and Roebuck in the fall of each year. If you're like many children from those decades, you pored over the catalogs with glee, circling items you wanted (especially in the toy section of the book) for Christmas, birthdays, or other special occasions.

As modern-day women, we tend to see things we never knew we needed when we shop in malls or big box stores. Also, we spend time surfing online and end up pinning wish list items to boards on Pinterest. While there's nothing wrong with dreaming and wishing, there's a fine line between making a wish list and becoming discontent with what God's given us.

How do you know if you've crossed that line? Next time you shop or pin, examine your heart. Ask yourself prayerfully: Am I coveting what others have? Do I feel discouraged by the age or size of my home/car/closet? Have I begun to grumble about what I don't have, instead of being thankful for what I already own?

If you find yourself becoming greedy and ungrateful for the blessings God has bestowed, take a time-out from shopping. Instead of looking online for things to buy, make a list of the things God has given you (both large and small). You might find that you don't really "need" anything, after all.

Heavenly Father, protect my heart from greed.
Give me eyes to see all the wonderful
blessings with which You've blessed me.

The Gift of Friends

*The seeds of good deeds become a tree of life;
a wise person wins friends.*
PROVERBS 11:30 NLT

During a long, boring presentation, Hillary saw the text from her friend LeeAnne and smiled. LeeAnne often texted funny pictures or silly quotes to Hillary on Wednesdays, because she knew Wednesdays were particularly stressful days for her best friend.

"Thank u!" Hillary replied. As she hit SEND, she thought of a joke she could send to LeeAnne after the meeting was over. She looked forward to their weekly lunch date, when they talked about their families, jobs, and relationship with the Lord.

Thank You, Lord, that You placed LeeAnne right in my path. Help me to be as good a friend to her and other women as she's been to me. And forgive me for not looking past the surface sometimes.

Hillary regretted that she had often misjudged other women. While the speaker droned on, she pondered how God had brought LeeAnne into her life. Before they'd met, Hillary thought LeeAnne was too pretty, wealthy, and successful to be real or down-to-earth. However, at a women's ministry event, they ended up sitting next to one another and discovered that they had quite a few things in common. Their friendship had been growing ever since.

*Dear Savior, give me an open heart toward
those women You want me to befriend.
Thank You that You created us for relationship.
Help me to glorify You by how I treat my
friends. And Jesus, I praise You for
being the perfect friend.*

Lean on Jesus

*"You and these people who come to you will
only wear yourselves out. The work is too
heavy for you; you cannot handle it alone."*
EXODUS 18:17–19 NIV

Holly put her head down on the desk as her tears flowed. Her supervisor had just given her another project—when Holly was still behind on her current assignment. "I'll never catch up," she said out loud, to no one in particular.

Over the last few months, ever since several staff had been laid off due to budget cuts, Holly's work had gotten more stressful. While she was thankful to still be in her position—and she'd actually gotten a small raise and more responsibility—she often felt stretched beyond her natural comfort zone.

What was it her pastor said? "More challenges mean more opportunities to lean on Jesus." She needed to remember that. Holly grabbed a tissue and dabbed her eyes. While she wanted to go home, crawl under the covers, and watch back-to-back episodes of *Downton Abbey* while ingesting copious amounts of chocolate, Holly had an important meeting with a client in ten minutes. She dried her cheeks, grabbed a mirror and some lip gloss from her purse, and said a quick prayer.

God had given her the job, she knew, and He would be her strength and support. He had always helped her in the past, and she knew He would again. She needed to trust Him to do for her what she could not do on her own.

*Creator, I praise You for being my trustworthy
Savior. Give me the courage and humility
to call on You when I feel overwhelmed.*

The Perfect Redeemer

*"Who are you?" he asked. "I am your servant Ruth,"
she replied. "Spread the corner of your covering
over me, for you are my family redeemer."*

RUTH 3:9 NLT

Ruth was a woman of faith. After suffering the loss of her husband, she could have wallowed in grief and misery. Instead, she chose to follow her mother-in-law, Naomi, to a place where she knew no one, in order to honor her late husband (and, perhaps, the God he had introduced her to).

Ruth was also a woman of action. She worked hard to glean in the fields, toiling with intention and consistency. The owner of the fields, Boaz, noticed her work ethic and was impressed. Later, Ruth followed Naomi's advice and found Boaz at night while he was sleeping. Because he was a relative of hers and a man of integrity, he agreed to spread his covering over her as her "family redeemer." This meant he promised to marry and take care of Ruth (and Naomi).

Ruth's story has much to teach us. Just as Ruth moved on from grief to action, we can ask for God's help to move past our own losses and not get stuck in bitterness or anger. With His help, we can honor others and not wallow in self-pity or destructive habits. Also, as His strength and forgiveness covers our weaknesses and failures, we can find peace and joy. He is the perfect Redeemer who takes care of us so we don't have to worry about providing for ourselves.

*My Rock and Redeemer, I praise and
thank You for Your covering over me.
You are a faithful provider.*

Blessing Our Families

God places the lonely in families;
he sets the prisoners free and gives them joy.
But he makes the rebellious live in a sun-scorched land.

PSALM 68:6 NCV

Maybe you're a single mom, an older person living with a younger relative, or a foster parent. Perhaps you're married to a disabled spouse. Whatever your situation, God created families to give community, consistency, and care in the midst of an often-hostile world. Though our homes aren't always conflict-free, we can choose to pray for those we reside with and strive to live as examples of godly love.

How could you show patience today? Try praying before you get out of bed, asking the Holy Spirit to remind you to think before you speak. Does your spouse need encouragement? Leave him a loving note on his coffee mug or briefcase. You might include a helpful scripture verse.

Small children can drive even the most selfless mom to frustration. Today, take a moment (maybe before or after naptime) to cuddle with your baby or toddler just a minute longer than is necessary. Breathe in their smell and pray blessings over them.

If you're alone and lonely, pray that God will bring you a family to minister to, whether it be a physical family or a spiritual one (a Bible study class or online group). God desires for all of us to have connection with others, because those relationships can mirror—and extend—His love and concern for us.

Loving Father, I praise You for providing
families for those who are lonely. Help me
to be a godly example of Your love to
those I live with.

The Hard Work of Humility

God has chosen you and made you his holy people. . . .
So you should always clothe yourselves with mercy,
kindness, humility, gentleness, and patience.

COLOSSIANS 3:12– NCV

Miranda spent her life in the shadow of her older sister. For many years, teachers compared her to Megan, saying, "I hope you're going to be as smart as her!" It discouraged and frustrated Miranda.

She chose a different college and career from Megan in order to get away from hurtful comments and unrealistic expectations. She also struggled with resentment and anger toward her sister, who had done nothing wrong. One weekend, however, at a discipleship conference for young singles, Miranda heard a sermon about humility that convicted and challenged her.

"Have you been overlooked and underappreciated?" the preacher asked. "Perhaps instead of bemoaning that fact, you could consider that in some small way, you've been identifying with Christ. He gave up heaven and all its rewards to come to earth as a tiny, human baby. Our own humiliations and lack of accolades can't really compare."

Humility is about surrender, the preacher continued, to the Lord's plan and ways. It's also about being gentle and kind with others who mistreat us, and about our perspective as servants of the Most High God. Miranda prayed as tears fell from her face: *Forgive me for letting my exasperation cloud my relationship with Megan. Thank You for a chance to see it all differently.*

Lord, forgive me when I let others' reactions,
comparisons, and comments unnerve me. Give me
the peace that comes from trusting Your plan
and surrendering. I know that the only
opinion that really matters is Yours.

Practicing Gratitude

*Everywhere and in every way, most excellent Felix,
we acknowledge this with profound gratitude.*
ACTS 24:3 NIV

"Jean didn't even acknowledge my gift," Dani told her husband. "At the very least, an e-mail would have been nice. Do people even write thank-you notes anymore?"

"I usually text people," Paul admitted.

"You tell people thanks, though. That's good!" Dani replied.

The couple talked for a few minutes about how they could encourage gratitude in their two young children. They decided on a few actions. First, they would buy fill-in-the-blank notes at the local stationery store. Second, Dani would sit down with her two little ones and show them how to write a thank-you letter. Third, the family would verbally share about that particular day's blessings at the table every time they gathered for dinner.

After a few months, Dani acknowledged (gratefully!) that she and Paul had begun the long process of teaching her children to be thankful to God—and to the people in their lives who spent time and/or money on them.

How can you express gratitude to someone today? Send a friend a social media message, thanking them for a kind word; write a note to someone who gives of their time (Bible teacher, committee member, volunteer); call a staff member at your church and tell them thanks for all they do; e-mail a relative and praise them for a stellar quality or an act of selfless service.

*Father God, You have given us so much.
Help us to show gratitude to You and others.
May we never take You—or Your
many blessings—for granted.*

His Love Never Fails

*As pressure and stress bear down on me,
I find joy in your commands.*
PSALM 119:143 NLT

Back-to-school stress is real. It's easy to fall prey to impatience, frustration, and anger in the midst of school supply shopping, teacher meetings, and activity sign-ups. Just think about 1 Corinthians 13 and apply it to this time of year:

Love is not proud—except when I gloat about my child's placement in a gifted class on Facebook.

It is not rude—except to the person at the mall, who is maddeningly slow.

Love is not self-seeking—but how many things do our kids want to sign up for, and how many do we want them to participate in?

It always trusts, always perseveres—but I doubt my kids' school and teachers will live up to my expectations.

Love never fails. Sigh. But we sure do. Perhaps you really, truly want a different kind of school year this year. Maybe you long to be a conduit of grace to your kids' teachers and administrators. How do we get there?

Let's pray for deep faith, born of our miraculous God, to settle our fears. His peace can calm our harried hearts and flood our anxious souls. Each day, let's spend a few minutes seeking His face in prayer and quieting our minds. His love, after all, never, ever fails.

*Gracious God, give me the desire to
spend time with You, especially when I
think I'm too busy. May I be a worthy
representative of You each day.*

Kick Envy to the Curb

*But if you harbor bitter envy and selfish ambition in your
hearts, do not boast about it or deny the truth.*

JAMES 3:14 NIV

For several weeks, Mandy noticed herself getting restless and
discouraged whenever she logged on to her computer. After
talking with her pastor-husband, Ron, she admitted that she felt
envious of several of her friends because they had more money
than she did. They seemed to be constantly acquiring expensive
possessions and traveling to far-off places. Some of her pals were
stay-at-home moms like Mandy, but those who worked full-time
often posted about awards banquets, business trips, and other
(seemingly) glamorous aspects of their jobs.

"Honey, why don't you take a break from social media?" Ron
asked. After praying about that suggestion, Mandy decided it
was a wise idea. Each morning, instead of immediately powering
up her computer and logging on to Facebook, she took out her
Bible and read the scriptures. She then spent time praying about
her contentment level and asking God to remind her of His
many blessings.

Within a few days, Mandy felt more peace in her spirit.
She also acknowledged that God had placed her in her current
role after she had prayed for years to have children and a family.
Ron encouraged her, too: "Hon, our life has less frills and more
fulfillment."

He's right, she thought. *Sure, I'm not making the big bucks, but
I am making a big difference in my children's lives by pouring
myself into them.*

*Lord, forgive me for envying what others have.
Thank You for the season I'm in right now and
for the financial situation You have me in.*

Jesus' Perspective on Priorities

*But Martha was busy with all the work to be done.
She went in and said, "Lord, don't you care that my sister
has left me alone to do all the work? Tell her to help me."*
LUKE 10:40 NCV

We often wear busyness as a badge of honor because busyness can equal productivity and usefulness. It's important to ask ourselves, however, whether busyness takes away from—or adds to—our faith journey.

When Jesus dined in the home of Mary and Martha, Martha prepared the meal for her special guest, while Mary (in a highly unusual move for a woman during biblical times) sat at Jesus' feet, listening to His teaching. Martha understandably felt frustrated that Mary wasn't helping her, and she asked Jesus to rebuke her sister. However, Jesus told Martha that Mary had chosen the "better part." The Bible doesn't say what Martha replied, or how she felt. Perhaps she felt relieved.

Picture yourself receiving a text that an important person was coming to your house. You might scurry around, tidying the bathroom and plumping the couch cushions. If your guest said, "Sit down. Relax! I don't want you to make a fuss over me. I just want to be with you," you would feel grateful. . .peaceful. . .and treasured.

Today, as you plan your to-do list, prioritize time to sit and reflect on God's Word. Instead of rushing around to accomplish things you feel should be done, ask God what He wants you to do. You might be relieved.

*Jesus, give me Your perspective today
as I plan my to-dos. Show me what's
important to You, and help
me to follow through.*

God's Mercy in Our Need

*Peace be to the brethren, and love joined with
faith, from God the Father and the Lord
Jesus Christ (the Messiah, the Anointed One).*

EPHESIANS 6:23 AMP

As soon as Marci got into her car, she began sobbing. She put her head on the steering wheel and cried until she couldn't cry anymore. "Lord, help!" she managed to whisper as the tears subsided.

A few minutes earlier, during a follow-up visit after her annual gynecological exam, Marci's doctor had revealed disturbing news. Several possibilities existed for the things going on in her body; none of them were good.

As a single woman with no family living nearby, Marci felt panic as she thought of the next few weeks. Doctors' visits, tests, and all sorts of treatments would eat up her time. When would she work? How would she pay her bills? She had no idea.

Suddenly, her phone rang. It was her prayer partner and best friend, Shellie. "Hello?" Marci said.

"Are you okay? I felt really strongly that I should call," her friend asked. Marci gasped, and then told Shellie everything.

"You're going to be fine," Shellie said. "Our Bible study class will bring meals, and I can help you drive to appointments. And God is going to carry you when you can't carry on." Marci's tears fell again as she murmured her thanks to Shellie. It was good to not be alone—and it was so kind of God to remind her of that, at just the right moment.

*Heavenly Father, thank You for the gift of Christ's
presence and peace. Give me courage when I am
afraid and strength when I am weak. Amen.*

He Equips Us

*Therefore, since we do hold and engage in this ministry
by the mercy of God [granting us favor, benefits, opportunities,
and especially salvation], we do not get discouraged
(spiritless and despondent with fear) or become faint
with weariness and exhaustion.*

2 CORINTHIANS 4:1 AMP

Lucy and her husband, Matt, looked at each other and grinned. They had just spent an hour and a half consuming a four-course meal, engaging in deep conversation, and looking into each other's eyes. It was pure gift. . .one that they did not take lightly.

The couple, who had adopted several foster children, often heard phrases such as "We don't know how you can take care of all those kids" or "I could never do what you do!" Because she heard those comments so often, Lucy now answered the same way every time. "We wouldn't last a week—or a day—without the Lord," she always admitted. "He has called us to this ministry, and He equips us with His energy and strength each day."

Some days were harder than others for the couple, who had no special training. However, some days were simply glorious. They both loved the feeling of being in the center of God's will, out on the edge of their own capabilities. They were also immensely grateful for people who gave them opportunities for nights away from their loud, high-maintenance brood.

"Ready to go back home?" Lucy asked Matt as she squeezed his hand.

"Ready," he said.

*God, thank You for equipping me for the
service You've called me to. Help
me never forget that it's You
doing the work through me.*

Inhaling His Word

*The word is very near you. It is in your
mouth and in your heart so you may obey it.*
DEUTERONOMY 30:14 NCV

God has given us His Word to encourage, strengthen, and
energize us. It lifts us up when we are down and prods us into
action when we feel incompetent. It gives us courage when we
are afraid and provides us with effective ammunition against the
enemy of our souls. With God's Word, we can replace Satan's lies
with God's truth. One woman who memorizes scripture says that
the practice helps her "take every thought captive immediately."

Are you intimidated by memorization? Pick two or three
scriptures and write them on index cards. Put them in the places
you will see them often, such as the car, bathroom mirror, or on
the fridge. Don't force yourself to memorize. Simply inhale them
like air (because they are life-blood for your soul). Sing them if
you want to; there are apps—like the "Fighter" App by Desiring
God ministries—which will put music to verses.

You'll be amazed how God will use those truths to shine the
light in dark places of your spirit.

Jenna Lang says she "accidentally" memorized scripture
by declaring promises of God out loud when she needed an
emotional and spiritual boost. It paid off in unexpected ways, she
says, because "being able to recall [verses] during times of intense
trial helped me not give in to utter despair."

*Lord, thank You for Your Word. Help me to never
take it for granted and to keep it in my heart
and mind and on the tip of my tongue.*

Sharing Jesus Naturally

*"But you are my witnesses, O Israel!" says the LORD.
"You are my servant. You have been chosen to know me, believe
in me, and understand that I alone am God. There is no other
God— there never has been, and there never will be."*

ISAIAH 43:10 NLT

Although Nonette became a Christian at age ten, as a teenager she was shy and afraid of what others thought of her. She became hesitant to talk about Jesus. Once, however, she boldly shared her faith. During a Bible study, Nonette became concerned about a girl in her youth group. Samantha wasn't born again, and Nonette knew God wanted Sam to accept Christ. Nonette decided she was the one to help her.

One night after the study, Nonette and a friend cornered Sam. Then Nonette went into the "spiel" she had practiced. But Sam yelled at her and ran away. *I tried too hard,* Nonette realized. *I scared her off.*

It was years before Nonette would verbally witness again. She doesn't know what became of Sam, but after several years of being a non-witness, Nonette realized that she wasn't being obedient to Christ's mandate to share the Gospel with the world, and she began to look for opportunities to talk about Jesus kindly and winsomely. When she does, Nonette feels God's presence and His approval—like a father who is proud of his daughter for "just trying."

*Precious heavenly Father, thank You for the
gift of Jesus. Help me to share Him in a
natural, authentic way. May others see
You through me in every action I
take and word I say. Amen.*

Encouraging Words

*Don't use foul or abusive language. Let everything
you say be good and helpful, so that your words will
be an encouragement to those who hear them.*
EPHESIANS 4:29 NLT

"Sticks and stones may break my bones, but words will never hurt
me," goes the old saying. It's not true, however. Words can—and
do—hurt. Ask anyone who was bullied as a child. Discouraging,
shaming words stay with a person for years, even decades.

As we spend more time texting and giving status updates—
and less time talking—we also need to be aware that whatever
we "say" online stays online, for good (we can delete things, but
others may have captured screen shots or printed our words out).
Did you rant on Facebook about a friend or political party? It's
out there. That comment belittling a coworker? It's out there.
When you left a nasty comment on a blog in a moment of
anger? It's out there.

As Ephesians 4:29 says, the words we choose are important. . .
especially as the world becomes more disconnected and dis-
interested in the things of God. The way we talk, both online
and off, can either attract people toward Jesus or turn them away
from Him. Today, think about the language you use and the tone
you're talking with. Are your word choices helpful? Are your
phrases kind? Is the tone you're taking sarcastic? Cynical? Bitter?
Ask God to help you think before you speak (or post).

*Father, may everything I say be helpful, kind,
and encouraging to others, and thank You for
forgiving me when I mess up, Lord—because I will.*

Our First Thought

*They even did more than we had hoped, for their
first action was to give themselves to the Lord
and to us, just as God wanted them to do.*

2 CORINTHIANS 8:5 NLT

Darlene listened to the radio as she drove to work. This morning, a popular women's Bible study teacher asked her listeners, "What's the first thought you have in the morning? Do you point your mind toward God to thank Him for your life and ask His guidance, or do you complain that you have to get up and grumble your way to the coffee maker?"

Ouch, thought Darlene. She switched off the radio so she could think. When was the last time she woke up and thanked God for anything? Since her recent unwanted divorce, if she prayed, it was a quick "emergency" prayer. She had gone back to work to support herself and her two young children, and most days she struggled just to get through the day. If anything, her conversations with God had become darker and more critical. *I'm talking with Him, but I'm not listening,* Darlene thought. *I'm mad at my husband and my "lot in life," and I'm taking it out on the One who could help me get through this.*

I need to make Him my priority again, Darlene concluded. As a woman of faith, she believed God would provide for and take care of her, regardless of what her circumstances looked like. It was time to start living that way.

*Father God, thank You for giving Yourself to me.
I give myself to You, wholeheartedly.*

Aging Well

*So refuse to worry, and keep your body healthy. But remember
that youth, with a whole life before you, is meaningless.*
ECCLESIASTES 11:10 NLT

Our society is youth-obsessed. As soon as movie stars get past
a certain age, they're offered fewer roles. Websites post pictures
of "past their prime" actors' sagging, wrinkled frames. Even
magazines touting the benefits of becoming seasoned often
airbrush and edit photos of their subjects.

Why are we reluctant to celebrate aging? It is a natural
process, and the alternative isn't good. Perhaps we are
uncomfortable with one day being less useful, dependent on our
loved ones, or feeble in body and mind. Maybe we're afraid of
death. Heaven seems far away at times.

However, God takes a different view of getting older. In
Leviticus 19:32, the scriptures say, "Stand up in the presence
of the aged, show respect for the elderly and revere your God"
(NIV). Job 12:12 says, "Is not wisdom found among the aged?
Does not long life bring understanding?" (NIV).

Look for godly women in your church or community who
have aged well. Ask them how they feel about getting older.
You'll probably discover they love the age they are and wouldn't
trade their hard-won wisdom for all the anti-wrinkle cream in
the world. As Audrey Hepburn once said, "And the beauty of a
woman, with passing years only grows!"

*Lord, show me Your perspective on getting older.
As I age, help me to become more in tune with
You and less in tune with the world. Thank You
for healthy role models. May I become one for
younger folks as I sail into my later years.*

The Power of Intercession

I exhort therefore, that, first of all, supplications, prayers, intercessions, and giving of thanks, be made for all men.
1 TIMOTHY 2:1 KJV

The group of thirteen women from all over the country met during a writer's workshop at a retreat center. Something spiritual and quite unexpected happened as they chatted about careers, families, and the Lord: God knitted their hearts together.

Coming home from the nurturing and surprising weekend, one of the ladies found out that her husband had had multiple affairs. She reached out to her new friends, and prayers began to flow. Another like-hearted woman from the retreat initiated a private social media group so the Bakers' Dozen could share prayer requests. They dubbed themselves the "Ninja Prayer Warriors."

Since that workshop a year and a half has passed. The women have endured health problems, financial difficulties, crisis after crisis with relatives, divorce, betrayal, job stress, and more. However, their common faith in Christ, kinship in using their talents to serve God, and bond of intercession has cemented them together.

When one sister has a concern, the others gather around her in spirit. The group has seen several miraculous answers to prayer, but the biggest miracle is that no matter how far apart they live, each sister feels supported and nurtured by a diverse network of big-hearted, faithful warrior saints. It's a stunning picture of the body of Christ in action.

*Lord, thank You for the prayers of
Your people. Please give me sisters
in Christ who will pray for me,
and help me to be a
prayer warrior for others.*

Hallowing the Sabbath

*For in six days the LORD made heaven and earth, the sea, and
all that in them is, and rested the seventh day: wherefore the
LORD blessed the sabbath day, and hallowed it.*

EXODUS 20:11 KJV

God created us to need rest, and He modeled that for us by
taking the very first Sabbath. He then commanded the Israelites
to follow His example and keep the Sabbath one day a week.

The Israelites had strict instructions about what they could
and couldn't do on their Holy Day. While Jesus' new covenant
with believers fulfilled the law and gave us freedom, modern
Christians seem to have thrown the proverbial baby out with
the bathwater. Now, we cram our Sabbath day full with sports
practices, shopping, and meetings (just like every other day of
the week).

However, we can't ignore the Sabbath without
consequences. God formed the world, our bodies, and our spirits
to have seasons of stillness. Our minds must be still so they
can reboot. Our bodies crave rest in order to recharge. And our
spirits must worship, so we can experience refilling. In *The Holy
Wild: Trusting in the Character of God*, Mark Buchanan writes,
"Most of the things we need to be most fully alive never come in
busyness. They grow in rest."

To be fully alive, we need relationships, wonder, silence,
peace, and the infilling of the Holy Spirit. All these things
benefit from rest. When we learn to truly take the Sabbath, we
will call it (as God does) good.

*Holy God, thank You for creating the Sabbath.
Help me to honor it and keep it holy.*

A Heart for Learning

*It is senseless to pay tuition to educate a fool,
since he has no heart for learning.*
PROVERBS 17:16 NLT

Jeanine tapped her pencil impatiently as she waited in the assisted living center's common area. A professor had given her the task of interviewing an exceptional older woman, and she had chosen her great-aunt May. She was looking forward to seeing May, who was one of her heroines. But mostly, Jeanine wished that she didn't have to complete the assignment. She was sick of school and tired of studying. She felt restless and burned out.

As the attendant wheeled May over to her, May exclaimed, "Jeanine! I've missed you!" With a bright smile, May gushed over Jeanine's long hair and new engagement ring. They chatted amiably for several minutes about May's late husband and Jeanine's fiancé before Jeanine took out her notepad, explained why she was there, and cleared her throat.

"How do you stay energized when you can't do as much as you once did?" Jeanine asked.

"Well, I sometimes get tired of the limits of this old body," May answered. "But my faith and a desire to learn keeps me young at heart."

"What do you mean?" Jeanine asked.

"I love to try new things. This last year, I took piano lessons. I enjoy playing hymns while the other residents sing along."

Jeanine shook her head and wrote down her aunt's answer: "Keep learning." God had used May to remind her of the importance of studying and growing. *Okay, I get it Lord*, she prayed, smiling.

*Father, give me the desire
to keep learning new things,
especially as my body ages.*

A Promised Healing

*Behold, [in the future restored Jerusalem] I will lay upon it health
and healing, and I will cure them and will reveal to them the
abundance of peace (prosperity, security, stability) and truth.*
JEREMIAH 33:6 AMP

Are you longing to be healed of an affliction? Mary Magdalene
suffered with seven demons before Jesus touched her and
restored her to life. Scripture doesn't tell us much about how,
when, or where Jesus healed Mary. It does tell us that Mary,
along with several other women, provided for and supported
Jesus so that He could do what God had called Him to do. After
Jesus healed her, she became one of His most ardent followers.

This woman, who had been tormented by Satan himself,
became a walking testimony of the power of the Light to dispel
darkness: "The light shines in the darkness, and the darkness has
not overcome it" (John 1:5 NIV).

Whether or not God chooses to cure you here on earth, one
day He will restore you to total health. In heaven, our bodies will
be perfect and no diseases will be allowed to touch us. We will
live in peace and prosperity.

Such a promise should make us rejoice. Jesus will strengthen
us for this life, whatever it may hold, and will one day turn
on the light that will make the darkness scatter for all time.
Hallelujah!

*Heavenly Father, thank You for Your promise
of healing. Strengthen me as I walk this earth,
and give me hope as I look toward heaven.*

Indescribable Grace

*I would like to learn just one thing from you:
Did you receive the Spirit by the works of the law,
or by believing what you heard?*
GALATIANS 3:2 NIV

Kristi accepted Christ at the age of twelve, but she spent her teenage years living in fear of "messing up" and not pleasing God. Perhaps her fear stemmed from a controlling mother, or maybe she misunderstood what her preacher taught. Whatever the reason, Kristi exhausted herself by trying too hard. She focused on what she didn't do, at the expense of peace and contentment in Christ.

Finally, during college, a mentor explained that she was trying to earn what was already hers. This mentor began walking Kristi through the scriptures and explaining to Kristi that God sees His children as righteous and holy because of Jesus' sacrifice on the cross. The concept of grace, once a dim, distant concept to Kristi, exploded in her mind and heart. Suddenly, she was filled with an unexplainable joy.

Ever since her second awakening, Kristi has been on a mission to spread the message of grace. She parents with purpose and loves her friends well, because she accepts God's approval of her through His Son. Even her non-Christian friends have noticed the difference—for which Kristi gives God all the glory.

*Lord, thank You for Your
indescribable, generous, and never-ending
grace. Help me to live in its light
every day, so that I may show
the world who You are.*

Our Highest Goal

Let love be your highest goal!
1 CORINTHIANS 14:1 NLT

For Sherry, the beginning of her children's school year brings an urge to set goals. Is it the smell of her son's new crayons or the crisp collar on her daughter's shirts? Maybe it's her childhood memories of fresh wardrobes and new locker assignments.

Whatever the reason, Sherry loves to sit down with her pen and journal and pray through the areas of her life.

As she's faithful to seek God's desires for her, Sherry feels the Holy Spirit encouraging her to work on certain things. First, she writes down a goal to "make mornings less stressful." She jots a note to herself about looking up tips about calmer mornings. Second, she decides to try memorizing several of her favorite psalms. She is sure that her son's foray into driving will tempt her to worry. Committing half a dozen psalms to memory will serve her well.

Finally, Sherry thinks about her husband, who provides well for the family. However, he doesn't help around the house as much as she would like, and when he's off work, he tends to engage his computer tablet instead of her or the kids. "Lord, show me how to love him well," she prays. She is sure that's a prayer God will approve of—and answer, in His time and way.

Jesus, show me the desires You have
for me, and help me to remember that
loving my family and those You put in
my path is the highest and best goal of all.

Constant in the Midst of Change

*In the beginning you made the earth, and your hands
made the skies. . . They will all wear out like clothes. And,
like clothes, you will change them and throw them away.
But you never change, and your life will never end.*
PSALM 102:25–27 NCV

Change is in the air as the summer sun wanes and the nights
grow cooler. Soon all the kids will be back in school. Some
moms will breathe a sigh of relief, welcoming the idea that
the children will no longer be constantly underfoot. Other
moms already miss the little darlings who filled the house with
laughter—and most likely a few tears—over the summer.

Whether a woman has children or not, it's likely she
remembers having had the anxious-yet-exciting thoughts and
feelings so prevalent at the beginning of each new school year:
Will she like her new schedule? Will she find the way to her
classrooms? Will she get along with her new teachers? Will the
classes be easy or hard? Will she make new friends?

Yes, there's no getting past the fact that some anxieties can
come with change and that all things must and do change. Well,
all things except for one: God. He is the one constant in the life
of each and every woman. He is the one person, power, rock, she
can count on. In Him, and only Him, she finds the comfort of
the unchangeable.

*Lord, I find peace in the fact that You
never change. Knowing You will always be
there for me gives me the strength and peace
to begin this day with Your joy.*

Step One: Vital Seeking

*Then Jehoshaphat feared, and set himself [determinedly,
as his vital need] to seek the Lord.*
2 CHRONICLES 20:3 AMP

The Bible says God was with good King Jehoshaphat, ruler of
Judah, because he followed His commandments. But that doesn't
mean Jehoshaphat didn't face trouble now and again. In fact, one
day, the king was told that some countries had formed a great
army that was on its way to attack his kingdom.

Jehoshaphat was scared. After all, who wouldn't be? But
instead of taking flight, he set his heart, mind, body, and soul
on seeking God. Following his example, his people also came to
seek God, "yearning for Him with all their desire" (verse 4 AMP).

God can't help but respond to His people when they make
Him and the seeking of His face a "vital need" in their life.
When they look to Him for all wisdom, comfort, strength,
peace, and grace. When they submit themselves to Him and wait
upon Him until they feel His presence.

In the midst of the seemingly impossible, spiritually
dedicated women—such as Hannah, Mother Teresa, Corrie
ten Boom, and Helen Keller—set the stage for the possible. An
amazing source of strength and miracle-working power is found
and established by obedient women who spend time upon their
knees, determined to seek their Lord.

*I come before You, Lord, upon my knees. In this
silence, my head is bowed, my mind engaged,
my heart offered, and my soul presented. Come
to me now as I yearn for Your
presence and seek Your face.*

Step Two: Truly Focusing

*We have no might to stand against this great
company that is coming against us. We do not
know what to do, but our eyes are upon You.*
2 CHRONICLES 20:12 AMP

Even with a great army coming against him, King Jehoshaphat of
Judah kept his faith in God. Even more importantly, Jehoshaphat
knew enough to humble himself and go to the "guy" who was
really in charge—his own King, the Lord God, the one whose
spiritual muscle was a tremendous force in the material world.

In his prayer, Jehoshaphat reminded himself and his people
of several things: (1) that no one can withstand God's power;
(2) that time and time again, God has saved His people—as
promised; (3) that God would hear his prayer and save Judah
from her aggressors; and (4) that although Jehoshaphat and his
citizens had no idea what to do, all would be well because their
eyes were on the Lord—front and center.

The same holds true to this day! With her eyes on God,
today's woman is not cognizant of the crashing waves. She no
longer feels the sting of the wind. She refuses to allow her mind
to wander with what-ifs. She looks away from storms, fears,
and enemies as she determines to keep her eyes on the prize she
knows is hers—the power, peace, and presence of God.

*Jesus, with You in my life I can walk on water.
With my eyes plunging into the depths of Your spirit,
nothing and no one can harm me—for everything
I truly need and desire is found in You.*

Step Three: Standing Still

*You shall not need to fight in this battle; take your positions,
stand still, and see the deliverance of the Lord [Who is]
with you. . . . Fear not nor be dismayed. Tomorrow go
out against them, for the Lord is with you.*

2 CHRONICLES 20:17 AMP

King Jehoshaphat made all the right moves when it came to a
major army rising up against him and his people. His first step
was to humbly seek God's face. His second, to keep his eyes on
his Lord. Because Jehoshaphat took these bold steps, God gave
him a good word. The king and his people need not fight this
great army but merely hold their positions and watch what God
was going to do! They were not to fear, nor freak out because
when they headed out to meet the enemy, the All-Powerful would
be with them!

When God's daughters, princesses in their own right, seek
their Father's face, focus on Him alone, then take a firm stance
with courage and conviction, knowing that God will fight
whatever challenge approaches, nothing can defeat them! Holding
this knowledge close to her heart, a woman remains calm,
empowered, and faithful—able to lead herself and others. This
"standing still" is evidence of God's unique and awesome power
in this frenzied, fast-paced society. How delightful to be a woman
firmly planted in faith, filled with the serenity of her Savior.

*Help me to stand still, Lord. Give me the confidence
to know You are with me every step of
the way. Calm the fast beating of my heart
as I lean back upon You.*

Step Four: Praising

Believe in the Lord your God and you shall be established;
believe and remain steadfast to His prophets and you shall
prosper. When he had consulted with the people, he appointed
singers to sing to the Lord and praise Him.
2 CHRONICLES 20:20–21 AMP

The threat against King Jehoshaphat and the country of Judah
was real and certain. The huge army was right outside their door.
But the godly king took the appropriate steps to meet this threat:
He sought God, focused on Him, and took comfort in the
fact that the battle before him was God's battle. As he and his
people marched out with the army to meet the enemy, he told
them that as long as they believed God, all would be well. More
than well, actually. They would prosper! Then Jehoshaphat did
something amazing. Before seeing God work His wonders, he
told the people to praise God, to give Him thanks for His mercy
and love. As they did so, God set ambushes against the enemy
armies, which destroyed each other! All Jehoshaphat had to do
was collect the spoil!

Praising God is a potent weapon against any and all
challenges. Whatever the obstacle, nothing can stand in the
way of the power of praise. It can move mountains, open prison
doors, destroy armies, and summon chariots to earth. What
more could a woman need?

Lord, You know what enemy has come
against me. You know how much I need
Your help. I put all in Your hands today,
as I begin praising Your name,
applauding Your power.

Clued In

This book of the law shall not depart out of thy mouth; but thou shalt meditate therein day and night, that thou mayest observe to do according to all that is written therein: for then thou shalt make thy way prosperous, and then thou shalt have good success.

JOSHUA 1:8 KJV

God clues Joshua in on a few things, things he'll need to know now that he's Israel's new leader. The Lord tells Joshua that everywhere he steps, whatever land his foot touches, God has already given him (1:3). It's a done deal! God also tells him that he will not be defeated, that God will be with him no matter what and that Joshua should never be afraid or discouraged. (God repeats that last one two more times in this chapter alone!)

But then God mentions success, a word that appears only once in the King James Version. To have good success and to prosper, Joshua needs to speak, think about, and obey God's Word. After hearing these instructions, Joshua remains true to them and becomes the conquering hero God created him to be!

Today's daughters of the King can have the same victory! God has already given His princesses all they need to be successful—as a mom, a career woman, a wife, a sister, a friend. Keeping that in mind, as well as God's Word on her tongue and obedience in her actions, she cannot be anything other than prosperous in everything she does!

*Thank You, Lord, for the gift—and challenge—
of Your Word. I know that as I live, move,
and have my being in You, I will have success!*

Godly Workers

*We hear that some of you are living idle lives, refusing to work
and meddling in other people's business. We command such
people and urge them in the name of the Lord Jesus Christ to
settle down and work to earn their own living. As for the rest
of you, dear brothers and sisters, never get tired of doing good.*

2 THESSALONIANS 3:11–13 NLT

God wants His children to be active, to be earning their daily
bread. When hands are busy with their own business, they are
less likely to delve into someone else's. In other words, working
keeps people out of trouble. Yet, there is another type of danger
that may crop up in the life of a worker—that of making work
her all in all, with no room to spare for helping others, including
those in her own family.

Yes, it's important for a woman to help earn the bread—
either by working outside or inside of the home. But it's even
more important to be doing that work in love. To be blessing the
lives of others in the midst of the working day. To be working for
God—not wealth.

Laboring for the Lord instead of working for wealth,
recognition, and power will keep women energized and able to
meet whatever challenges come before them. Such efforts make
this a true and worthwhile celebration of Labor Day!

*I know I do not labor in vain when I focus
on working for You, Lord. I, too, want to be
about my Father's business. Show me where
You can use me today—and every day.*

Heaven Set

For as he thinketh in his heart, so is he.
PROVERBS 23:7 KJV

*The thing which I greatly feared is come upon me,
and that which I was afraid of is come unto me.*
JOB 3:25 KJV

These two verses are amazing insights into the power of the mind.

According to Proverbs, whatever a woman thinks in her heart, that is what she will become. In other words, she is what she thinks! If she is thinking doubt in her heart, that's what she is—doubting. If she's thinking about sad things, that's what she becomes—sad. On the other hand, if she's thinking about joyous things, she cannot help but smile. If she's thinking love, she cannot help but beam with light.

The verse from Job reveals that when a woman is fear-filled, her mind and spirit are focused on her circumstances. Instead of having her eyes on Jesus, she looks at the waves and wind around her and begins to sink. What she feared is what she is focused on and thus what she gets, what she drowns in!

It takes the same amount of energy to think of good things as it does bad. But the effect of each is very different. God would have His daughter have a heavenly mind-set—thinking of Him, His blessings, His love, and His light. For that not only brightens her outlook and day but shapes her and the world surrounding her.

*Lord, help me to be more aware of what I
am thinking. Keep my mind set on heavenly
matters. Raise me up—mentally, emotionally,
and spiritually—to You!*

The Deep End

*I truly believe I will live to see the LORD's goodness. Wait for the
LORD's help. Be strong and brave, and wait for the LORD's help.*
PSALM 27:13–14 NCV

A woman is often caught off guard when grief crashes upon her
with the loss of a deeply loved one. In those times, she can look
to God, her major consolation, her refuge, her true and steady
rock. For His Word has an amazing power to reach out, to heal,
to catch her heart—and breath.

The words of Psalm 27:13–14 contain such power. They are
an amazing balm to help heal a woman's heart torn by loss. For
her, they serve as a reminder that good times will one day come
again. That God is working in this life, on this earth, among these
people. That the pain will subside, and then God can begin the
healing.

Her part? To not give in to despair. To remain strong and
brave. That doesn't mean not shedding a tear, for there will
be plenty. But to know, deep down, where deep calls to deep,
that she is not alone. That Jesus, sitting right beside her, is also
weeping. And that one day, she and her loved one will both
rise again. That one day, she will bear a lighter heart and the
beginning of a smile.

*Thank You, dear God, for comforting me
when the hurt is so deep, and healing me
when I am ready. Help me to memorize
these verses so that I can call upon
them in a moment of need.*

The Voice

*[The Lord] will still be with you to teach you. You will
see your teacher with your own eyes. Your own ears will
hear him. Right behind you a voice will say, "This is the
way you should go," whether to the right or to the left.*

ISAIAH 30:20–21 NLT

It's a fact that women hear better than men! But to whom are
the ladies listening?

God wants to be the supreme Voice in the life of each of His
daughters. For when she follows His direction, she will not be
misled. She will not be deviating from His path.

Yet today's world holds so many competing voices, people
shouting for attention. So how does a woman of the Way know
which voice is God's? By staying deep in His Word. By not just
reading that Word but obeying it. By using that Word to filter
all her circumstances to determine the real truth. By using that
Word as a litmus test to prove all other theories, opinions, and
observations.

Then, and only then, in the quiet, secret place, alone with her
Savior, can she sense God's familiar presence, discern His voice,
seek His direction, and determine her next step, confident that
the Teacher is with her and giving her the best guidance she could
ever ask for or imagine, saying, "This is the way you should go."

*May You continue to speak words into my life, Lord.
I thank You so much for where You've brought me
thus far. And I am excited about the roads to come.*

Selfless Sister

*"Love your enemies! Do good to those who hate you. Bless those
who curse you. Pray for those who hurt you. If someone slaps
you on one cheek, offer the other cheek also. If someone demands
your coat, offer your shirt also. Give to anyone who asks. . . .
Do to others as you would like them to do to you."*
LUKE 6:27–31 NLT

These five verses contain a myriad of selfless verbs—love, do
good, bless, pray for, offer (twice), give—all of which culminate
with the amazing phrase, "Do to others as you would like them
to do to you." Oh, if only life were that simple! . . . But it is!

God loved His children before they loved Him. So why
should His daughters be any different when it comes to their
fellow humans? How different would this world be if each
woman, mother, wife, sister, daughter, and girlfriend were
demonstrating love, even to the unlovable. Doing good, even to
those who don't like her. Blessing and praying for those who hurt
her feelings. Offering her other cheek to a (hopefully figurative)
slapper and giving to anyone who asks for anything—regardless
of the person's race, creed, color, or reputation.

It's easy to be loving and selfless to those a girl already loves.
The challenge comes in applying those attributes to perceived
enemies. But there is a bonus to such behavior. Although a
woman may not be rewarded here, her "reward from heaven will
be very great" (verse 35 NLT).

*Ever merciful God, fill me with
Your compassion, light, and love
so that I can do unto others as
You do unto me.*

Heart Check

*Why are you cast down, O my inner self? And why should
you moan over me and be disquieted within me? Hope in
God and wait expectantly for Him, for I shall yet praise Him,
Who is the help of my countenance, and my God.*
PSALM 42:11 AMP

A woman can be going through her day, minding her own
business, and suddenly find herself frowning, discontent. At
such times, she would do best to stop whatever she's doing and
perform a heart check by asking her inner self, "What's up?
What's the matter? Why so down?" She may come up with a
specific instance when someone slighted her. Or maybe it's the
anniversary of a tragedy in her life. Or maybe it's the holidays,
and her mind is filled with voices of those no longer among the
living. Or maybe she's just plain blue, for no reason at all.

Whatever the cause of her being down, the remedy is
certain: She is to tell her inner woman to hope in God. To wait
for Him. Because no matter how she feels today, or may feel
tomorrow, she will in all certainty "yet praise Him"! There's no
doubt about it. So, after allowing herself one quick moan, she
can turn her "phaser" to "expectation of praise," and squeeze the
trigger. Before she knows it, praises will be bubbling up from her
heart and come streaming through her lips, turning her frown
upside down.

*Help me to remember to check my heart each day,
Lord, making sure I'm tuned out of hopelessness
and in to great expectations in You.*

A Living Faith

*I am calling up memories of your sincere and unqualified
faith (the leaning of your entire personality on God in Christ
in absolute trust and confidence in His power, wisdom, and
goodness), [a faith] that first lived permanently in [the heart
of] your grandmother Lois and your mother Eunice and now,
I am [fully] persuaded, [dwells] in you also.*

2 TIMOTHY 1:5 AMP

One of the greatest things a woman can hand down to her
children and her children's children is the gift, the example, the
wonders of her faith.

Timothy, born of a Greek father and a Jewish mother, had
a great faith. So great that he totally relied upon and had an
unparalleled trust in Christ. Paul writes that this same faith had
been evident in Timothy's grandmother and mother.

From Timothy's childhood, these two women had trained
him in the Scriptures. Because of that knowledge, Timothy
totally understood and came to believe in Jesus Christ (see 2
Timothy 3:14–15).

From Lois to Eunice to Timothy, a strong faith was read,
spoken, lived, handed down, and inherited. Would that each
woman, whether mother or grandmother, sister or aunt, friend
or girlfriend, spouse or stranger, approach life with a living
faith, open, powerful, and used for training up all children in
the way of God.

*You have told us, Lord, to walk as Jesus
did, to imitate Him. Help me be faithful
in doing that, as the eyes of children
are watching me live my faith.*

The Measure of Your Faith

*Go thy way; and as thou hast believed,
so be it done unto thee.*
MATTHEW 8:13 KJV

The centurion humbly approached Jesus in this one and only biblical account wherein a master came to Christ, pleading for Him to heal his servant.

Jesus must have recognized the soldier's compassion, for He responded immediately, saying He would go to the man's home and heal the boy. But the man humbled himself even more, telling the Christ that he, the centurion, was not worthy to have Jesus come to his home—and finally admitting all Christ needed to do was "speak the word only, and my servant shall be healed" (verse 8 KJV).

Hearing this, Jesus actually "marvelled" (verse 10 KJV), remarking He had not found such great faith in all of Israel! And in the same hour in which He said, "Go thy way; and as thou hast believed, so it be done unto thee," the centurion's servant was healed.

Might every woman have this measure of the centurion's faith. May she bring not only her own child, but all children before Jesus, humbly pleading with Christ to heal them of mind, body, spirit, and soul. And then go her way, knowing that it will be done for her just as she believed!

*I bring before You one of Your children, Lord. I know
there is nothing impossible to You. You need only
speak the word, Jesus, and this child will be made
whole. May it be done as I believe!*

A Potent Paradox

*Do not let yourself be overcome by evil,
but overcome (master) evil with good.*
ROMANS 12:21 AMP

There's an old adage that says, "Don't get mad, get even."
Unfortunately, that's going expressly against what Romans
12:21 would have Christ followers do. So if revenge is out, what
other ways of dealing with evil could a woman take? Well, she
could either allow it to taint and dictate everything in her life,
or she could run and hide in fear. None of these ways seem very
empowering, do they?

Jesus and New Testament writers give Christians many
paradoxes. And the above verse is no different. Like the text
about turning the other cheek (see Matthew 5:39), Romans
12:21 instructs God's people not to bow down to, hide from, or
return evil for evil, but to conquer it by doing good. Amazingly
enough, it works! And, as a bonus, it will not only stop evil (and
evil doers) in its (their) tracks but will relieve the flesh-filled
human desire of revenge.

What a glorious day it would be if, instead of taking revenge
for or hiding from evil, every daughter of the King faced the
dark beast head on. Neither cowering in fear or wallowing in
self-pity, God's girls can count on His power to step boldly,
repay evil with a kindness, and move on. What a paradox! What
a Godsend!

*Lord, it seems natural for me to want
to return evil for evil. But I want to do
the supernatural. Help me to conquer
evil by doing something good!*

Rock of Escape

*Saul quit chasing David and returned to fight the
Philistines. Ever since that time, the place where
David was camped has been called the Rock of Escape.*

1 SAMUEL 23:28 NLT

Hearing that Saul was after him, David fled to a great rock and
hid there. Just as Saul was about to capture David, Saul had to
give up the chase and return to fight the Philistines. Ever since
then, David called his hideout "the Rock of Escape."

Unsure of her footing, longing to find peace and rest,
desperate for protection from circumstances, yearning for the
silence only God can provide, woman also has an escape: God.
"For who is God besides the LORD? And who is the Rock except
our God?" (Psalm 18:31 NIV). In Him, as nowhere else, is she
safe from pursuers, be they in the form of family or friends,
strangers or enemies, thoughts or circumstances, things seen
or unseen. Here in her "sanctuary [a sacred and indestructible
asylum]" (Isaiah 8:14 AMP), she can rest easy, soak up the quiet,
gather her forces together, remember the power of the spiritual
over the material, and revive herself.

But how does she get to her Rock of Escape? By stilling
her mind and approaching God. By trusting in Him alone. By
calling out, "My Lord! Save me!" By faithfully camping herself
in His presence. By basking in His precious words of peace,
comfort, and solace.

*I come to You, my Rock, my God,
my Refuge, my Lord. It is in You
alone that I may rest in peace and safety.*

Powered Up

*With God's power working in us, God can do much, much more
than anything we can ask or imagine. To him be glory in the
church and in Christ Jesus for all time, forever and ever. Amen.*
EPHESIANS 3:20–21 NCV

One day two blind men yelled out to Jesus. People tried to tell
them to be quiet. But the men kept shouting, asking Him to
have pity on them. Suddenly Jesus stopped in His tracks, then
asked them, "What do you want me to do for you?" (Matthew
20:32 NCV). The blind men said they wanted to see. And so, God
honored that request. But the men got so much more in return.
Not only did they obtain their vision, but they were also given
the eye-opening opportunity to follow this Man of Miracles!

God is asking each of His daughters the same question:
"What do you want me to do for you?" He wants her to not let
others dissuade her from telling Him exactly what she wants—
no matter how impossible or improbable the request may seem.
He wants her to be specific, yet also to dream big—for He is a
limitless God, ready to do so much more than one woman could
ever ask or imagine! He wants her to then begin expecting the
unexpected as she continues to travel with Him down the road
with a lighter, more joyful step.

*Lord, You have planted dreams within me.
Power me up. Help me bring them to
fruition beyond anything I could ever
ask or imagine. To be specific,
Lord, here's what I'd like. . . .*

Loving All

Beloved, let us love one another, for love is (springs) from God; and he who loves [his fellowmen] is begotten (born) of God and is coming [progressively] to know and understand God [to perceive and recognize and get a better and clearer knowledge of Him]. . . . For God is love.

1 JOHN 4:7–8 AMP

Love. What an amazing force! It is the greatest power of all—in heaven and on earth. Love cannot be defeated, lost, or destroyed. Why not? Because love is God—and God is love.

The love a newborn has for his mother is incredibly strong. In his eyes, she is the sun, moon, and stars. As a newborn views its mother, God's daughters are to view their God, looking at Him with total adoration, expectation, and inspiration. He alone nurtures the nurturer. It is His dedication to her in every way, shape, and form that gets a woman through the day. It is His Word that helps her to rise above the material pain and plain. It is His death-defying adoration that will never leave nor forsake her—in this life or the next. It is His love that flows out from her to all others. And the more she allows herself to be the conduit of His love, the more she understands the source of that love— the one and only God and song of her life.

*I want to know You more and more, Lord.
Show me how to love all people, no matter what.
Help me to see them with Your loving eyes.*

The Expectant

*The Lord [earnestly] waits [expecting, looking, and longing] to
be gracious to you. . . . Blessed (happy, fortunate, to be envied)
are all those who [earnestly] wait for Him, who expect and
look and long for Him [for His victory, His favor, His love, His
peace, His joy, and His matchless, unbroken companionship]!*
ISAIAH 30:18 AMP

God is looking for women to bless. He's waiting for His
daughters to look up and seek His face, to spend some quality
time with Him. But some women are staring at their path, their
thoughts miles away from heavenly happenings. Carefully they
walk, heedless of God's direction, their eyes glued to the ground
so they don't trip up. Their ears are plugged into a smartphone,
so they cannot hear God's whispered, "Pssssssssssst! Look up!
Look up here!" And in the evening, when they should be more
receptive to His call, they turn on the TV. Once tuned in, they
become tuned out—spiritually and physically.

To break the cycle, women of today need to stop and look
around for God. To yearn for His presence and all that comes
with it—His victory, favor, love, peace, joy, and friendship. To
live a life certain of the knowledge that with their eyes on, ears
open to, and heart centered on Jesus, they can expect to be
blessed.

*Help me keep my eyes on You, Lord. And
allow me to loosen whatever earthly
things I am holding on to. I want my
hands, mind, spirit, heart, and soul
to be open to receive all Your
blessings—in heaven and on earth.*

A Wonderful Cord-Ship

*A person standing alone can be attacked and defeated,
but two can stand back-to-back and conquer. Three are
even better, for a triple-braided cord is not easily broken.*
ECCLESIASTES 4:12 NLT

Alone a woman may be beaten down spiritually, emotionally, or physically. But when one woman teams up with another, the two have a better chance of standing firm together! Like Ruth who refused to leave Naomi, a woman who pledges herself to a female friend not only pulls up and strengthens herself, but her friend as well. Their fates forged together, they seek to help each other in every manner of ways—building each other up, sharing life experiences, bearing each other's burdens, sharing each other's sorrows, celebrating each other's successes, seeking wisdom in the quest to understand the opposite sex, discussing methods of child rearing, exploring new employment avenues, challenging and comforting one another, and keeping each other firmly footed on the spiritual path.

When two women who are bound in such a friendship add love and fellowship with God to their "cord-ship," they become even stronger. With Christ in the mix, this now "triple-braided cord" will not easily fray.

May all women on this National Women's Friendship Day find a special way to honor their girlfriends, their God, and their special cord-ship.

*Thank You, Lord, for my girlfriend and
for Your presence among us. Help me to be as
good a friend to her as You are and
have been to me.*

Thankful Peace

Pray continually, and give thanks whatever happens.
That is what God wants for you in Christ Jesus.
1 THESSALONIANS 5:17–18 NCV

Jesus commanded His children: "When you hear of wars and insurrections (disturbances, disorder, and confusion), *do not become alarmed and panic-stricken and terrified*" (Luke 21:9 AMP, emphasis added). This seems a somewhat hard-to-swallow directive for today's women living in a society where there are school killings, marathon bombings, terrorist attacks, and mass shootings in the most common of places. Yet a prayerful presence of peace is what Christ commands.

Instead of expecting the worst, daughters of God are to have faith in the Father who has control of every situation. But how does she grow that faith? By praying continually and thanking God for each and every situation. Amid this gratitude, a sense of peace will prevail for she is reaffirming to herself (and God) that He means to use every situation for her ultimate good.

Thus, there is no reason for a princess to become alarmed. For she knows there is more to this life than what is seen, heard, and felt on this physical plane, and that her God the Father, the King, has a bigger and a better plan and kingdom for her. Based on that fact, a continual prayer for peace and a never-ending stream of thank yous no matter what happens are two of a woman's most powerful tools on earth—and in heaven.

Jesus, keep my heart and mind focused
on the peace that You bring me. May my
praise of Your peace be continually on
my lips and sent forth upon my breath.

20/20, 20/20 Vision

*[Elisha] answered, Fear not; for those with us are more
than those with them. Then Elisha prayed, Lord, I pray You,
open his eyes that he may see. And the Lord opened the young
man's eyes, and he saw, and behold, the mountain was full
of horses and chariots of fire round about Elisha.*

2 KINGS 6:16–17 AMP

One morning Elisha and his servant were surrounded by an
enemy army with its horses and chariots. Having seen the odds
against them, his servant man, who apparently only had earthly
vision, freaked out, asking Elisha, "What will we do?"

The prophet seems rather calm with his reply of, "Don't
worry. Our army is bigger than theirs." But then he prayed that
God would open the servant's eyes so that he could see how well
protected he and the prophet were. So God honored Elisha's
request—and the scales from the servant's spiritual eyes fell away,
revealing a mountain full of charioted cavalry.

When women of the Way open their eyes of faith, the
shadows of this world shrink away and fear abates. The more
they understand the absolute and awesome power of their God,
the better their 20/20, 20/20 vision and the less terror this world
holds for them. And with the fading of the darkness of worry,
dread, and anxiety comes the Son's brilliant light of peace, faith,
and serenity.

*Lord, help me to throw open the shades and let
the Son Light in. Give me the eyes of faith
so that I have 20/20, 20/20 vision.*

Upholding the Next Generations

I urge you, first of all, to pray for all people. Ask God to help them; intercede on their behalf, and give thanks for them. Pray this way for kings and all who are in authority so that we can live peaceful and quiet lives marked by godliness and dignity.

1 TIMOTHY 2:1–2 NLT

When God moves, His people move with Him. Such was the case with the beginning of the See You at the Pole movement. Back in 1990, a small group of Texas youth felt a burden to pray for their friends. So they drove to three schools that night, stood around the flagpoles, and prayed for their leaders, fellow students, and schools. What started out as a small group of teens being obedient to God's call has turned into an annual international movement that takes place on the third Wednesday of September. That's great, but how can today's woman help to empower this movement and the children who hold the future of tomorrow?

By every woman—whether or not she is a mother or grandmother—praying for all the students gathering at the poles today. Perhaps some ladies can even start a movement of their own, not just helping the kids annually prepare for See You at the Pole but by actively pre-praying for the day itself. Either way, the key is women gathering up their mantle and upholding the next generation by interceding for it today.

Lord, I pray for the children—those standing around the poles this morning and those who do not yet know You. May many turn to Your powerful, all-encompassing presence.

God, the Ultimate Fashionista

*Therefore, as God's chosen people, holy and
dearly loved, clothe yourselves with compassion,
kindness, humility, gentleness and patience.*

COLOSSIANS 3:12 NIV

Yesterday was the first day of fall. In some regions, the air will soon become quite frosty, and old fall jackets and sweaters will be making their way out of closets and drawers. Although such garments are one sure way to physically protect any woman from the colder weather, what can she wear to keep herself spiritually warm?

Colossians 3:12 contains a God-tailored list for His daughter. She is to clothe herself with the exact same characteristics her brother Jesus exuded when He walked this earth. First, she is to don compassion and kindness, the same emotions that moved Jesus to heal so many of the suffering. Then to apply humility, as Jesus did, being humble all the way to the cross. Next, she is to dress in the same gentleness Jesus displayed with the little children. Then to wear and bear His inexhaustible patience. And finally, on top of all of these great virtues, she is to "put on love, which binds them all together in perfect unity" (Colossians 3:14 NIV).

It's great to have nice, warm clothes in the house. But it may be time to get the spiritual garments out of the mothballs and try them on for size—today and every day.

*Jesus, it's more important to follow You than the
latest trend in clothes. Remind me each and
every day to put on compassion, kindness,
humility, gentleness, and patience, all
stitched together with love.*

The Insistent Woman

*She came and, kneeling, worshiped Him and kept praying,
Lord, help me! . . . Then Jesus answered her, O woman,
great is your faith! Be it done for you as you wish.*
MATTHEW 15:25, 28 AMP

This Canaanite woman is a wonderful example of perseverance in the midst of discouragement. After she made her first urgent plea to Christ, for Him to heal her possessed daughter, He did not answer. As if that weren't bad enough, the disciples begged Jesus to send her away. In response, He gave the disciples the reason He was ignoring her: She was not an Israelite. Yet the Canaanite woman continued, now upon her knees, worshiping, crying, praying, pleading. When Jesus again refused, her woman's logic served her well, as she gave Him a reason why He should grant her request (see Matthew 15:26–27). As a result, not only was the insistent woman's request granted, but Jesus commended her for her great faith—and her daughter was healed at that moment.

How insistent is God's daughter today? How much discouragement will she ignore? How far will she go to intercede with God for the ones she loves—no matter who they are, no matter if they are saved or unsaved? How ready is she to get down on humbled knee? How great is her faith?

*Lord, I come to You on bended knee today. I know
You can and do answer prayer. Help me have
the same great faith as the insistent woman,
to look discouragement in the face and
keep moving closer and closer to You until
I reach the hem of Your gown.*

Sowing Seeds

*So let's not get tired of doing what is good. At just the right
time we will reap a harvest of blessing if we don't give
up. Therefore, whenever we have the opportunity, we should do
good to everyone—especially to those in the family of faith.*
GALATIANS 6:9–10 NLT

Many years ago there was a man named John Chapman. He
walked around the United States, planting seeds for apple trees,
and so earned the nickname Johnny Appleseed. At the end of
his long life, it's reported that he was able to leave his sister over
1,200 acres of nurseries! What a harvest!

In Galatians, the apostle Paul writes that Christians
should not get tired of doing good things whenever they have
the opportunity. For someday, if they do not give up, they will
reap a harvest of blessing. The key word in the verses above is
opportunity. God's daughters are to do good to everyone, every
chance they get. But to seize that chance, a woman's eyes must
be off herself. She must be actively looking around, seeking
an opportunity to help someone. When she makes it a habit
to survey situations and then serve others—especially fellow
believers—she will, like Johnny Appleseed, leave an amazing
legacy behind. Not only that, she'll find herself noticing where
she can help more and more, all the while reaping a sweet-as-
apple-pie reward of God's blessings.

*Jesus, show me where I can sow the seed
of Your Word today. Then give me the
words You want me to say.*

Harvesting Appreciation

*Sing praise upon the harp unto our God: who covereth
the heaven with clouds, who prepareth rain for the earth,
who maketh grass to grow upon the mountains.*
PSALM 147:7–8 KJV

Everything that is seen in nature is a result of the handiwork
of God. His power is exhibited in the little mustard seed as
well as in the gigantic, blazing sun. He is the one in charge of
the seasons and is the impetus for making things grow. And
although God's children may plant the seeds and harvest the
grain, it is God who waters the crops and the grasslands. He
is the one that has engineered the nourishment of wheat and
designed the breath taking beauty of roses.

Even though they are surrounded by the beauty and splendor
of God's works, His children often go through life with blinders
on, watching more traffic than sunrises, eating more processed
foodstuffs than naturally whole, and watching *American Idol*
instead of glorying in the wonder of the moon and stars.

To show God His handiwork is beyond compare and
acknowledge that His works are appreciated, His daughters can
easily stop their frenzied pace for a few moments each day and
take in the beauty of God's creation, one cloud, one petal, one
planet, one leaf at a time. Would woman but "Stand still and
consider the wondrous works of God" (JOB 37:14 KJV), she would
grow in admiration and wonder of all God has made for her.

*Not only is Your grace amazing, but so is
the beauty of Your creation, Lord.
I praise You and thank You for
all Your wondrous works.*

Interesting Endeavor

*Don't look out only for your own interests,
but take an interest in others, too. You must
have the same attitude that Christ Jesus had.*
PHILIPPIANS 2:4–5 NLT

In this world, it is so easy for women to get caught up in their own little universes, never looking to the right or left, but continually checking to see if they are on the right road and, if not, what adjustments might be necessary. But God would have His daughters looking beyond their own interests by investing themselves into the lives of others. After all, isn't that what Jesus did time and time again? In fact, the only time Jesus was not investing Himself in others was when He was away somewhere in a quiet place, either communing with His Lord or sleeping.

So, if a sister in Christ wants to adopt Jesus' attitude, she is to be looking to help others. And in this day and age, it shouldn't take her too long to find someone who needs a helping hand, a lift out of the mire, or just plain loving kindness.

Like the Good Samaritan, may God's girl not pass others by but seek to understand their situation and, if needed, bind their wounds, whether they be physical, mental, emotional, or spiritual.

*I want to have a Christlike attitude when it
comes to looking out for others. Help me, Lord,
not to be so consumed by my own needs
and wants but to help others
in every way possible.*

Safe Place

*O God, be merciful and gracious to me, for my soul takes
refuge and finds shelter and confidence in You; yes, in the
shadow of Your wings will I take refuge and be confident
until calamities and destructive storms are passed.*

PSALM 57:1 AMP

Where can a woman run when the thunderclouds begin rolling
in? Where can she hide when feeling blue? Where can she find
sleep when the night seems endless? Where can she go when
there is danger? To God.

God is the only really safe place to go when threatened, sad,
troubled, or in need of safety. In Him, a woman of the Way has
a true sanctuary. Beneath His precious, soft, silky, massive wings,
her soul can rest in comfort. In the midst of that wingspan, no
destructive force can touch her. In that safe place, she can regain
her confidence, rethink her game plan, consult God, glean His
wisdom, and come away with a new perspective.

God says, " 'I carried you on eagles' wings and brought you
to myself" (Exodus 19:4 NLT). He has done so over and over
again. That is part of God's character. That wingspan is real. That
feathery fortress can hold each and every person. There, and only
there, are His daughters safe during the worst of storms.

*Thank You, Lord, for being my safe place.
I come to You now, ready to find shelter,
love, protection, and confidence before,
during, and after the storms of this life.*

Good & Plenty

*Then Jesus called his disciples and told them, "I feel sorry
for these people. They have been here with me for three days,
and they have nothing left to eat. I don't want to send them
away hungry, or they will faint along the way."*
MATTHEW 15:32 NLT

There they were. Four thousand men—not including the women
and children. They'd been hanging with Jesus, watching the
miracles of healing the mute, the crippled, the lame, and the blind.
Now the crowd was hungry. But where, the disciples asked, would
they get enough food to feed all these people—especially since
they were in the wilderness (no takeout available)? Jesus never
answered that question. Instead He asked the disciples what they
had on hand. The response: "Seven loaves of bread and a few small
fish." Amazingly enough, after Jesus thanked God for that food,
broke it into pieces, and gave it to the disciples to distribute, there
was enough food for all of those people—plus leftovers!

The point of the story? Jesus will never let any of His people
go away hungry. He will always find a way to give His daughters
what they need—and more! This limitless God can do anything,
anywhere, with anything! He's the Lord of not only good—but
plenty!

*Sometimes, Lord, I cannot see or understand how You
are going to provide for me. But then, miracle of miracles,
You find a way of making the most of what I
have—and more! Thank You for offering me
so many good and plentiful things. Help
me to see things with the eyes of
Your abundance.*

Stand Firm as a Woman of God

"The Lord lives! Praise be to my Rock!
Exalted be my God, the Rock, my Savior!"
2 SAMUEL 22:47 NIV

Carol sees advertisements everywhere showing beautiful, smartly dressed, confident women. They lead her to believe she should be able to balance time for work, family, church, and friends while having adequate time left for a beauty regimen. Unfortunately when Carol looks in the mirror, she sees a frumpy woman struggling to balance her responsibilities with little time for herself. Some days Carol actually feels like she's stepped off solid ground and into quicksand. She can literally visualize herself being swallowed by all the demands of her life.

Carol understands how some people become depressed. Her confidence plummets and her footing falters when responsibilities overwhelm her. When Carol feels herself beginning to sink, she reaches out to God in prayer. With His support she can emerge from the quicksand of her problems. Carol may never see herself as one of those beautiful women from popular ads. But, she can see herself as a woman of God when her feet are on solid ground making progress one step at a time. When Carol looks to the Lord for guidance, He will be her Rock, the foundation she needs to be a beautiful, confident woman of God.

Lord, although I am just a regular woman,
I know You are my dependable partner.
Thank You for being my Rock, the
solid foundation I need. Amen.

God's Will Is Perfect

*Do not conform to the pattern of this world, but be transformed
by the renewing of your mind. Then you will be able to test and
approve what God's will is—his good, pleasing and perfect will.*
ROMANS 12:2 NIV

Their employer was going out of business; they were losing
their jobs. When Lucia worried aloud about the future, Connie
insisted the Lord would open other doors for them. Lacking
Connie's confidence, Lucia told her friend she would just
become a homeless bag-lady.

Connie responded as always. "When you get your spiritual
life in order, God will give you the desires of your heart." Connie
truly believed Lucia first needed to accept Christ as her Savior
and seek His will. Once Lucia had a personal relationship with
Jesus she would become the woman God wanted her to be.

When the doors closed on this chapter of their life, Lucia
moved out of state while Connie found work locally. Over a
year had elapsed when Lucia called pleading for Connie to fly
down for a visit the second weekend in April. When Connie told
Lucia she couldn't make it, Lucia shared her good news. "As you
predicted, once I got right with the Lord He gave me the desire
of my heart. You have to be here for my wedding to Marvin."

Connie attended the April wedding. When she met Marvin,
Connie knew he was the godly man that would help Lucia with
her Christian journey.

*Lord, thank You for Your perfect will for
our lives. Help me to look for Your good
and pleasing direction. Amen.*

Communication through Prayer

*Then the LORD reached out his hand and touched my mouth
and said to me, "I have put my words in your mouth."*
JEREMIAH 1:9 NIV

At Women's Fellowship a request was made for a volunteer
to offer a prayer. Lila immediately looked down. She prayed
regularly but, not out loud in front of a group. Her friend, Rose,
raised her hand and poured out a sincere prayer which touched
on needs within the group, guidance for the meeting, and
blessing for the refreshments.

Lila was in awe that Rose could do that. Lila knew she
would never have been able to pray so eloquently, even if she had
prepared with note cards.

That day their program was on childhood development. The
speaker explained receptive vs. expressive language development.
She said receptive language skills are developed first—the ability
to understand words. As we grow we then develop expressive
language skills—the ability to communicate with words. Each
child's ability to understand and communicate is unique to them
alone and develops at different rates.

When Lila applied this concept to herself, she was thankful
God gave her the ability to understand and communicate words.
Although God hadn't given Lila the ability to pray in front of
a crowd, she knew the Lord had put silent, heartfelt words of
prayer in her mouth. Apparently He chose to bless others, like
Rose, with words of prayer to be spoken aloud.

*Lord, thank You for understanding
my prayers. I trust You to touch
my mouth with Your
words. Amen.*

Gems of Wisdom

*"Do you hear what these children are saying?" they asked him.
"Yes," replied Jesus, "have you never read, "'From the lips of
children and infants you, Lord, have called forth your praise'?"*
MATTHEW 21:16 NIV

Nicole stood at her father's grave. It had been a year since the
Lord had taken him home. Although the official cause of death
was leukemia, Nicole knew her father had left this world to be
with his heavenly Father.

"Dad, I miss you every day. You would be surprised at how
many times I hear your words in my mind, or maybe I hear them
with my heart. Your rambunctious granddaughter frequently
reminds me that you live in our hearts. As you would have said,
'out of the mouths of babes oft times come gems.'"

For Nicole, gems had oft come from her father's mouth.
The advice he most frequently gave was measure twice and cut
once. Although that gem was a carpentry saying, her dad had
applied it to making careful decisions. And he had been right.
When Nicole took the time to check things twice before taking
action—she made better decisions and had fewer regrets.

"Dad, I'm proud to be your daughter. Although I didn't
always appreciate your gems of wisdom when you shared them
with me, now each is a treasure. And Dad, you live on each time
I pass along one of your gems to my daughter."

*Lord, thank You for sending my dad to be
the earthly father I needed. The dad that
shared his heart with me. The dad
I now carry in my heart.*

Prayer, Hands, and Healing

*His father was sick in bed, suffering from fever and
dysentery. Paul went in to see him and, after prayer,
placed his hands on him and healed him.*

ACTS 28:8 NIV

"Medical advances have created miracles," Wilma told her daughter.

Tracey wanted God to send her a miracle. But God hadn't
healed her last year with chemotherapy. Now the oncologist said
a second chemo program might address her remaining cancer
cells. Why should she believe God would heal her through more
chemo? With the side-effects she suffered last year, Tracey didn't
think she could do it again.

Wilma surrounded Tracey's right hand with both of hers.
"Tracey, I will hold your hand again for each treatment. More
importantly, God will be holding your hand each step of the
process. He wants you to have faith that you can be healed."

"Mom, I do believe God can heal me—if He chooses to. I'm
just not sure more chemo will heal me."

Wilma squeezed Tracey's hand. "I know this is a difficult
decision. Just know your church, family, and friends will pray
for your healing. But then, God may need you to let the medical
community lay their hands on you for His healing to occur."

"Okay, Mom. Tell the doctor I'm ready to set up chemo
appointments."

"Tracey, I'll call and start the church prayer chain. Then I'll
ask the doctor to come back in."

*Lord, thank You for telling me that
physical healing can come from
hands guided by prayer. Thank You for
the hands of doctors and those in
health care that help me. Amen.*

A Good Name

*A good name is more desirable than great riches;
to be esteemed is better than silver or gold.*
PROVERBS 22:1 NIV

Samantha's father had frequently lectured her about maintaining a good name. As a teen, it had seemed he harped on the importance of her reputation. Now he was telling her kids— when all the extraneous stuff is taken away, all a person really owns is his or her good name. She smiled as her kids gave her that here-grandpa-goes-again look.

Samantha was glad her dad had loved her enough to emphasize the importance of a good name. Of course when she had been the age her kids were now, she hadn't understood why it was a big deal. Now, as a thirty-eight-year-old wife, mother, and career woman she was very thankful that she had learned to consider how her decisions might affect her reputation. Whether she was working for her employer, her church, or a charity, people trusted Samantha to make good on her commitments. She felt like her good name went before her. People just seemed to know that Samantha's word was as good as gold.

After giving her mother-knows-best look Samantha said, "You need to listen to your grandpa. He loves you and wants you to understand one of God's truths. Having a good name is more desirable than great riches."

*God, please help me pass on to my children
a good name. Help me also pass on to them
Your desire for them to value their
good name. Amen.*

God Equips the Called

I will instruct you and teach you in the
way you should go; I will counsel you.
PSALM 32:8 NIV

As Patricia approached retirement, she asked the Lord for
direction. She expected Him to give her peace about spending
more time with her grandkids—which He did. What she hadn't
expected was to feel the Lord leading her to write Christian
fiction.

Patricia had done a fair amount of technical writing
throughout her career. And she had been successful in writing
grants and newsletters as a volunteer. What she didn't have was
expertise writing inspirational stories.

Patricia didn't understand why the Lord was asking her
to do something outside her comfort zone. Could she do it?
After talking with her family, Patricia enrolled in online writing
classes and joined a Christian writing organization. Three years,
four classes, and five workshops later Patricia received a writing
contract. She still lacked confidence in her ability to write for
Him, but Patricia was confident that her writing journey was
being led by the Lord.

When Patricia saw her work in a bookstore, she felt a peace
that could only come from God. Patricia hadn't been equipped to
write for Him when He called her. With God as her counselor,
she had been able to develop the skills needed.

Lord, thank You for calling on me, even
when I am not equipped to do Your
work. I trust that You will help
me learn the skills I
need to serve You. Amen.

The Fellowship of Believers

*They devoted themselves to the apostles' teaching and to
fellowship, to the breaking of bread and to prayer.*
ACTS 2:42 NIV

Melanie and Judith worked together to provide needed meals
for the Light of Christ. Church members always came through
whether for funeral dinners or meals to be delivered to homes.

Today, Melanie and Judith were planning for their sixth
funeral dinner in twelve months. They dreaded having to once
again ask the ladies in their small congregation to help. But ask
they did. After filling all their needs, Pastor Jacob walked in with a
request for a meal to be delivered to the Thompsons' that evening.
They glanced at each other, not knowing who to call now.

Pastor Jacob asked, "Will this be a problem?"

Melanie said, "We just finished calling ladies to help with
the funeral dinner."

"Well that's two days from now. That shouldn't interfere
with doing this today."

Judith said, "It's kind of short notice."

"Our church is devoted to Bible-based fellowship. I've
already started the prayer chain over this injury so I'm sure
someone will want to take them a meal."

As Pastor Jacob walked out the door, Judith's cell phone
rang. Penny called to see if the Thompson family could use some
of the beef stew she had simmering. The power of prayer was
truly amazing.

*Lord, thank You for the fellowship
You provide through Your believers.
Through prayer we know that You will
help us meet needs as they arise. Amen.*

God Loves Us

*For God so loved the world that he gave his
one and only Son, that whoever believes in
him shall not perish but have eternal life.*
JOHN 3:16 NIV

Susan's family was asked to light the fourth candle on the
Advent wreath. She was thrilled. Growing up as an army brat,
Susan never lived in one place long enough to feel like a real
part of a church family. Families with roots in their church light
Advent candles.

Susan read that the fourth candle is purple and is called the
angel candle or candle of love. In the Christmas story, the candle
of love represents the good news of our Savior's birth announced
by the angels; the good news that God loved us enough to send
His only Son to live among us and die for us.

When Susan thought about lighting this symbol of God's
love, she was humbled. As a wife and mother, she saw herself as
a caregiver for her family of five. Compared to God who is and
will be the caregiver for all people throughout all time, she felt
insignificant. To God though, even she was important. He loved
her enough to know even this small desire of her heart. He knew
lighting this Advent candle would show her that she was deeply
rooted in His love.

*God, thank You for loving me enough
to send Your only Son to earth to
save me. I am just a regular person, but
I see Your love for me
each day. Amen.*

Standing My Ground

*Therefore put on the full armor of God, so that when the
day of evil comes, you may be able to stand your ground,
and after you have done everything, to stand.*
EPHESIANS 6:13 NIV

While cleaning her patio doors, Leah gasped at the sight of a
German shepherd bounding toward her. The large dog skidded
to a stop when he saw her cat, Panther, crouching on the deck.
Panther turned his body sideways to the interloper, arching his
back and raising his fur. While they stood frozen, staring at each
other, Panther held up a paw, threatening to swipe with claws
extended. The dog was the first to break eye contact. He looked
down, slinked back a few steps, and ran off.

Although a wild thumping remained in Leah's chest,
Panther recovered quickly. He sat up and started grooming
himself as if nothing had happened.

Leah had just watched her eight-pound cat stand his ground
with an eighty-pound dog. She realized just as God's armor
equips people, animals also receive special armor. Through
God's love Leah receives multiple armors of protection: belt
of truth, breastplate of righteousness, shield of faith, helmet of
salvation, and sword of the Sprit. God's same love also extends to
providing Panther with unique armors of protection.

*Lord, I know when I put on the full
armor of God, like Panther, my feet will
be fitted with readiness when the
day of evil comes. Help me to stand firmly
when my ground is threatened. Amen.*

Winning with Words

*Praise be to the LORD my Rock, who trains
my hands for war, my fingers for battle.*
PSALM 144:1 NIV

As director of the charity distributing food and donated items
to those in need, Genevieve was driven to provide a hand up to
families struggling to meet basic needs. Although times were
tough, somehow the charity survived.

Unfortunately, they were now facing vandalism and safety
issues. Some mornings Genevieve arrived to find rubbish heaped
in front of their building. The cost of trash disposal was twice
what had been budgeted. Plus, women had begun to mention
being uneasy about people loitering outside.

Genevieve knew they needed security cameras. She also
knew there was no extra money in their budget. They would
need to find a way to fight this battle without cameras.

Genevieve's zest for the charity reached a new low as she
slumped into her chair with the mail. Upon arrival she had found
a Dumpster-full of trash, including a stained mattress. And now
she had strangers hovering near their entry.

When Genevieve opened the mail she found a check from
a foundation. Without her knowledge, their board secretary
had written a grant request for security cameras! Their safety
problems were going to be overcome by the power of words. She
called and thanked the secretary.

"You're welcome. The words just flowed once I put my
fingers on the keyboard."

*Lord, thank You for showing us
how to use our hands to
fight Your battles. Amen.*

Pray, Plan, and Enjoy

Wait for the LORD; be strong and
take heart and wait for the LORD.
PSALM 27:14 NIV

Are you a take-each-day-as-it-comes person or a long-range
planner? If you like to have a plan for what you want to do—
today, this month, this year—you're like me. We feel "in control"
when we're working toward our goals. But, those take-each-
day-as-it-comes people also feel "in control" as they handle
each challenge that meets them. They find regular satisfaction
a little bit at a time. We long-range planners may find ours less
frequently, in bigger chunks.

So which way is a better approach to the life God has given
us? Does He care how we choose to control what we need to do?

He does care. Whether we are a short-term or long-range
planner, He wants us to seek Him first and let Him be "in
control." If we pray as we go, God will help us accomplish
everything we do. He wants us to be happy. As long as we ask
Him to guide our actions, He will enjoy walking with us. He
will rejoice with long-range planners when they crest another
mountain. And He will rejoice with the take-each-day-as-it-
comes people as they sprint over hurdle after hurdle.

Lord I will wait for You to guide my life.
With Your help, I will use my unique style
to accomplish the work You
send my way. Amen.

A Father's Love

*Follow God's example, therefore, as dearly loved children and
walk in the way of love, just as Christ loved us and gave
himself up for us as a fragrant offering and sacrifice to God.*
EPHESIANS 5:1–2 NIV

When her daughter was called in to work unexpectedly, Maggie
was asked to care for her infant granddaughter. Maggie's son-
in-law, Tim, had taken the baby with him to the six-year-old
grandson's soccer scrimmage.

If the truth were known, Maggie had never truly respected
Tim. Her daughter, Michelle, seemed quite happy, but Maggie
thought she could have found a more refined husband, at least
one whose huge hands weren't continually stained from working
on smelly diesel truck motors.

When Maggie arrived at the soccer field with her grandma-
to-the-rescue-hat firmly in place, she was shocked when she
saw Tim. While giving a bottle to his warmly wrapped daughter
held close to his chest, he was coaching the soccer players. He was
giving them gentle direction, encouraging words, and smiles. The
young players seemed to respect him and look to him for guidance.

Instead of seeing the hulking mechanic that wasn't good
enough for her daughter, Maggie saw a glimpse of what Michelle
sees in Tim. A gentle man who loves his wife and children
enough to give himself up for them just as Christ did for us.

*Lord, thank You for sending loving
fathers to care for children in
the same way You love
and care for us. Amen.*

Blaze Your Trail in Life

*"His master replied, 'Well done, good and faithful servant!
You have been faithful with a few things; I will put you in
charge of many things. Come and share your master's happiness!'"*
MATTHEW 25:21 NIV

At preschool graduation Clara announced she just wanted to play when she grew up. Clara's fun-loving style gave her a true zest for life. Her lively charm was recognized throughout her school years. No one was surprised when Clara was voted prom queen as a senior.

But being popular was not a plan for the future. Clara needed to decide what to do after graduation. Although she applied to universities, Clara didn't know what she wanted to do with her life.

Clara went to see her grandmother, who was said to have been a trailblazer in her day. "Grandma, how did you know you wanted to study engineering back when it wasn't a popular field for women?"

Her grandmother smiled. "I studied engineering so I could get a job doing what came naturally to me. The Lord gave me talents; it was up to me to make the most of them."

Clara knew God had given her a talent for working—or maybe playing—with people. With that firmly in mind, she was confident she could find a path to develop her talent and blaze her own trail in life.

*Lord, I want to use the talents You
have given me. Help me to blaze a trail
that will be pleasing to You. Amen.*

Pray for His Will

*For this reason, since the day we heard about you, we have
not stopped praying for you. We continually ask God to
fill you with the knowledge of his will through all the
wisdom and understanding that the Spirit gives.*

COLOSSIANS 1:9 NIV

Catherine didn't normally worry about her children. They had
received a solid Christian foundation and as adults had wisely
chosen paths suited to them. Then Cindy brought Seth home.
Cindy had always been a self-starter with high personal goals.
Cindy with Seth was another story. He appeared to manipulate her.

Catherine had always prayed for supportive Christian
spouses for her children. Now Catherine became unyielding in
her prayers for Cindy to find the husband God planned for her.
Neither Catherine nor her husband felt Seth was that man.

Cindy and Seth dated for six years while finishing college
and beginning careers. They were discussing marriage when Seth
ended their relationship. Cindy took time off work and came
home to lick her wounds.

Catherine listened sympathetically to Cindy's anguish while
privately celebrating the relationship's end. Catherine believed
the Lord was working in Cindy's life. The following week when
Seth called to get back together, Cindy said no.

Two years later, Catherine was lighting a wedding candle
for Cindy's marriage to Isaac. Catherine believed her unyielding
prayers—for God to lead Cindy to the husband He intended—
had been answered. Only through His grace could Cindy have
walked away from Seth's controlling ways and found Isaac.

*Lord, thank You for listening when I pray continually.
With Your help, my family has
been filled by Your spirit. Amen.*

Do Not Worry

*"Therefore I tell you, do not worry about your life, what you
will eat or drink; or about your body, what you will wear.
Is not life more than food, and the body more than clothes?"*
MATTHEW 6:25 NIV

Suzanne watched her daughter preening. Lucy was making her
last mirror check before her prom date arrived. The stylist had
achieved a soft up-do for Lucy. With her hair out of the way, the
glitter on Lucy's shoulders highlighted her movements. Suzanne
might be prejudiced, but she thought the deep green chiffon
dress perfectly accented Lucy's figure and complexion.

As Suzanne started telling her daughter how lovely she
looked, Lucy interrupted with worries about her appearance.
Lucy turned to her mom and said, "I'm too fat. I won't be able
to eat dinner without every mouthful showing in this dress."
She continued on, fretting that her date wouldn't like how she
looked. Lucy was even convinced that her friends would look
much nicer than her.

Suzanne put her hands on those lovely glitter-covered
shoulders and looked Lucy in the eyes. "Sweetheart, you are the
young woman God intended you to be. You are perfect in His
sight. You know that you are so much more than how you look.
God is interested in the person you are, not the clothes you wear
and certainly not what you eat tonight. Put your worries away
and have a wonderful time at prom."

*Lord, please help me not to worry
about appearances. Inside I want to be
the person that pleases You. Amen.*

The Sun Will Come out Tomorrow

*Therefore do not worry about tomorrow, for tomorrow will
worry about itself. Each day has enough trouble of its own.*
MATTHEW 6:34 NIV

Noah and Anita wanted to have their wedding and reception at
his parents' home. Their five-acre yard outlined with trees would
be the perfect setting.

Kathy and Mike were excited to host the nuptials. However,
the three weddings of their older children (in churches with
receptions at halls) did not prepare them for Noah's simple outdoor
wedding. He gave them an eighteen-page plan—complete with
CAD drawings laying out everything, even trash receptacles.

Kathy tried to follow the detailed plan. She knew having a
plan was important, but meeting the demands of Noah's detailed
pages actually limited her ability to focus on the needs of each
day. When a rainy week (which was not part of the plan) led up
to the wedding, Kathy put the plan aside. She decided to only
worry about each day as it came. When Friday's storm clouds
hovered over them, she refused to worry about the forecast of
more rain for Saturday. Kathy knew the Lord would help her
manage what needed to be done each day, if she let go of worries
about tomorrow.

Even when Saturday began with a gray sky, Kathy trusted
the Lord to see them through the wedding and reception. By
noon, the sun came out, creating a spectacular fall
backdrop for Noah and Anita's wedding.

*Lord, I will let You handle
tomorrow. With Your help, I
will only worry about what
I can do today. Amen.*

Prayer Brings Hope

Be joyful in hope, patient in affliction, faithful in prayer.
ROMANS 12:12 NIV

Fern was at a new low in her life; always the bridesmaid and never the bride was a fitting description. She was happy that Sally had found a godly husband. It was just hard to see the last of her four high school best friends walk down the aisle. And it was even harder to see two of them at the wedding as glowing expectant mothers.

Did God plan for her to marry? She had always wanted to be a mom. When would her turn come? Since Prince Charming hadn't shown up to whisk her onto the dance floor, Fern decided to stop moping and go sit at the table with her grandmother.

Fern's grandma grabbed her hand. "Why don't you tell me why your smile seems a bit wobbly?" Fern shared how distraught she was to be the only "unmarried" of her friends.

"Fern, we both know the Lord has a special plan for your life. When you feel the most vulnerable, God needs you to let go of your fears through prayer. He has promised you joyful hope if you wait on His plan for your future. Young lady, is your cup half-full or half-empty?"

Grandma could always lift Fern's spirits. "Yes, Grandma, my cup of patience is still half-full. I'll remain optimistic about His plan for me as long as I know you're praying with me."

Lord, I know my patience will never
run out as long as I go to You in prayer.
Help me find joy in the hope You offer. Amen.

Silence Can Be Golden

*Then they sat on the ground with him for seven
days and seven nights. No one said a word to him,
because they saw how great his suffering was.*
JOB 2:13 NIV

Since Doris loved her cat, she had learned to accept what
affection Dynamite chose to give her. She knew if she patted the
spot next to her he would come only if he wanted to be there.
The opposite was also true. When Doris was reading, Dynamite
might decide to sit on her lap and command center stage.

When Doris went through a sad time in her life, she slowly
became overwhelmed with feelings of ugliness and isolation. She
became self absorbed. She stayed home more and didn't reach
out to friends or family.

Awaking from one of her frequent naps, Doris again found
Dynamite lying next to her. As always, Doris enjoyed petting
Dynamite and hearing his steady purr. But today, Doris began
to wonder if God had sent Dynamite to patiently stay with her
during her time of suffering. Doris smiled—for the first time in
days—once she realized she wasn't alone. Dynamite loved Doris
as only he could. He comforted her without speaking a word.

Like Job's three friends, without speaking a word Dynamite
gave Doris sympathy and comfort when he saw her suffering.

*Lord, when I know a friend is suffering, help me
to be like Job's friends. Help me show Your love
without words. Help me offer my presence as a
symbol of Your comfort. Amen.*

Wisdom through a Child's Eyes

*Choose my instruction instead of silver, knowledge rather
than choice gold, for wisdom is more precious than rubies,
and nothing you desire can compare with her.*
PROVERBS 8:10–11 NIV

Although Linda didn't have children of her own, she had taught
Sunday school for many years. Linda knew she had learned more
from her students than they had learned from her. Recently,
though, she had decided a younger teacher might be better for
her rambunctious class.

Sunday morning Linda added pieces to her felt board as she
taught the story of the angel who appeared to Moses from within
a bush that was on fire but didn't burn up. After completing the
story, Linda asked her class what they had learned.

June blurted out, "Miss Linda I learned that God talked
through the angel."

Holly added, "I learned that Moses had faith that God
would save the Israelites from the bad Egyptians."

Wanting to encourage her reluctant boys, Linda asked if
they had any thoughts. She smiled and nodded at Kenneth when
he glanced at her. "Um, Miss Linda, you're kind of like that
angel, you're old and you tell us about God. You're like the bush
on fire, too. For some reason, God doesn't want you to burn up."

Renewal flowed through Linda's teaching spirit. She knew
the Lord spoke to her through Kenneth. She heard God tell her
to continue sharing His lessons as a Sunday
school teacher.

*God, thank You for the instructions
You have for me. Your wisdom reflected
through a child is my jewel. Amen.*

Others Need Our Prayers

*And pray in the Spirit on all occasions with all kinds of
prayers and requests. With this in mind, be alert and
always keep on praying for all the Lord's people.*
EPHESIANS 6:18 NIV

Cheryl hadn't been able to pray since her mother died. After she
passed, Cheryl's father seemed to be adrift without an anchor.
Within six months he joined his wife in heaven. In quick
succession, Cheryl's family then experienced the death of her
aunt, father-in-law, and teenage niece.

Although too embarrassed to admit it, Cheryl could barely
function. She knew she should give her pain to the Lord through
prayer, but Cheryl just couldn't.

The good news was Cheryl's family, church, and friends were
praying for her. They lifted Cheryl up when she couldn't do it
herself. Whenever she felt the lowest, the Lord sent her a message
of support. She received hugs, cards, notes, calls, food, and offers
of assistance. Regardless of who the angel was or how they
worked, the message was always the same—I'm praying for you.

The Lord knew Cheryl's needs even when she couldn't take
them to Him in prayer. And Cheryl heard the Lord speaking
to her through all those who offered her support. When Cheryl
was once again able to pray, she began with a lengthy message of
thanks for her lifeline of intercessory prayers.

*Thank You, Lord, for the prayers others give
for me when I'm not able to pray. Help me
be alert to the prayer needs of others. Amen.*

Clothes Are Not the Person

"And why do you worry about clothes? See how the flowers of the field grow. They do not labor or spin. Yet I tell you that not even Solomon in all his splendor was dressed like one of these."
MATTHEW 6:27–29 NIV

Lily feared her teenage daughter placed more value on being accepted by a clique of girls than she did on her values. Kristen had just flopped on the sofa after pleading for the famous brand jeans all her friends were wearing. Kristen's drama-queen-theatrics centered on needing the right clothes to fit in, to be loved by her friends.

"Kristen, I'd like to ask you a question on a different topic. Do you love your pets?"

"Mom, you know I do!"

"Kristen, as a shelter volunteer you could have picked perfect animals. Doesn't it seem strange that you've adopted a cat with half an ear missing and a three-legged dog?"

"Mom, they're perfect for me. They're as loving as any of the shelter's adorable kittens and puppies. My cat and dog just have their own unique look."

"Kristen, God would be happy with your choice of pets. He wants us to measure worth by looking inward to see the natural beauty of a loving heart. What would God think about your friends who worry more about the clothes you wear than the beautiful person you are?"

With a sigh Kristen said, "He wouldn't approve."

Lord, thank You for loving me for who I am.
Help me to look beyond clothes to find
friends filled with Your beauty. Amen.

Prayer Strengthens

*I pray that out of his glorious riches he may strengthen you
with power through his Spirit in your inner being,
so that Christ may dwell in your hearts through faith.*
EPHESIANS 3:16–17 NIV

While walking to yoga Justine said, "I never pray for strength, Karen. God gives us strength through adversity. And I certainly don't need any more adversity in my life."

"Justine, my God is merciful. He wouldn't heap more adversity on me when I pray for His strength to help me handle the problems I'm already facing.

"If I want to build muscle strength, I progressively increase exercise to accomplish that goal. I'm not saying God would just dump more adversity all at once. I think He would build our strength over time, adversity by adversity.

"Justine, I know we attend different churches, but we believe in the same God and read the same Bible. When I pray for strength, our God renews me from within, through the power of His Holy Spirit."

"It sounds like how yoga strengthens us."

Karen said, "Somewhat. In yoga we calm our mind and focus inward as we move through poses to increase flexibility and strengthen our core. When we quiet ourselves and pray, God strengthens our inner being and keeps us flexible to face our problems with confidence."

"That makes sense. Our God uses our faith to progressively build the inner strength we need, step by step."

*Lord, thank You for rewarding my
faith with the strength to handle
each adversity I face. Amen.*

Hospitality Shows Love

Let no debt remain outstanding, except the continuing debt to love one another, for whoever loves others has fulfilled the law.
ROMANS 13:8 NIV

For Bella's twelfth birthday, she invited four classmates to a Friday night sleepover. To be ready for her guests, Bella's mom said she needed to help out by doing extra chores. Bella tried to talk her way out of helping. "After all," she said, "I'm the birthday girl so I shouldn't have to lift a finger on Friday."

Bella's mom said even though she was the birthday girl she needed to show hospitality to her guests. She said, "Hospitality begins when you invite someone to our home. Before their arrival you show love for your guests by preparing. Once they arrive, you show them love in everything from the warmth of your greeting to the food served and activities planned. Showing hospitality is one way to fulfill God's law to love one another. "

"I guess that makes sense, Mom. If I want my friends to enjoy my party, I need to first show them I appreciate having them celebrate with me."

"Bella, you're getting older and wiser."

On Friday, Bella pitched in and helped her mom clean house. She even volunteered to give her two younger siblings their baths. As her friends arrived, Bella greeted them and helped tote their things to the family room. Her actions spoke of the love she felt for her guests.

Lord, let me show Your love through my hospitality. I want to love others as You have commanded. Amen.

Dance with the Joyful

*I will build you up again, and you, Virgin Israel,
will be rebuilt. Again you will take up your
timbrels and go out to dance with the joyful.*
JEREMIAH 31:4 NIV

Tonya's family attended Living Water Church. The pastor was dynamic. The music led by the praise team inspired them to worship. And they loved the positive energy that flowed between church members.

Unfortunately a negative current had developed over children dancing at the front of the church during the praise songs. Tonya's two children were often inspired to leave their seats and join other children moving with the music. Tonya didn't want her children to be a distraction from worship; neither did she want to dampen her children's enthusiasm for worship.

The pastor took a firm stand. He announced that children were welcome to gather and dance during praise music. Then he corrected his statement—all were welcome to praise God joyfully with their voices and their movements. He told the congregation that dance is mentioned as part of worship in the Bible. He said, "We are and will continue to be a Bible-based fellowship."

Tonya and her husband were tempted to keep their children in their seats. But when they discussed the pastor's direction, they agreed they should follow the teachings from the Bible. They would let their children go out to dance with the joyful.

*Lord, thank You for the children who dance
with joy. Help me to let You lead as
You and I dance through my life. Amen.*

Persistently in Prayer

*Rejoice always, pray continually, give thanks in all
circumstances; for this is God's will for you in Christ Jesus.*
1 THESSALONIANS 5:16–18 NIV

Georgia was struggling with Pastor Wayne's sermon about
prayer. From the time her parents taught her to pray, she always
started by thanking God for her blessings and joys. What she
couldn't wrap her mind around was how to pray continually.

Georgia opened her dictionary. She met the first definition.
She prayed with her morning devotions, at meals, and at
bedtime. That surely qualified as praying habitually. After
reading the second definition she decided to stop by the church
and talk with Pastor Wayne. She asked him what it meant to
pray continually—unceasingly; always.

Pastor Wayne suggested continually meant praying
persistently or without yielding. He said, "The Lord didn't
intend for us to pray every waking minute. He wants us to pray
often and with persistence. It isn't enough to take some issues to
the Lord just once."

"How can I pray persistently about a problem I need to let
go of and give to the Lord?"

"Praying to the Lord is a process. Georgia, you'll know in
your heart when you need to be persistent about a request or
problem. Just as you'll know in your heart when you're ready to
yield a burden and give it to the Lord."

Georgia agreed; prayer was a process. A process she would
need to continually develop throughout her
Christian walk.

*Lord, thank You for listening to my habitual,
and my persistent, prayers. Help me to discern
how often I need to talk with You. Amen.*

Excited for the Next Chapter in Life

*But you, dear friends, by building yourselves up in
your most holy faith and praying in the Holy Spirit,
keep yourselves in God's love as you wait for the mercy
of our Lord Jesus Christ to bring you to eternal life.*

JUDE 1:20–21 NIV

Danielle was baffled by her friend's enthusiasm. Noelle and her husband, Bryce, seemed to thrive on moving. Danielle was a nester. She liked knowing she and her husband had secure jobs, well secure for this economy. She liked knowing they would pay off their mortgage in nine more years.

Bryce's employer was "rewarding" him with another "opportunity" to relocate for advancement. Danielle didn't think being uprooted was a "reward." Noelle said this move would only take them from Nebraska to Iowa. In Danielle's mind, once you packed everything you own on a truck and move to a new community you were starting over.

"Noelle, aren't you worried about having to find another new job? I know these moves are good for Bryce, but what about you and what you want?"

Noelle said, "I can't wait to see what the Lord has planned for me with this move! Every move we've made has been an exciting new chapter for Bryce and for me. God has always rewarded our faith and prayers."

*Lord, thank You for rewarding each of us for
our faith and our prayers. Help me to be excited
for each new chapter of my life. Amen.*

One for Me, One for You

*And do not forget to do good and to share with
others, for with such sacrifices God is pleased.*
HEBREWS 13:16 NIV

When Keith and Sandra said "I do," their family included her
cat, Racer, and his Sheltie, Tab. Keith believed each pet would
view the other as a trespasser and not get along.

When Sandra took them for their annual checkups, the vet
said, "I suspect Tab really enjoys living with a cat. The weight
he's gained is probably from enjoying Racer's tastier, higher-
calorie food."

When Sandra returned home, she moved Racer's food up
onto a cabinet in the laundry room. Racer could access his food,
but it was out of Tab's reach. Problem solved.

Then one day Sandra walked into the laundry room and
caught Racer sharing his food. She watched as her cat swiped
some kibbles out of his bowl. He munched on a piece as he
turned and batted a kibble down to Tab who sat with tail
wagging. The one for me, one for you process continued until
Racer had had his fill and jumped down.

Watching her cat share his food with the dog he barely
tolerated reminded Sandra of God's instruction to do good and
to share with others. Watching Tab and Racer, it was evident that
sharing some of what we have not only pleases God, it also brings
pleasure to those involved.

*Lord, help me to be generous with others.
Help me to find pleasure, like You do, when I
sacrifice some of what I have for others. Amen.*

Trust the Lord with Your Problems

*Cast your cares on the LORD and he will sustain you;
he will never let the righteous be shaken.*
PSALM 55:22 NIV

Dawn has her fair share of problems. With an elderly father, husband, four children and their spouses, and ten grandchildren there is always something going wrong. She tries to be a prayer warrior for her family. However, even as she hands the Lord today's problems, she knows that some of them will follow into tomorrow. In addition to the problems that carry over, Dawn knows that tomorrow will also bring new problems.

Dawn knows her faith is the lifeline that sustains her. Dawn needs daily spiritual energy just as her body needs energy from food. She needs both types of energy to face life's problems. Without adequate energy, Dawn's ability to cope would shrivel and her emotions would become raw. Dawn could literally be drawn into a downward spiral. Without God, life could be overwhelming.

The only healthy way Dawn has found to face her problems is with God's help. She casts her cares on the Lord. After letting go, Dawn trusts that God will be with her family as each challenge is faced.

Although God never promised life would be easy, He did promise to sustain us.

*Lord, You know the large number of problems
I face. I trust You to hold my cares in Your
hands. I know You will walk with me
through each challenge. Amen.*

Hope for the Future

*"For I know the plans I have for you," declares
the* LORD, *"plans to prosper you and not to harm
you, plans to give you hope and a future."*
JEREMIAH 29:11 NIV

Debra was discouraged. She had been so hopeful when she
received her college diploma. A year later with only a part-time
job, she still needed to live at home to make ends meet.

Although Debra wasn't musically talented, she agreed to
help coordinate the children's Christmas production at church.
Her reluctance turned to enthusiasm as she was able to lead
improvements using her organizational skills.

Debra received positive feedback from people each week.
She was happy the Lord was using her talents.

After the organized chaos of getting the right costumes on
each child, Debra started the dress rehearsal. She was thrilled when
everything came together and the children were able to shine.

Then during the cast party, a stern older man asked to talk
privately with Debra. She braced herself for criticism. Instead
the man asked if she would be interested in interviewing to
be his office manager. His daughter had told him, "Debra can
organize anything and always keeps a cool head." Debra agreed
to the interview.

When she became a volunteer, Debra never dreamed her
efforts would become a stepping stone to her future.

*Lord, thank You for working in
amazing ways to prosper me and
give me hope for the future. Amen.*

You Are the Light of the World

In the same way, let your light shine before others, that they may see your good deeds and glorify your Father in heaven.
MATTHEW 5:16 NIV

Edna, an elderly widow, frequently received family help with "the heavy work." She figured that just gave her more energy for the Lord's work. Edna was a tireless prayer warrior for her church and family. She baked and gave away cookies every week. She was committed to loving others however possible.

When a sixty-year-old lady with health issues from church lost her job, Edna offered her a home. Although she knew the Lord led her to make the offer, theirs was not a match-made-in-heaven. Edna tried to reflect God's love to her guest, even though the lady wasn't outwardly appreciative. Edna thanked God for letting her show the woman Christian love—even though she looked forward to again living alone.

Fast forward ten years. Edna has joined God in heaven. Now a thirty-year-old lady with health issues at Edna's church is going through a divorce. Her job is secure, but the direction for her life is not. Alice, a recently widowed friend of Edna's, invites the young lady to move into her home. Alice believes she's reflecting God's love the same way she had seen Edna do. She knows through Edna, God prepared her to make this invitation a decade ago.

*Lord thank You for letting me shine
the light of Your love before others
as others have done for me. Amen.*

Going in the Right Direction

*Your commandments give me understanding; no wonder I
hate every false way of life. Your word is a lamp to guide my
feet and a light for my path. I've promised it once, and I'll
promise it again: I will obey your righteous regulations.*

PSALM 119:10–106 NLT

As Maggie turned right, her friend, Jenna, sitting in the
passenger seat, squealed, "Oh, no! That was supposed to be a left
turn, not right." Maggie let out a deep sigh. "It seems like I'm
always headed in the wrong direction—not just physically—but
with my life!"

She quickly made a U-turn that set them in the right
direction based on the instructions they'd been given to the
birthday party. "Well, we left early, so we have plenty of time,"
Jenna encouraged. "We'll be all right."

Maggie didn't respond. Jenna knew she was still thinking
about the wrong turns she'd made in her life. Her voice softened.
"Maggie, now that you are back in church and really looking to
God for wisdom and direction, you can trust that He will show
you the way."

"Yes, I know you're right," Maggie mused. "Each time I
open the Bible, I discover something new. I feel encouraged
when I read it, and I'm learning to make decisions based on what
God's Word says is good and right for me." She smiled at Jenna.
"Thanks, friend!"

*Heavenly Father, thank You for Your Word. Help
me to receive and understand Your direction for
my life as I study the Bible. Give me insight
into the wisdom You have in all the decisions
I make. Amen.*

Following God's Schedule

*The blessing of the LORD, it maketh rich,
and he addeth no sorrow with it.*
PROVERBS 10:22 KJV

Shelley pulled into Kaitlyn's driveway. She was right on time but prepared to move as slow as necessary since Kaitlyn was a new mom and it never seemed their plans ever came together "on schedule" anymore. She had even brought an extra shirt, just in case the baby "erupted" onto her shoulder sometime throughout the day.

Forty-five minutes later Shelley clipped the car seat into place and dropped the diaper bag behind the driver's seat of her car. Although she had somehow avoided the spit-up, mom and baby had changed clothes twice.

Finally on their way to the mall for shopping and lunch, the six-lane road slowed to a crawl. The entire intersection was blocked with fire trucks, ambulances, and tow trucks. The accident included a motorcyclist and several cars. Firefighters and police officers had formed a line around someone laying on the ground, a clue that the accident had probably resulted in at least one fatality.

As Shelley steered the car around into the detour, she said a prayer for everyone involved in the accident. Then she looked at Kaitlyn. "We could have been in that accident if we'd come along much earlier. I was sure we were on the baby's schedule, but apparently, we are on God's schedule.

*Heavenly Father, thank You for divine interruptions
that keep me on Your schedule instead of my own.
Remind me that my time is in Your hands when
I'm tempted to become agitated with delays.
Thank You for protecting me and keeping
me in all my ways. Amen.*

Speak Up with Your Vote

*Let every person be loyally subject to the governing
(civil) authorities. For there is no authority except
from God [by His permission, His sanction],
and those that exist do so by God's appointment.*
ROMANS 13:1 AMP

The lines were longer than Penny expected. She had hoped she
could run in and out of the polling place quickly by going early
this morning and still get to work on time. Her employer gave
her time to vote, but she was in the middle of a project and
wanted to get it done.

As she tried to be patient, she recognized Michael, a
young man in her community who had just returned from
Afghanistan. He would still be over there if it had not been for
an accident that took his right arm. She watched as this young
man struggled to mark his voting card using his left hand. It was
apparent he was right-handed before the accident.

Several news cameras and reporters were there to capture
this young man's determination to vote. He placed his card in
the voting slot and then turned and faced the cameras. "I hope
everyone will take time to speak up with your vote today," he said.
Then he smiled, turned, and walked out of the polling place.

Penny was so thankful she'd made the effort to vote today.
She decided she would never again let an opportunity slip
by to let her vote speak for what she believed.

*Lord, I am thankful to live in a country that
provides me with a voice. Help me to use this
opportunity to bring glory to You. Amen.*

From Pain to Peace

This day I call the heavens and the earth as witnesses against you that I have set before you life and death, blessings and curses. Now choose life, so that you and your children may live.
DEUTERONOMY 30:19 NIV

Kimberly's feet dangled off the edge of the tailgate of her step-dad's pickup truck. "So, Dad, you've never told me your story," she pressed him as she patted the tailgate, motioning for him to take a seat beside her.

Sweaty, Ken struggled to get comfortable on the tailgate and begin. "I had a daughter only six weeks older than you; she drowned. After that it seemed the whole family nearly drowned in our own way. . ." His voice trailed off.

Kimberly urged him on with a nod. "Somewhere between 'why did this happen' and 'where are you, God,' I found the Son of God. I wasn't looking for Him—He just appeared. That night I was drunker than a skunk, but came straight to my senses when I saw Jesus standing there. I gave my life to Him."

Ken slid off the tailgate and wiped his eye with his index finger. "Before then, I never really liked people much. Now, well, you know. . ."

"Yes, I know." Kimberly smiled. "The love of God changed you. You use the pain you felt and the peace you have now to help others reach out of the pain and find peace through God."

Lord, You know my pain and hurt. You see my tears. I trust You to turn my pain to peace as I grow in my relationship with You. Amen.

In His Presence

*Enter into his gates with thanksgiving, and into his
courts with praise. Be thankful unto him, and bless his
name. For the LORD is good; his mercy is everlasting;
and his truth endureth to all generations.*

PSALM 100:4–5 KJV

Anna's cell phone rang, and when she answered, her friend
Sarah's voice sounded a bit frantic. Anna could hear Sarah's
five-month-old son, Marshall, crying in the background. "I put
him in the car seat and was going to start toward the airport, but
he's spent. I don't think he's going to settle for another minute in
this car seat, let alone handle the drive to the airport to pick up
his dad. I overdid it today—it was our first time running errands
alone and he's just not going to stop."

"Bring him over and we'll watch him," Anna said. In the
last few weeks, Marshall had become aware of the absence of
his mother. Whenever she was out of his presence, he was very
difficult to console. Anna and her husband tried everything to
console him, but nothing distracted him very long from the fact
that his mother was gone.

As soon as Sarah returned to Anna's front door, Marshall
recognized her. He wiggled and squirmed until Sarah took him
into her arms. Miraculously, all was well. His tears dried, and
a big smile appeared on his chubby little face. Nothing could
match his desire to be in his mother's presence.

*Father, give me an overwhelming
desire to spend time in Your presence.
I desire to know You more. Amen.*

My Hero

"The LORD your God is with you, the Mighty Warrior who saves. He will take great delight in you; in his love he will no longer rebuke you, but will rejoice over you with singing."
ZEPHANIAH 3:17 NIV

Dayna had known the Lord all her life. She asked Jesus to come into her heart as a young child. Her childhood memories were filled with God's intervention. He had always been there. There were times she deliberately cut Him out of the picture, or didn't invite Him to weigh in on her decisions, but she knew He never left her side.

When her mother was drunk, and her parents fighting, she slipped into her bedroom closet and talked to God. When her parents divorced and her mother disappeared, God comforted her and brought new friendships into her life. Even the times she put herself in unsafe situations as a teenager—going places and doing things she knew He would rather her not go and do—God provided a way of escape. From the small hurts to the big, breathtaking grief in the deepest parts of her heart, her bigger-than-life hero, God, reached in and pulled her out of the mess she found herself in.

She took a sip of her coffee and began a conversation once again with the one who had always been there for her.

God, thank You for being my hero. Thank You for being with me—even when I have pushed You away. You always come to my rescue. Amen.

You've Got God's Attention

I will bless the LORD who guides me;
even at night my heart instructs me.
I know the LORD is always with me.
I will not be shaken, for he is right beside me.
PSALM 16:7–8 NLT

Phone calls, text messages, children shouting your name from down the hall—they can all interrupt and completely end a conversation with someone. Worse yet, once you've regrouped from the distraction, you find that the person you were talking to wasn't even listening in the first place.

Have you ever been in a crowd desperately trying to get someone's attention? Maybe you were telling someone something very important, while they looked over you to see who else was in the room. It can make you feel worthless.

Your heavenly Father would never do that. He loves you and values every moment you are willing to give to Him. You are His focus. His eyes are constantly on you; His ears are tuned to your every word. He's seen every tear you've cried and celebrated every joy of your heart with you.

Even when you feel most alone, you can trust that He is there. He is your constant audience. The more time you spend with Him, the more you will realize that He has a lot to share with you. If you return the favor by giving Him your attention, He will lead you, guide you, and show you things that you'd never discover on your own. He wants to share your life today.

God, thank You for giving me Your
undivided attention. Show me the
plans You have for me today. Amen.

Letting Go of the List

*It teaches us not to live against God nor to do the evil
things the world wants to do. Instead, that grace
teaches us to live in the present age in a wise and
right way and in a way that shows we serve God.*
TITUS 2:12 NCV

Molly stood in line at the concession stand, deep in conversation with her friend Katrina, when she caught a glimpse of Erica out of the corner of her eye. She stopped talking mid-sentence as the list under Erica's name began to play. *She was so horrible to you How can she call herself a Christian? She doesn't act like she should. . . .*

Katrina interrupted. "You're doing it again. Don't you see what's happening? The list is stealing your life. It isn't hurting anyone but you—and my relationship with you."

Molly bit her lip. "You are right. I am judging Erica, saying she doesn't act like a Christian when I'm not being Christ-like either."

"I have an idea," Katrina said. "You could write out the list, cross off each offense with a pencil, confess aloud that you forgive the person who hurt you, and then toss that piece of paper in the trash. Just like God let your list go, you've got to let the list you have for each of these people go."

Molly smiled. "I really think I can do that!"

*Lord, I have a list of hurts that I need to let go of.
Help me to release those pains and find Your grace
to forgive those who have hurt me. Amen.*

The Gift of Listening

*My dear brothers and sisters: You must all be quick
to listen, slow to speak, and slow to get angry.*
JAMES 1:19 NLT

When Ginger lost her job, it became a huge blessing for her
and for her family. Financially she was concerned as each month
doors remained closed to opportunities for employment. But in
the middle of a financial challenge, she discovered what she'd
been missing each day with her children.

Now that her schedule was clearly flexible, she scheduled her
job interviews and other errands around the boys' school drop-off
and pick-up times. The first afternoon she picked up her third
grader, she discovered he was full to overflowing with the details
of his day. He shared things on the ride home about his day, what
he hoped and even imagined. Once he arrived home, his desire
to talk turned off and he went on about his afternoon. The same
seemed to be true for her seventh grader. Time in the car became
a wonderful exchange with each of her boys.

When she had the opportunity to go back to work full time
or work two part-time jobs from home, she kept the flexible
schedule so she could continue the afternoon conversations in
the car with her sons. She was careful to really listen and hear
their hearts.

Give your children your undivided attention
sometime during the day.

*Lord, help me to give the gift of listening. Help me
not to become distracted but really tune in. Amen.*

Merciful Heart

*You will be judged in the same way that you judge others,
and the amount you give to others will be given to you. . . You
hypocrite! First, take the wood out of your own eye. Then you
will see clearly to take the dust out of your friend's eye.*
MATTHEW 7:2, 5 NCV

"It's been weeks. . ." Natalie told her mother over coffee. "She
keeps calling me, texting me, and I haven't responded to her. She
just doesn't get it."

"Obviously your friendship is important to Shelley," her
mother began, "or she wouldn't keep trying to speak with you.
Maybe you need to take a step back."

Natalie fumed. "Mom, she doesn't act like a Christian; even
though she says she is one."

Mom hit a nerve. "And your response to her has been
Christ-like? Honey, we can't have a double standard. When we
hold others accountable to reflect Christ and they fail us, we
want to judge them. When we fail, we give ourselves a pass. This
causes division in the church and confusion for those who do not
share the faith.

"Jesus called us to a life of grace and mercy. Shouldn't we
also extend that grace to others as He did? Perhaps you should
give Shelley the opportunity to share her side of the story."

Natalie nodded. She knew her mother's words were truth.

*Father, help me to have a merciful heart and
respond with Your love when relationships are
difficult. Show me how to live a life that pleases
You with those I know and love. Amen.*

See the Invisible Ones

*Since God chose you to be the holy people he loves, you must
clothe yourselves with tenderhearted mercy, kindness, humility,
gentleness, and patience. Make allowance for each other's faults,
and forgive anyone who offends you. Remember, the Lord
forgave you, so you must forgive others.*

COLOSSIANS 3:12–13 NLT

Ginger's grocery cart was full as she pushed it out to her car. She
was thinking how thankful she was that she had some extra time
before she had to pick up the kids from school. Returning her
cart to the front of the store, she noticed the older man sitting on
the bench outside the commissary. He wore a cap with a WWII
emblem on it. She checked her watch and walked back toward
the man, sitting down beside him.

She thanked him for his service. He smiled appreciatively.
Then she asked him his name, followed by when and where he
served. He seemed excited to share with her. He began to tell her
about "some of the shenanigans" he and several of his buddies used
to play on each other. He laughed; and she laughed with him.

After half an hour, she thanked him again, especially for
sharing a part of his life with her, and let him know she needed
to go on to the school to pick up her children. He responded
with tears in his eyes. "Thank you for seeing me—and letting me
know I'm not always invisible."

*Lord, there are so many I see each day that must feel
invisible. Give me the opportunity to acknowledge
them and show them Your compassion. Amen.*

Time to Laugh

*Then were our mouths filled with laughter, and our
tongues with singing. Then they said among the nations,
The Lord has done great things for them.*

PSALM 126:2 AMP

Becky replayed the phone call in her mind and her actions
immediately following. The unexpected death of her father had
left her entire family numb. How would they get through the
upcoming holidays? Random thoughts poured over her mind:
What would Mom do with his car, his boat, his clothes, his
fishing gear? Dad always carved the turkey on Thanksgiving and
Christmas. Tears came again; nothing would ever be the same.

Tim, her husband, interrupted her thoughts. "Babe, come
outside. Quite a few of your dad's friends are here." Reluctantly
she followed him and was surprised to find the front yard full
of friends and family. Her father's best friend, Don, was grilling
hamburgers and hot dogs—outside, in November!

Don said, "Dex was my best friend! If he was still with us
he'd be doing this instead of me—and telling us a big story about
days gone by. So, in his honor, let's tell stories on him." One by
one different friends stepped up next to Don and started "telling
on" her dad.

The stories were extravagant but definitely believable.
Joyful laughter began to spill out as the stories grew more
and more funny. Becky began to laugh. With each story, her
laughter became louder and deeper. For the
moment grief lifted and laughter erupted in
remembrance of her father.

*Heavenly Father, when I am overwhelmed
with difficult times, help me to remember
how to laugh. Amen.*

Determined to Win

*Fear not [there is nothing to fear], for I am with you; do not
look around you in terror and be dismayed, for I am your God.
I will strengthen and harden you to difficulties, yes, I will help
you; yes, I will hold you up and retain you with My [victorious]
right hand of rightness and justice.*

ISAIAH 41:10 AMP

God loves you and desires to bless you; your adversary, the devil,
wants to convince you to give up on ever receiving the promises
of God.

Think about the last time God showed up and turned
your circumstances around. Most likely in the midst of your
celebration of the blessing, another challenge or difficulty hit you
head on. It's the enemy's attempt to steal what God did for you
and even convince you that God wasn't in it.

He wants to bring disappointment in the hope that you'll
just give up. When John the Baptist baptized Jesus, God blessed
Jesus by declaring Him as His Son. From there Jesus went into
the desert to fast and pray for forty days. Immediately the devil
came to tempt Jesus, trying to get Him to give up His blessing.
Jesus refused to give up. Like Jesus, you can hold tight to the win
God has promised you.

Satan, your adversary wants you to give up and quit. But if
you remain determined to win—refusing to let go of God's
promise—you will always win.

*Heavenly Father, help me to keep my focus on You.
I will not let the enemy talk me out of anything
You have for me. I am determined to win!*

It's Not about the Dos and Don'ts

Who hath saved us, and called us with an holy calling, not according to our works, but according to his own purpose and grace, which was given us in Christ Jesus before the world began, but is now made manifest by the appearing of our Saviour Jesus Christ, who hath abolished death, and hath brought life and immortality to light through the gospel.

2 TIMOTHY 1:9–10 KJV

More than six hundred Jewish laws are derived from the Ten Commandments that God gave Moses. Before Jesus the Messiah came, they had to follow a list of rules in order to live a life that pleased God and assured them of His continued blessing in their lives.

Jesus came to the earth; gave His life; and defeated death, hell, and the grave, so you could choose eternal life. You are not saved because of a list of dos and don'ts you follow. Instead, it's all about surrendering your heart to God. You are His child by His grace. Once forgiven, He doesn't remember your sins.

Our world is moved by conditional love: I will love you if you do this or that. Thankfully that has no place in your relationship with God. His love is unconditional. You don't have to work from a list for God to accept you. His grace has already made you lovable and acceptable to Him. There is nothing you can do to make God love you any more or any less.

*Lord Jesus, I surrender my heart to You.
Thank You for the gift of eternal life. Amen.*

Promises Delivered Right on Time

God is not a man, so he does not lie.
He is not human, so he does not change his mind.
Has he ever spoken and failed to act?
Has he ever promised and not carried it through?

NUMBERS 23:19 NLT

Paige put the final touches on her daughter, Avery's, birthday cake and then carried it into the dining room, placing it in the center of the table. The balloons danced in a colorful assortment behind the table, floating up to the ceiling. All her tasks were done and ahead of schedule. Even her daughter was completely dressed, hair combed, and ready to receive her guests.

She glanced over to the living room window where her precious five-year-old stood. She'd been there for a good twenty minutes filled with anticipation, waiting for signs of her friends' arrival. "Honey, it's going to be a little longer. . ." Paige encouraged.

"I know, Mommy! I just don't want to miss seeing them get here," she replied.

Waiting for God's promises to become a reality can be similar to a long-awaited celebration. Once you've done everything you need to do, all you can do is wait. You know the promise He dropped into your heart. You've prayed and believed with great expectation. It can be a test of patience to stand and wait for His special delivery. You can rest and rely on Him. When God promises, He delivers—not always in your time frame—but always right on time!

God, I believe the promises You've dropped
into my heart. Help me to wait with
patience for Your perfect timing. Amen.

Put Your Hope in the Lord

*Love the LORD, all his faithful people! The LORD preserves
those who are true to him, but the proud he pays back in full.
Be strong and take heart, all you who hope in the LORD.*
PSALM 31:23–24 NIV

Jamie poured herself an evening cup of decaffeinated coffee
and then carried the pot into the den where her husband,
John, was watching the news. She knew he also liked a warm
cup on a chilly evening. As she filled his cup up her eyes fell
on the evening news. "John, why do you have to watch all that
bad news? It really hurts my heart to see so much pain and
devastation. Just the things people do to each other. . ." Her
voice trailed off.

John muted the TV and looked into his wife's beautiful
blue eyes. "We live in a fallen world and the earth is filled with
darkness. I know our hearts break when we hear all the tragic
things that are happening around us. I know it hurts your heart
sometimes so much that it takes your breath away. But we need
to be aware of what's happening so we can know how to pray."

Jamie nodded, and John continued. "The enemy of our souls
wants us to give up and lose our hope in God. We have to hold
on and believe in God's ability to keep His promises."

*God, instead of looking away from the things
going on in my world, give me a desire to grow
my hope in You as I read my Bible and
spend time in prayer. Amen.*

. . And the Walls Came Tumbling Down

*When the people heard the sound of the rams' horns,
they shouted as loud as they could. Suddenly, the walls
of Jericho collapsed, and the Israelites charged
straight into the town and captured it.*

JOSHUA 6:20 NLT

Five-year-old cousins Jane and Piper marched from the dining room, through the den, into the kitchen, and back around—making a complete circle. Their mothers, Ann and Sharee, were in the kitchen putting a family meal together and catching up on family news. Ann stopped and said, "What are they singing?"

Sharee laughed. "They're singing 'and the walls came tumbling down.' Remember that song?"

"Oh my goodness!" Ann exclaimed, and the mothers dropped what they were doing and got in line with the little girls, marching and singing the song with them. The little girls stopped when they realized their mothers knew their special song.

"How do you know that song?" Piper asked with her hands on her hips. "Gammy gave us that song."

"We sang it when we were your age." Sharee laughed, as she sat down on the floor to catch her breath. "Your Gammy taught it to us. It's from a Bible story we learned a long time ago. The song is fun, and it helps us remember what God has done for others and can do for us when we believe." But the little girls weren't listening. They were marching and singing again.

*Remind me, God, that I am extraordinary
by Your grace. I choose to follow as You direct
me so that Your miraculous power can
work in my life today. Amen.*

Joy Anyway

*We believe with our hearts, and so we are made right
with God. And we declare with our mouths that we believe,
and so we are saved. As the Scripture says, "Anyone
who trusts in him will never be disappointed."*

ROMANS 10:10–11 NCV

Connie and Josh had made three offers on three different
houses in three months. There wasn't a lot of inventory in their
price range, and people wanted to purchase before Christmas.
Although they felt God had impressed on their hearts they
would be in this community for a long time, it seemed He had
other plans for them for a permanent home.

They had moved their family several times throughout their
marriage as the Lord led them and Josh's career grew. "We've never
had a problem buying a house—until now," Connie questioned.

"We have to trust that God will lead us to exactly what He
wants us to have. He's always exceeded our expectations," Josh
replied in an attempt to comfort Connie. Their prayer with each
contract they signed was God's perfect plan be revealed to them.
And each time the contract fell through—closing the door to
their dream of owning their own home again.

When believing for God's very best, disappointment
can come to steal your joy during the times of waiting.
Disappointment can wear away your faith and enable your doubt.
Instead, you can choose joy in the midst of your disappointment.
God never fails—His best is yet to come.

*God, You are good to me. I am determined to find
joy when I am disappointed. I will trust You
for Your very best for my life! Amen.*

Flex a Little

But we all, with open face beholding as in a glass the
glory of the Lord, are changed into the same image
from glory to glory, even as by the Spirit of the Lord.
2 CORINTHIANS 3:18 KJV

Claire was struggling at work. The recent restructure of the
organization had been a surprise for everyone except for a few
in leadership. Twenty percent of her colleagues had lost their
jobs, departments had been completely closed, and she had been
reassigned to a new boss—one she had experienced conflict with
in the past. While she was thankful to still have a job, she was
nervous about the transition.

At lunch with a close girlfriend, she tried to be positive. "I
admit I'm set in my ways. I don't like change, but I realize I'm going
to have to be flexible—and you know that is really hard for me."

Her coworker replied, "Change isn't easy for anyone. But as
Christians we are called to bend and flex. God has been making
changes in us since we invited Him to be the leader of our lives."

Back at home that night, Claire thought about her lunch
conversation. She took some time to get alone with God and ask
him to help her change. She knew it was required for her success
in business and, more importantly, in order to become more of
who He created her to be.

Heavenly Father, thank You for teaching me that
Your ways are higher. Show me how to embrace
change when it comes from You and open my heart
to something new and different. Amen.

Dependent on God

*Keep on asking and it will be given you; keep on
seeking and you will find; keep on knocking
[reverently] and [the door] will be opened to you.*
MATTHEW 7:7 AMP

"Do you ever feel like you just want to help God out?" Candy asked her friend Dan. "I mean, sometimes I just feel like there are things I should be able to handle on my own. I see challenges and think, I can do this. I ask Him for help with so much."

Dan smiled. "How does that usually turn out for ya?"

Candy squished her face up. "You know it doesn't turn out well most of the time. Something that seems little in the beginning somehow becomes a big, fat mess before it's all done. There's always more to the situation than what I can see."

"And that's why it's important to include God in everything. He can see it all, He knows it all, and He has plans for your life that you have no idea about. You don't have to look at your life, you can learn from the lives of those recorded in the Bible: Abraham and Sarah tried to help God out with His promise to them for a son and made a huge mess."

"Yes, you are right," Candy replied. "I am learning that He wants to be included in everything. And when I turn to Him, things turn out much better."

Without prayer, we resort to trying to do things in our own strength when in fact God wants to work in us and through us, accomplishing more than we could ever ask or think on our own.

*Father, I know I can count on You. You
created me to trust, rely, and depend on You.
Help me to look to You for counsel, help,
and guidance in all things. Amen.*

The Overflow

You prepare a meal for me in front of my enemies. You pour oil
of blessing on my head; you fill my cup to overflowing.
PSALM 23:5 NCV

Amy and her husband, Clark, bought a house, and one of her
delights was the beautiful swimming pool out back. When the
water in the pool dropped below a certain level, it was necessary
to open the manual valve and fill it up.

Early one Saturday morning, Amy stepped outside with
coffee in hand and realized the pool was pretty low. She turned
the water on and then went back inside to get breakfast for
the kids. Hours later, upstairs cleaning, she suddenly realized
she never went back to check on the water level. She rushed
outside to find the pool full to the very top of the pool edge, and
she shut the water off. *Well, that will be a big fat water bill*, she
thought.

She hurried back inside where it was warm and bumped
into Clark, who was peering out the sliding glass door at her.
Knowing her thoughts about the water bill, and what she had
done, he laughed and tried to encourage her. "The pool is
overflowing just like the blessing of the Lord in our lives. He is
always good to us. He cares for us with more than enough."

Lord, help me to recognize Your hand of blessing
in my life and soul. No matter what I'm facing I
trust You to bring an overflow of blessing
for whatever I need. Amen.

A Matter of Conscience

Good people will be guided by honesty;
dishonesty will destroy those who are not trustworthy.
PROVERBS 11:3 NCV

Donna had been so excited the last three weeks about her newest and most prominent client, but this morning something had changed. The owner of the company she now represented had asked her a difficult question as he sat across from her desk. He had asked her to "fudge a little" and say that "they had been with her organization three years, instead of three months" when others inquired about their business relationship. He even went as far as requesting she "doctor up" a few dates.

The client immediately recognized that his question made Donna uncomfortable, yet he pressed her for an answer. She squirmed a little and thought, *This is the biggest client I've ever brought on board.* She took a deep breath and looked her client in the eye. "No," she told him. "That's not the way I do business. If I fudged for you; then you could not trust anything that ever came out of my office. If you can't work with me, then I understand."

Her client smiled. "Good! I like that answer. I want to be able to trust you and this company to represent me in honesty and truth!" Donna relaxed. It had been a test—a test of her ethics and of her faith. She stood to shake her client's hand. "It will be a pleasure doing business with you, sir."

Lord, help me to do what is right in every
circumstance. May I represent You in all
I do with honesty and integrity. Amen.

Not So Invisible

*The earth trembled, the heavens also poured
down [rain] at the presence of God; yonder Sinai
quaked at the presence of God, the God of Israel.*
PSALM 68:8 AMP

The weather was much cooler, but Shannon didn't care. Her
work schedule had kept her way too busy to get any time for a
morning run on the short trails close to her home. The work
continued to pile up with no end in sight; so this morning she
decided not to jump on her computer first thing or even look at
her long list of to-dos. It could all wait. She was determined to
spend some time with the Lord.

As she stepped outside, she noticed each time she exhaled
her breath was visible in the morning air. When she reached the
end of the neighborhood and stepped off the sidewalk and onto
the trail, she began to pray quietly. Just minutes into the wooded
area, a small jackrabbit ran quickly across her path. She stopped
for a moment to drink in the beauty of her surroundings.

The sun caught the dew on the few remaining fall leaves,
and they sparkled. Just as the air escaping her lips was normally
unseen during her run in other seasons, winter seemed to expose
the presence of God. Those things that often were invisible
seemed to shout out God's presence with each step she took. In
these quiet moments, He was reminding her that He was always
there.

*Lord, forgive me for being distracted. I will make
time for You—especially today. When I am
distracted, give me a visible glimpse of You. Amen.*

Thankful for the Little Things

Give thanks to the LORD and pray to him.
Tell the nations what he has done. Sing to him;
sing praises to him. Tell about all his miracles.

1 CHRONICLES 16:8–9 NCV

Trish got up early and was surprised to find her cousin, Tracey, sitting at the kitchen table in her housecoat. "I thought you'd sleep in this morning since you're on vacation." Tracey got up to pour herself another cup of coffee. "I was just excited for our families to finally have some time to spend together, a few extra days before Thanksgiving."

"You know," Tracey continued, "I was just sitting here thinking about how sometimes I really miss the simple things. Our lives are so busy."

"Like what?" Trish asked.

"Remember the times we were all together at Grandpa and Grandma's house for holidays? Like the fresh eggs Grandma let us gather from the chicken coop for breakfast and drinking the fresh milk from their cow just after Grandma strained it?"

"Oh and the blackberry cobbler from the vines in the front yard," Tracey added. "And I loved those late nights when we'd hear Grandpa in the kitchen and he would share his cornbread in milk with us?" The cousins continued to reminisce about their time together at their grandparents' house with stories of growing up together during their visits to the farm, each one expressing thanks for each other and to God for the little things that meant so much.

Lord, remind me of the little things in my
life that are special to me. I never want to
take Your gifts of friendship and family for
granted. Amen.

Discover Your Dream Once Again

Restore unto me the joy of thy salvation;
and uphold me with thy free spirit.
PSALM 51:12 KJV

Have you ever looked at a small child and caught a glimpse of the possibilities of success that lay dormant within him or her? Perhaps you even picture just a little of who that child might later become. Did you have a dream as a young person that has not yet been realized?

Life happens, and often those big dreams seem impossible. Maybe you went to school and started your career, maybe got married and started a family. Today that dream may be packed away in the garage, sitting on a shelf in the attic, or buried deep in a quiet, seldom touched part of your soul.

God has a plan. Even though you may have changed and gone in a different direction—that desire that He put within you can still be realized. The dream was still in there, and the ability to do what you once were passionate about can grow in your heart again. Dreams that God put in your heart are what make you who you were created to be. When you trust God to take your life and do with it what He purposed, He'll make your dreams a reality in His time. Just trust Him!

Heavenly Father, remind me of the dreams
that I have set aside. Those are not destroyed—
just forgotten. They are still within me,
and I am trusting You to restore them. Amen.

Remembering with Thanks

> *Your statutes are my heritage forever;*
> *they are the joy of my heart.*
> PSALM 119:111 NIV

Esther sat down at the long dining room table. At eighty-nine she still got around pretty well, but her granddaughter, Emily, was insistent that she go on in and find her seat at the table while she called the rest of the family together for Thanksgiving dinner.

She could hear the great-grandchildren squealing and laughing as they made a line from the bathroom sink into the hall as each took a turn to wash their hands. She smiled as she raised the tablecloth up a little and peeked at the worn hardwood. Her beloved husband's father had made the table when his own family needed a big table to gather around. She closed her eyes and thought about the generations who had sat at this very table—precious family like her husband who had left the earth many years before.

"Grand-mom," Emily said, "What are you thinking about?"

Esther smiled. "I was lost in the many yesterdays of Thanksgiving, remembering the many who have sat right here year after year."

Emily smiled. "Maybe you should say grace today and remind us of what a beautiful heritage so many before us have given us."

Esther smiled. "I'd be honored."

> *God, thank You for giving me a godly heritage. You*
> *have blessed me with the truth of Your Word.*
> *Help me to live each day according to Your*
> *truths so that I can pass that heritage on*
> *to others. Amen.*

Sing—Even If You Don't Feel It

*Come, everyone! Clap your hands!
Shout to God with joyful praise!*
PSALM 47:1 NLT

Nikki noticed Pam wasn't her normal, bubbly self. She watched
as her friend walked slowly into the sanctuary and sat down.
Normally she was bouncing around, talking to their friends
and sharing stories of what God had done in her life that week.
Nikki slid into the seat next to her. "So what's up? Why are you
bummed out today? It's not like you."

"It was a horrible week at school; work didn't go well either.
It just seemed like everything that could go wrong this week, did,"
Pam confessed. Nikki knew that Pam's husband had been away on
business for most of the month as well, and that added pressure.

"Well, you made a good decision by coming to church
today," Nikki told her. "The Lord's house is the best place to be
when you're bummed out, and the best thing to do is worship!"

Pam hugged her friend and said, "Yes, I am going to sing my
heart out."

When worship began, Pam didn't feel anything different,
but she sang anyway. Then halfway through the second song, she
fully surrendered her emotions to the Lord. Before the pastor
came to the platform to share his message she realized her heart
had changed, there was a real smile on her face, and faith started
to rise and carry her above her circumstances of the past week.

*Lord, I know there's something exciting about
spiritual worship. Help me to worship by faith,
because it's when I feel like worshiping least
that I need it the most. Amen.*

Can Others Count on You?

*The Lord does not delay and is not tardy or slow about
what He promises, according to some people's conception
of slowness, but He is long-suffering (extraordinarily
patient) toward you, not desiring that any should perish,
but that all should turn to repentance.*

2 PETER 3:9 AMP

Jessica grew up in a home filled with lies. Her parents made promises and very seldom kept them. Trusting others was extremely difficult for her. When someone broke a promise, the childhood wounds caused her heart to bleed once again.

There was a time when a person who made a promise refused to break that promise—even if keeping it cost them large sums of money. For the most part, society sees a lie as a normal, everyday part of life. In general, white lies are acceptable because there is a misconception that no one gets hurt. Lies are lies, and when promises are broken, someone suffers the consequences.

The Bible says that Satan is the father of lies and there is no truth in him, but that God will keep all of His promises. You are born again to reflect God's character and nature. People should be able to count on you like you count on God. Carefully consider the cost before you make a promise—and then keep it at all costs.

*Father, forgive me for the times that I have broken
promises to You and to others. Help me to count the
cost of my commitment before I make it. I want
others to see Your character in me. Amen.*

For This Very Purpose

*"But I have raised you up for this very purpose,
that I might show you my power and that my
name might be proclaimed in all the earth."*

EXODUS 9:16 NIV

In 1952, Dr. Virginia Apgar designed and introduced the Apgar Score, an unbiased score of the baby's condition after birth used to evaluate his or her transition to life outside the womb. A baby's score is calculated by the heart rate, respiratory effort, muscle tone, skin color, and how they respond when a catheter is used in the nose. A low Apgar Score alerts doctors to the need for life-saving intervention for newborns.

Virginia knew she wanted to become a doctor by the time she graduated from high school. The death of her oldest brother from tuberculosis and another brother's chronic childhood illness may have influenced her determination to help others.

Leadership discouraged Dr. Apgar from continuing in her dream to become a surgeon because other women had failed to establish successful careers in the surgical field. Despite this, she pressed to step outside of the social norm by completing her surgical residency in 1937. She was the first woman recognized as a full professor at Columbia University College of Physicians and Surgeons in 1949.

God has given you a purpose and a desire to fulfill your destiny. What is your dream? Trust God today to put His plans in motion.

*God, You created me with a specific purpose. I have
a dream, and I believe You will show me how to
take the necessary steps to realize it. Amen.*

A Picture from the Inside

*But the LORD said to Samuel, "Don't look at how handsome
Eliab is or how tall he is, because I have not chosen him. God
does not see the same way people see. People look at the outside
of a person, but the LORD looks at the heart."*

1 SAMUEL 16:7 NCV

Penny sat next to her good friend, Louise, waiting for service
to start. "Years ago, people dressed up for church," Louise
commented. "When I was a little girl, getting ready for church
started on Saturday night. It was quite an ordeal at our house.
My mother washed three heads of hair—mine, my younger
sisters', and hers. Then she rolled our hair on sponge rollers, and
as uncomfortable as it was, we slept all night that way. She set
out our church shoes, frilly socks, and dresses the night before."

Penny nodded. "And now it's so casual even some pastors
wear jeans on the platform—and that's all right with me! I think
it reminds me that people examine us based on our outward
appearance, but God isn't concerned with that. His focus is deep
within our hearts. We can be dressed up, with every hair in place,
and be a total wreck on the inside."

"Been there; done that," Louise replied. "I've pretended
to have everything together, but God knew that my heart was
full of sin and rebellion. God knew the real me, and I was only
deceiving myself."

*God, I don't want to pretend anymore.
Show me the places of my heart that need to be
cleaned up so I can live my life transparent
before You and others. Amen.*

Shine the Light

*For God, who said, "Let light shine out of darkness," made
his light shine in our hearts to give us the light of the
knowledge of God's glory displayed in the face of Christ.*

2 CORINTHIANS 4:6 NIV

December. Winter has come in all its blustery glory. It's cold and
dark. If it weren't for the Christmas season, December would be
downright dreary. But few think of this month as a bleak time,
because everywhere we look lights shine through the darkness,
carols are being sung about a blessed gift of love, and people seek
to find—and share—the true meaning of Christmas.

Indeed, God made His light shine out of darkness by
sending Christ. Hopeless without Him, we now have a hope
and a future because of Him. But the light doesn't end with our
salvation. No, that's just the glorious beginning. Once Christ's
light has spread its warmth into our lives, we're to carry that light
into the dark places of this world. His love in us, not electric
Christmas lights, will illuminate all in our paths. When we carry
that light well, others will be drawn to the sweet comfort of
His wisdom, His compassion, and His love in our hearts. And
their hearts will be kindled, and on and on until the entire world
shines with His glory. At least, that's how it should be.

*Dear Father, help me to do my part in carrying the light
of Your love into this world. I want to shine for You
and spread the warmth of Your kindness, compassion,
and acceptance to those around me. Amen.*

Overshadowed

*The angel answered, "The Holy Spirit will come on you,
and the power of the Most High will overshadow you.
So the holy one to be born will be called the Son of God."*
LUKE 1:35 NIV

Mary must have felt overwhelmed in that moment she learned she, of all people, had been chosen to be the mother of God's Son. She was just a simple Jewish girl. There was nothing impressive about her, as far as the world could see.

But God didn't want impressive. He's impressive enough. He didn't need credentials, either. After all, who could top His credentials? What God wanted, what He had searched the world for, was a simple, humble heart. He wanted a woman who knew she wasn't up to the task, but who recognized that He was up to any task.

He found that humility in Mary. Through that humility, through that recognition that she wasn't enough, God poured out his power. The Holy Spirit came upon her. The power of the Most High overshadowed her. And God's glory shone through the plain, quiet frame of her meekness.

God wants to work that way in each of our lives. The Holy Spirit waits to come upon a humble heart that recognizes she can't do it on her own. God longs to display His power through the lives of people who don't claim power of their own. When we recognize our weakness, we allow room for God's strength to shine.

*Dear Father, I can't manage this life without You.
I'm not up to the task. Holy Spirit, come upon me.
Overshadow me with Your power. Amen.*

Insignificant

But you, Bethlehem Ephrathah, though you are small among the clans of Judah, out of you will come for me one who will be ruler over Israel, whose origins are from of old, from ancient times.
MICAH 5:2 NIV

Funny how we always look to the big, important places for our news. We tune our televisions to Washington, DC, or the Kremlin or some other such significant spot. But more often than not, the stories that get our attention happen in small towns, even in our own neighborhoods.

The same is true of people. We expect great men and women to graduate from Harvard or Princeton. We expect them to be tall and beautiful and have impressive social connections. We watch with bated breath to see what these qualified youngsters will contribute to our world.

Yet, we're often surprised when truly great men and women come from our own city block or from the local farm up the road. What? A farmer? What can he possibly know?

God loves surprises. He likes to work through seemingly insignificant people. That way, when a truly humble person with truly humble circumstances accomplishes something great for God, He gets the credit. And if He chooses insignificant people from insignificant places, I suppose that means He may choose me. Or you. Any one of us can be great for God, when we recognize the greatness is only from Him and not from ourselves.

Dear Father, thank You for choosing insignificant people. I want You to have Your way in me. Amen.

Nothing Is Impossible

"For nothing will be impossible with God."
LUKE 1:37 NRSV

A virgin birth. Wow. Mary may have been young and innocent, but she wasn't stupid. She'd been well-brought-up in the ways of, well, men and women. She knew her place. She'd been prepared since birth, practically, for the role of wife and mother. And she knew how babies were made.

So when the angel told her she, a virgin, would carry God's Son, of course she questioned. Of course she was skeptical. Intelligent questions don't show a lack of faith. Rather, they demonstrate a longing to understand.

But God's ways aren't always our ways. Sometimes we must accept things on blind faith, simply because we know God is God and we'll never fully understand Him. That's when we rely on the great things God has already done, and we trust Him.

In response to Mary's question, the angel told her that her cousin Elizabeth—a woman far beyond child-bearing years—was also with child. "For nothing is impossible with God."

Sometimes, our circumstances seem impossible, and we question God. Life doesn't make sense, just as being pregnant didn't make sense to Mary. Our questions are okay, as long as we're willing to accept God's answers. His response to us won't always make sense in the moment, but we can trust Him. We can trust His love for us, and His great plan. We can place our hope in the knowledge that miracles are commonplace to Him, and He may just be including us in a miracle.

*Dear Father, help me to trust You. I know
nothing is impossible with You. Amen.*

Peace on Earth

*"Glory to God in the highest heaven,
and on earth peace to those on whom his favor rests."*
LUKE 2:14 NIV

December brings peace. Or at least, it's supposed to, according to the Christmas card photos and television messages. During this month, we're supposed to set aside differences, love everyone, and just be happy. It's all so warm and fuzzy.

But peace isn't a Hollywood-generated theme that goes away when the movie—or the month—is over. Peace is a real, almost tangible quality that God sends to those He favors. It has less to do with our circumstances than with our relationship with our Father.

Think about it. We can find ourselves in a serene mountain resort with soft music in the background, luxurious furnishings, and servants to cater to our whims. But if our own thoughts aren't at rest with our Creator, we won't have peace. Or we can be in the middle of a battlefield, bullets and cannons zinging overhead, yet with the knowledge that we're not alone, that God is with us and He'll take care of things. Right there, we can have peace.

God's peace is a gift He gives to those He favors. And He favors those who love Him with their whole hearts and who want to please Him. Next time we find ourselves needing peace, we can simply focus on our relationship with our Father. Despite our circumstances, the closer we are to God, the more we will find our spirits are at peace.

*Dear Father, I want to live in Your favor
so I can know Your peace. Amen.*

A Child Is Born

*For to us a child is born,
to us a son is given.*
ISAIAH 9:6 NIV

It's such a joyful occasion when a child is born into a family.
When that child is strong and healthy, that's even more reason to
rejoice. And when the family has waited and longed and prayed
desperately for that child, the jubilation and delight can't be
contained.

Christ's birth was just such an occasion. Only the joy wasn't
confined to His parents and grandparents, aunts and uncles. The
birth of this particular baby boy was—and is—an occasion for
intense celebration and grateful exuberance for all mankind.

Ever since sin separated us from God, we've been striving to
bridge that separation. But try as we may, we're not able to cross
the chasm between sin and holiness. God saw our dilemma,
had compassion on us, and sent the one who could serve as the
connection point.

Yet our celebration was, in some ways, God's heartbreak.
He gave up His Son so we could have a chance at the abundant
life sin destroyed. The good news is, Christ now sits next to His
Father in heaven, waiting for us—His family—to join Him.
All we have to do is embrace what was done for us that day and
celebrate the gift of this wonderful Son who came to heal the hole
sin placed in our hearts. That's a pretty good reason to celebrate.

*Dear Father, thank You
for sending Your Son. Amen.*

Coming Soon

*For to us a child is born, to us a son is given,
and the government will be on his shoulders.*

ISAIAH 9:6 NIV

There's some disagreement among scholars about whether this
verse refers to Christ's first coming or His second coming. It's a
popular Christmas verse, so most people believe it refers to the
day He was born in a stable. Angels sang, shepherds rejoiced . . .
It makes a really pretty Christmas card cover.

But the nation of Israel didn't receive Christ the first
time. He was rejected. Was the government on His shoulders?
Maybe, if you consider the government came down on Him and
ultimately had Him killed.

When He comes again, though . . . wow. That will be a sight
to behold. At that time, Christ will be well received. He will ride
forth in royal splendor and create a real version of the mythical
Atlas, carrying the government of the world on His shoulders.
The shoulders are a symbol of strength, and Christ will certainly
rule in strength and power and will wipe out the forces of evil in
this world.

Any way we look at it, Christ was, is, and always will be a
gift to us. This season and every day of the year, we celebrate His
first coming and look forward with excitement to the day He
will come again.

*Dear Father, thank You for
sending Your Son the first time.
Please send Him again soon. Amen.*

Life Coach

And he will be called Wonderful Counselor.
ISAIAH 9:6 NIV

There's a new title for an old profession: life coach. The phrase was first used in 1986 and refers to an advisor who helps people set and reach goals, deal with problems, and make decisions. Professionals can be trained and receive a certification to be a life coach.

While this is a worthy, fulfilling profession, we need to remember we already have a life coach. God sends His Holy Spirit to anyone who asks, and He guides us. He gives us wisdom. He shows us the best way to live.

The problem is, many of us don't want to listen to His counsel. We want what we want. We want to live the way we think is best, the way that seems easiest or most comfortable for us right here, right now. But God is more concerned with the big picture than our current circumstances. Oh, He will guide us through today, but if we listen to Him carefully and follow His direction, we will end up on the best path for eternity.

Our Wonderful Counselor isn't in it for the paycheck or to build a résumé. He loves us and only wants what is best for us. When we are confused about which way to go, which decision to make, we can go to our Life Coach. We can trust that He will always lead us in the right direction.

Dear Father, thank You for being my Life Coach.
Help me to heed Your counsel. Amen.

Power and Might

And he will be called . . . Mighty God.
ISAIAH 9:6 NIV

There wasn't much about that tiny baby, born in a borrowed room shared with animals, that could be called, "mighty." Humble, lowly, meek . . . all these words describe that prince-become-pauper. But mighty? No.

Then He grew in wisdom and stature. He healed the sick. He calmed the storm. He fed the hungry, forgave sinners, and took on the hierarchy of religious zealots. Then, He was mighty. But they killed Him.

Fortunately, that wasn't the end of the story. From the dark side of the tomb, He overcame death in a display of power and might that had never before and would never again be matched. He conquered all the powers of sin and hell, and won. Yet, that still wasn't the end.

Jesus' power and might continue to this day. It pierces through our every circumstance, making us more than conquerors through Him. No matter what we face, we don't have to face it in our own strength. We can simply be still, trust in His might, and let Him fight for us.

One day, He will come again in all His mighty glory. On that day, His power will be unfurled for all to see. Until then, we can hide in His shelter and rely on the power of the Mighty God.

*Dear Father, remind me of
Your power and might today.
Help me trust in You. Amen.*

Perfect Love

And he will be called . . . Everlasting Father.
ISAIAH 9:6 NIV

There seems to be a newly recognized realization in our culture about the power fathers have on their children's lives. Whether by their presence or absence, by their nurturing or neglect, fathers have a profound influence on their children. Unfortunately, many men did not have good role models in their own fathers. So they do the best they can, often using their own flawed father as the default model.

As women, we gather much of what we believe about ourselves from our fathers. If he thought we were beautiful, deep inside, we know we're beautiful. If he was loving and nurturing and present, we feel worthy of love, worthy of others' time. But if he was highly critical or distant, we can carry around a deep sense of shame and low self-esteem.

No matter what kind of earthly father we had, he was imperfect. In God, we find a perfect, Everlasting Father, who has perfect, everlasting love and acceptance for us. Never again should we gauge our value by what our flawed, human fathers may have made us feel. We can look into the mirror of God's eyes and see ourselves through the reflection of the One who made us, who adores us, and who loves us beyond measure. He will never leave us. He will never forsake us. And no matter what we do, He will always welcome us into His presence with open, loving arms.

*Dear Father, thank You for loving me perfectly.
Help me to see myself through Your perfect,
accepting, adoring eyes. Amen.*

Finding Peace

And he will be called . . . Prince of Peace.
ISAIAH 9:6 NIV

We all long for a peaceful place. The desire for peace is etched into our genetic code . . . perhaps because we're made in God's image and He is full of peace. When we think of peace, our minds fill with images of calm, quiet serenity. We picture a hilltop, surrounded by lovely gardens, with birds singing and the gentle laughter of loved ones.

While it's good to seek out a peaceful, tranquil existence, that's not always possible. In this world, stress finds us. War happens. People can be mean and selfish. Diseases appear, accidents occur. So how can we have peace when the pressures and tensions of life seem to hunt us down?

It's possible to have peace in the midst of chaos when we understand where peace is found. God's peace isn't confined to a specific location or a specific set of circumstances. His peace isn't something we have to maneuver and create. Jesus Christ is the Prince of Peace. Peace is His kingdom, and as long as He lives within us, that is where His peace dwells.

It's important to walk away from stress when we can. But when stress finds us, we can extinguish it—or at least diminish it greatly—by calling on the Prince of Peace within our hearts. When we respond with the calm, quiet assurance that comes from Christ alone, we will find peace.

> *Dear Father, thank You for sending
> the Prince of Peace. Help me to call
> on Him when I need peace. Amen.*

Joy and Peace

*May the God of hope fill you with all joy and
peace as you trust in him, so that you may overflow
with hope by the power of the Holy Spirit.*
ROMANS 15:13 NIV

December brings the season of joy and peace. Those words are
written all over Christmas cards, painted on storefront windows,
and sung about in carols. What a lovely tradition to focus on
these qualities for an entire month of our year.

But truly, joy and peace aren't seasonal. They're timeless
and eternal gifts, given by our Creator, the God of hope, when
we trust Him. That one little word—trust—holds the key to
unlocking joy and peace in our lives every single day of the year.

When things happen that we don't understand, will we
trust Him? That's when we'll find joy and peace. When life is
hard, people are mean, and we feel abandoned and alone, will
we trust His love for us? When money is tight, disease attacks,
relationships are broken . . . can we trust that He is good and His
plans for us are good? Can we really trust Him?

No one said trust is easy. But when we choose to trust God
in the midst of dire circumstances, He sends a calm assurance
that somehow, everything's going to be okay. He gives us hope
in a future filled with beauty and love and happiness. And in the
midst of that hope, we find joy, and we find peace.

*Dear Father, thank You for being the God of hope.
Thank You for offering joy and peace.
Help me to trust You. Amen.*

Unexpected Plans

*This is how the birth of Jesus the Messiah came about:
His mother Mary was pledged to be married to Joseph,
but before they came together, she was found to
be pregnant through the Holy Spirit.*

MATTHEW 1:18 NIV

What an exciting time for Mary and Joseph. Planning a wedding, dreaming of their future home, future children, future joys. Mary may have tucked things away in a hope chest; Joseph probably worked and saved and prepared to support his future bride. And then . . . oh, my.

Sometimes, God's plans for us are unexpected. Even when it seems we're going along, following the right path, doing everything as best we can according to God's policies, all of a sudden, bam! Something hits out of left field.

God's plans for us don't always make sense, in the moment. We feel overwhelmed. We may even feel betrayed by God. But in moments like these, we must fall back on our faith. We draw on the experiences we've had, which show us that He loves us, and that He is always good. We pull from the stories of those who've come before us, who have lived through similar crises, and who have seen from beginning to end that God's love never changes, never fails.

If Mary and Joseph's plans hadn't been interrupted by this unexpected event, they wouldn't have gotten to parent the Son of God. Next time some unforeseen calamity strikes, take a deep breath and a deeper dose of faith. Then, sit back and wait for the blessing.

*Dear Father, help me to trust You even
when circumstances surprise me. Amen.*

The Fall Guy

*And her husband Joseph, being a just man and unwilling
to put her to shame, resolved to divorce her quietly.*
MATTHEW 1:19 ESV

Joseph was a good man. He loved Mary, and he'd worked and
planned and prepared to spend the rest of his life with her. He
was an honorable man, and all he wanted was to live a quiet,
productive life and raise a family.

Imagine the depth of confusion and sorrow when he learned
his beloved Mary was pregnant . . . and he knew it wasn't his
child. His heart was broken. He felt crushed and betrayed. Still,
he didn't want to humiliate the woman he loved.

But then an angel told him to marry her. Marry her? People
would know! A rushed wedding . . . a baby born too soon . . .
why, they'd think he had compromised Mary.

Joseph had to swallow his pride. He chose to ignore the
whispers of everyone who mattered to him and obey the One
who mattered most. He knew that trying to please people is
futile. Pleasing God, though it may take us on a rocky path at
times, will eventually lead to the ultimate peace we all desire.

Like Joseph, there will be times when our obedience to God
will cause others to misunderstand us. But like Joseph, we can
hold our heads high and move forward, knowing that despite
what others may say, we know we are on the right path.

*Dear Father, help me to
obey You even when others
question my motives. Amen.*

The Highest Calling

*Let us not become weary in doing good, for at the proper
time we will reap a harvest if we do not give up.*
GALATIANS 6:9 NIV

A lot of good is done in December. We shop for gifts. We cook
big, delicious meals for our families. We give to charities and go
out of our way to show compassion and kindness to those around
us. And by the time the holiday season ends, we are bone-weary.

But sharing love, kindness, and compassion shouldn't be a
seasonal habit. Of all our reasons for inhabiting space on this
planet, our highest calling, our most noble purpose is this: we
were placed here to show love to other people.

Weariness never stems from living out our purpose. Rather,
it seeps in when we get distracted from our purpose and pour
our energy into things that don't elevate that calling. When we
stay committed to our most virtuous reason for existence, we are
energized.

That's not to say we won't need to rest. It takes a lot of
energy to pour ourselves out for other people. But when we
understand our purpose of love and we cater our actions to that
purpose, the weariness is the good, hard-night's sleep kind of
weary. The stress, the anxiety, the depression that come when
we don't live our purpose seems to dissipate when we continue
doing good and living out our highest moral function: to love.

*Dear Father, help me to live out my
purpose today and every day. Teach me
to love the way You love. Amen.*

Ordinary People

And Mary said: "My soul glorifies the Lord and my
spirit rejoices in God my Savior, for he has been
mindful of the humble state of his servant.
From now on all generations will call me blessed."
LUKE 1:46–48 NIV

God chose Mary, a young girl, to do a very important job. Of all
the polished, regal princesses, of all the educated, high-society
women He could have selected, He chose Mary. Nothing special
about her, at least not according to the world's standards. But for
all Mary may have lacked in importance, she had the qualities
God wanted most. She was humble and pure, and she loved God
with all her heart.

God doesn't play the political card when choosing people to
do His work. He cares nothing about looks or money or position.
God often chooses the simple, ordinary people of this world to
carry out His great tasks. Then, from their obedience, He will
elevate them to a position of importance.

We should never seek recognition for our great works. If we
are to be recognized, God will take care of that in a much greater
way than we ever could. When we humbly go about our lives,
doing our best to serve Him and please Him, God notices. And
like Mary, He will bless those who love Him with a pure heart,
and with those blessings will come great joy.

Dear Father, thank You for loving me.
Thank You for seeing me, even though there's
nothing special about me. I love You,
and I want to please You. Amen.

A Long Journey

*After they had heard the king, they went on their way,
and the star they had seen when it rose went ahead of
them until it stopped over the place where the child was.
When they saw the star, they were overjoyed.*
MATTHEW 2:9–10 NIV

Those men followed that star a long, looooong time. For more than two years, they watched the sky, and when the star moved, they followed it. They trusted their gut feeling that it would lead them to a newborn king.

But despite the signs and their gut feelings and their trust, two years is a long time to follow a dream they had no assurance would ever become reality. Surely they grew tired. Surely they became weary and discouraged.

Sometimes, our journeys seem long. We become tired and weary and discouraged, and our faith wanes. We wonder if our hopes will ever become reality or if we're just chasing stars. But we should never give up when it comes to following the path God has set before us. Oh, the road may be long and curvy. But the same God who led those wise men to the Christ child is leading us. The same God who whispered into their spirits and promised them that if they'd just believe, they'd receive a special blessing—He whispers those same promises to us. If we follow Him and don't give up, we will be blessed.

*Dear Father, I get tired sometimes.
Help me to follow You and
not give up. Amen.*

An Ordinary Night

*And the angel said unto them, Fear not, for behold
I bring you good tidings of great joy, which shall be to
all people. For unto you is born this day in the city
of David a Saviour, which is Christ the Lord.*

LUKE 2:10–11 KJV

For the shepherds, it was probably a night like any other. They counted sheep and made sure they were watered and fed. They sat on the hillside and tried not to doze as they scanned the area for predators. All in a day's work.

Yet on that ordinary night, God did something extraordinary. He sent angels to fill the sky and to proclaim good news to all who would listen. On this night, His promise was finally fulfilled. On this night, hope met reality.

Imagine what those shepherds thought when they looked into the sky. Confused, dazed, frightened . . . these are just a few of the emotions that probably swirled through their minds. They could have run and hidden. They could have rejected the message of hope and credited the hallucination to some bad barley. Instead, they set aside their discomfort and fears and embraced the promise fulfilled.

We never know when God will deliver a miracle. Often, He performs His greatest works in our lives when we're least expecting it. If we're not careful, we'll overlook His signs, or reject them as ridiculous. But God is alive and working. As we go about our daily tasks, we must remember to watch the skies. God may be getting ready to deliver a miracle.

*Dear Father, help me to expect
great things from You. Amen.*

Talk about It

*And when they had seen it, they made known abroad
the saying which was told them concerning this child.*
LUKE 2:17 KJV

When the shepherds finally found the baby wrapped in
swaddling clothes and lying in a manger, there's no telling what
went through their minds. But we know one thing for certain:
they didn't keep this miracle to themselves. Despite possibilities
that people would think they were certifiably nuts—seeing
angels, of all things!—they told everyone who would listen. The
promised Messiah had come at last.

God is still busy working miracles, large and small, in our
lives every single day. Whether it's helping us find our missing
car keys or healing us from some terrible disease, God is at work
in the lives of His people. And like those shepherds, He wants us
to tell everyone we know about how great He is.

Despite modern technology and its ability to send
information around the world at the click of a button, the
best advertisement is still word of mouth. When we talk
about God, when we give personal testimony about the great
things He's done in our lives, people listen. And some of them
will remember our words and ponder them in their hearts.
Eventually, a few of them will seek out this great God for
themselves. And their lives will be changed and touched and
blessed, all because we told people about the great things God
has done in our lives.

*Dear Father, help me talk about
You in a way that seems natural, in a
way that will draw others to You. Amen.*

Good Gifts

And when they were come into the house, they saw the young child with Mary his mother, and fell down, and worshipped him; and when they had opened their treasures, they presented unto him gifts: gold, and frankincense and myrrh.

MATTHEW 2:11 KJV

The wise men gave expensive gifts to Jesus—rare treasures, fitting for a king. The gifts themselves didn't really matter, though. The important thing was that they realized the value of the One who received the gifts. They wanted to give their best, because He was worthy of the best.

We may not be able to give large amounts of money or expensive gifts to God. But since He's God, He doesn't really need our treasures. More than anything, He wants us to recognize Him as God. He wants our gifts to Him to be the best we can give, because that shows we understand who He is. He wants our offerings to Him to be an outpouring of our love for Him and our worship of Him.

Whether we give Him our time, our talents, or a portion of our money, God is pleased when those gifts come from a pure heart. And when we offer our lives to Him—every aspect—He smiles. He accepts our gifts, humble as they may be, when He knows we offer them out of sincere worship of the One true God.

*Dear Father, I understand
who You are, and I worship You.
Please take my life as an offering. Amen.*

Storing up Treasures

*And all they that heard it wondered at those things
which were told them by the shepherds. But Mary kept
all these things, and pondered them in her heart.*
LUKE 2:18–19 KJV

In many ways, Mary wasn't any different from any other mother.
She watched her baby and treasured all the sweet things he said
and did. She watched others' reactions to him and tucked those
memories away in her heart. She knew her baby was extraordinary,
just as every mother knows her child is unique and special.

Later, when her son went through some very difficult times,
her mother's heart must have broken. She may have consoled
herself with those sweet recollections of better times, as she
watched her son suffer and die. Because she took time to savor
the sweet moments as they came, she had those memories to
hold onto when she needed them.

Sometimes, life gets so busy we forget to pay attention to
the sweet blessings God sends our way. We let all the special
little minutes slip by, and we forget to save them. We don't even
notice them.

It's important to take time and appreciate all the unique
moments God allows us to experience. He fills our days with
good things, if we just pay attention. When we take time to
notice God's gifts to us, and treasure them in our hearts, those
memories will sustain us during difficult times.

*Dear Father, help me to notice the good things You've
placed in my life. Remind me to treasure them and
save them up for when I might need them. Amen.*

Great Expectations

*Now there was a man in Jerusalem called Simeon,
who was righteous and devout. He was waiting for
the consolation of Israel, and the Holy Spirit was on him.
It had been revealed to him by the Holy Spirit that he
would not die before he had seen the Lord's Messiah.*

LUKE 2:25–26 NIV

Simeon was an old man. He was righteous and devout. But surely there were other old men hanging around the temple who were righteous and devout. Of all the Pharisees and Sadducees nearby, of all the truly devoted, religious people of that day, why Simeon? Why did God choose this man to welcome His Son into the temple and proclaim His coming to all who would listen?

One key phrase offers a clue: "He was waiting for the consolation of Israel." In other words, Simeon knew God's promises, and he was looking for good things to happen.

What a lesson we can learn from this old saint! God has promised many good things to His people. But often, we mope around, stressed and anxious, worried that things won't go well for us. Why do we do that? Like Simeon, we should wake up each morning looking for God to do great things. We should greet each new day expecting God to work, to fulfill His promises.

*Dear Father, thank You for Your promises.
I know You have good things in store. Help me to
watch and wait, expecting You to do great
things each and every day. Amen.*

Staying Close

There was also a prophet, Anna, the daughter of Penuel,
of the tribe of Asher. She was very old; she had lived with her
husband seven years after her marriage, and then was
a widow until she was eighty-four. She never left the temple
but worshiped night and day, fasting and praying.
Coming up to them at that very moment, she gave thanks to
God and spoke about the child to all who were looking
forward to the redemption of Jerusalem.
LUKE 2:36–38 NIV

Talk about commitment. Anna had been widowed since she
was a young woman. There's no mention of her having children.
Instead of finding another husband, she decided to live out her
days serving God.

Anna's years of commitment paid off when she was very
old. God made sure that Mary and Joseph brought Jesus to that
particular temple so Anna could see Him, hold Him, and declare
His presence to all who would listen.

If we want to catch God in His work, in the middle of His
most exciting acts, we must stay close to the place He's working.
In that day, it was the temple. Today, it might be at church or in
the middle of a particular ministry project. But when we put our
own schedules and agendas first and disregard God's work, we
miss out on His most thrilling exploits.

Like Anna, we should do all we can to serve God and
stay close to His work. When we do, we'll witness
some amazing feats.

Dear Father, show me where You are working,
and help me to stay close to You. Amen.

In Control

*And while they were there, the time came for her to give birth.
And she gave birth to her firstborn son.*

LUKE 2:6–7 ESV

Joseph took Mary, his betrothed wife, to Bethlehem for political reasons. He didn't really have much choice in the matter; if he'd failed to register them, he'd have broken the law. But even though it looks like politics ruled their circumstances, we know better. God orchestrated everything—including the time and place required for the census—in order to fulfill His plan.

Sometimes it may feel like we're controlled by our jobs, our schedules, or somebody's political agenda. But God is in control! He knows what He's doing, and we can trust that He's working all things together for our good and His glory.

Just as the prophets foretold Christ's birth in Bethlehem, God already knows every step of our lives. He knows tomorrow and next week and next month and next year, and He is lining things up to do something great in our lives. Like Mary and Joseph, all we need to do is follow Him, do our best each day, and trust His plan. Just as He brought everything together on that night, He is pulling all things together to fulfill His purpose in our lives.

*Dear Father, thank You for having a plan for my
life. Remind me that You're in charge, even when it
feels like other things are controlling my life. Help
me to trust You and follow You. Amen.*

Excuses, Excuses

*And she gave birth to her firstborn son and wrapped
him in swaddling cloths and laid him in a manger,
because there was no place for them in the inn.*

LUKE 2:7 ESV

The inn Mary and Joseph stayed at was called Geruth Kimham,
or in more modern terms, Kimham's Bed and Breakfast.
Hundreds of years before Christ's birth, Kimham was a servant
of King David. The king gave him this little piece of land near
Bethlehem as a retirement gift, so to speak, for years of faithful
service. The inn may have been full that night, but the owner—
probably one of Kimham's descendents—was kind enough to let
Mary and Joseph stay with the animals. At least they'd be out of
the cold.

The funny thing is, David didn't originally want Kimham
to be his servant. He wanted Barzillai, who had been a faithful
friend to the king during some difficult times. But Barzillai said
no. He said, "David, I'm too old. My family is here. My job is
here. Take my servant Kimham with you instead." Barzillai could
have had the eternal honor of having Christ born in his inn,
but he made excuses. So someone else—Kimham—received the
blessing.

When God gives us opportunities to serve Him, we can
accept the job or make excuses. If we make excuses, He'll find
someone else. But when we turn down the opportunity
to serve our Lord, we also turn down the blessings that
come with it.

*Dear Father, help me not to make excuses,
but to serve You at every opportunity. Amen.*

Pressing On

*I press on to take hold of that
for which Christ took hold of me.*
PHILIPPIANS 3:12 NIV

We all need a lot of work when it comes to fulfilling God's perfect plan for our lives. We get sidetracked, we mess up, life distracts us . . . and progress is slow. No matter how sincere our desire to live out God's purpose for us, we fall down again. And again.

But that's okay. God knows us better than anyone, and He knows we're not perfect. He knows we'll make mistakes and have setbacks. All He asks is that each time we fall down, we get back up and keep moving forward.

Think about it. Christ saw potential in us—so much that He died for us. He didn't say, "Oh good grief, look how slow they are! Look at how many times they goof up. Never mind. It's not worth it." Nope. He paid such a high price for us because He knew we were made in His image. And He knew that as long as we trust Him and don't give up and keep pressing forward, our likeness will become closer and closer to His.

That's what He wants for us—for our spirits to mirror His. He wants us to love, for He is love. He wants us to be kind and gentle and compassionate, for He is all those things. He longs for us to be His representatives in this world. And we will be, as long we keep pressing on.

*Dear Father, help me to press
on to become more like You. Amen.*

Eye on the Prize

Brothers and sisters, I do not consider myself yet to have taken hold of it. But one thing I do: Forgetting what is behind and straining toward what is ahead, I press on toward the goal to win the prize for which God has called me heavenward in Christ Jesus.

PHILIPPIANS 3:13–14 NIV

The Olympic games began in seventh century BC in Olympia, Greece, and were held every fourth year for nearly 1,200 years. In the third century BC, Alexander the Great required every region he'd conquered to speak Greek. Because of this, Paul and the people of that time were very familiar with Olympic terminology.

Paul uses the image of a marathon runner pressing onward, straining ahead, not looking back as he strives for the prize—a crown of laurel leaves. It was a great honor to wear that crown, and each participant kept his eye on that prize as he ran forward with all his might.

In the same way, we must keep our eye on the prize—the crown God will give each of us who have lived a life pleasing to Him. We can't look back, or we'll surely stumble. Each day, each moment, we must press ahead as we make choice by choice to live for Him.

The good news is, we're not competing against anyone but ourselves. It doesn't matter where the people around us are on the track. All that matters is where we are, and that we keep moving forward.

Dear Father, help me to press on in my journey to fulfilling Your purpose for my life. Amen.

Like Glue

*Surely your goodness and love will follow me
all the days of my life.*
PSALM 23:6 NIV

Sometimes it's scary to look out into the great unknown. As we stand on the threshold of a new year, we don't know what to expect. Will good things be in store, or do terrible things await?

We don't have the ability to see the future. But we do know one thing for certain. As long as we remain close to our Father, His goodness and love will stay close to us. No matter where we go, no matter where our circumstances may force us, His love and goodness will follow us.

Even when we wander away from His perfect plan for us, He is only a breath away. He promised in Romans 8 that nothing will ever separate us from that love. When life is good, He is there. When life is hard, His love and goodness are right there. Nothing—no sickness or disease, no foul circumstance, no financial difficulty will remove His love from us. It sticks like glue.

The challenge lies in finding His presence in tough situations. Sometimes we may have to look a little closer or search some odd places. But these things will never change: He is there. He loves us. He is good. And He will never leave us.

*Dear Father, thank You for sticking with me, no
matter what. That knowledge gives me confidence
to move into whatever the future holds. Amen.*

The Next Step

*Your word is a lamp for my feet,
a light on my path.*
PSALM 119:105 NIV

Change is unsettling. It doesn't matter who we are—old or young, rich or poor, married or single. Change can be exciting, but it also brings with it the unknown. And that can be a little unnerving.

When we face changes, the path ahead often looks dark and twisted. We squint and strain to see down the road, but we just can't see clearly. But we don't always need to see into the distance. We only need to see the step ahead of us. Then another step. Then another step.

When the path ahead is obscure, we can go to God's Word for guidance. His Word will light our way. Oh, it may not tell us exactly what's coming a year from now, or even a month from now. But if we depend on Him and follow the guidance He's given us, His Word will act as a road map for the step ahead. It will light the pathway at our feet, so we know we're not stepping off a cliff.

When we rely on His Word and follow it consistently, we can trust His goodness. Even when the future is unclear, we can move ahead with confidence, knowing He will lead us to the best place for us, and His goodness and love will stay with us every step of the journey.

*Dear Father, thank You for lighting
my way. Help me to follow You today
and trust You for my future. Amen.*

Stinkin' Thinkin'

Finally, brothers and sisters, whatever is true, whatever is noble, whatever is right, whatever is pure, whatever is lovely, whatever is admirable—if anything is excellent or praiseworthy—think about such things.

PHILIPPIANS 4:8 NIV

Studies have shown that New Year's resolutions are rarely kept. Within a few weeks, most New Year's goals have fallen by the wayside, replaced by a pan of brownies. But research has also shown that if the goals are small and achievable, they are more likely to be kept.

In the verse above, Paul urges us to turn our thoughts to positive things. Easier said than done, especially in a society where we're bombarded by negative images, negative language, and negative attitudes. We put up our own shells of negativity, just to survive.

While it may be unrealistic to say, "I'm going to stop thinking negative thoughts," we can still make a conscious, achievable effort to think gentler, more noble thoughts. If we determine to replace each bad thought with a kinder, love-filled thought, we will find our stress reduces and our peace increases.

Next time we catch ourselves thinking something negative about our job or our neighbor or a politician, let's try to replace that thought with a positive one. Before long, we'll re-train our brains to naturally turn to truth, purity, and excellence.

Dear Father, thank You for teaching me to focus on positive thoughts. Help me to think about things the way You do, with love, gentleness, kindness, and compassion. Amen.

New Things

"Look, I am about to do something new;
even now it is coming. Do you not see it?
Indeed, I will make a way in the wilderness,
rivers in the desert."

ISAIAH 43:19 HCSB

Sometimes it seems like we're standing in the middle of a thick forest. Lost. No way out. No path, no help to be found. Trees block the sunlight, we have no cell phone reception, no idea which way to go. At least, that's what it feels like, right?

But God says when we're in a wilderness with no clear path, He'll make a path. He'll clear a way for us, if we'll just keep looking to Him and moving forward. If we turn around and try to live in the past, we'll lose our way. But if we follow Him, He'll show us a better way.

At times, it feels like we don't have the provisions we need. We struggle to pay bills, or we long for friendship or lost love. We feel physically, financially, or spiritually destitute. But even then, God will provide. When we find ourselves in a desert, God will bring a river! But in order to find that river, we can't return to our former way of life. We must keep moving forward, keep following Him, keep trusting His love for us. He is good, and all His plans for us are good. In faith, we can leave the past behind and step forward into a future filled with His bountiful provision.

Dear Father, I trust You with my future.
I can't wait to see what You have in store. Amen.

Contributor Index

Emily Biggers is a Tennessee native living in Arlington, Texas. She loves to travel, write, spend time with family and friends, and decorate.

Renae Brumbaugh lives in Texas with two noisy children and two dogs. She's authored four books in Barbour's Camp Club Girls series.

Dena Dyer is a writer who resides in the Texas Hill Country. She has contributed to more than a dozen anthologies and has authored or coauthored three humor books.

Patricia Grau, a Michigan resident, is a retired engineer, who spends her winters in Florida. Pat's husband, George, went to be with our Lord in 2012. She has four children and ten grandchildren.

Shanna D. Gregor is a freelance writer, editor, and product developer who has served various ministries and publishers. The mother of two young men, Shanna and her husband reside in Tucson, Arizona.

Eileen Key, freelance writer and editor, resides in San Antonio, Texas.

Shelley R. Lee is the author of *Before I Knew You, Mat Madness,* numerous magazine and newspaper articles, contributor to 2014 *Daily Wisdom for Women,* and several other Barbour projects. She resides in northwest Ohio with her husband of twenty-nine years, David, and their four grown sons.

Donna K. Maltese is a freelance writer, editor, and writing coach as well as a pastor's prayer partner. She lives in Pennsylvania with her family.

Iemima Ploscariu currently lives in Citrus Heights, California, and works as a tutor for ABC, Inc., and American River Community College. She is also an independent history researcher.

Karin Dahl Silver is a former air force kid, voracious reader, and rock-climbing novice (getting braver!). She and her husband, Scott, live in Colorado Springs, Colorado.

Janice Thompson, a full-time author living in the Houston, Texas, area, is the mother of four married daughters.

Marjorie Vawter is a professional freelance writer and editor. She and her husband have two adult children.

Scripture Index